Anonymous

The Fern Manual

Being a description of all the best stove, greenhouse, and hardy ferns, cultivated in British gardens

Anonymous

The Fern Manual
Being a description of all the best stove, greenhouse, and hardy ferns, cultivated in British gardens

ISBN/EAN: 9783337069056

Printed in Europe, USA, Canada, Australia, Japan

Cover: Foto ©Lupo / pixelio.de

More available books at **www.hansebooks.com**

THE FERN MANUAL:

BEING A DESCRIPTION OF ALL THE BEST

STOVE, GREENHOUSE, AND HARDY FERNS.

LONDON:
PRINTED AT THE HORTICULTURAL PRESS,
17, JOHNSON'S COURT, FLEET STREET.

THE
FERN MANUAL:

BEING

A DESCRIPTION OF ALL THE BEST

STOVE, GREENHOUSE, AND HARDY FERNS,

CULTIVATED IN

BRITISH GARDENS;

WITH INSTRUCTIONS FOR THEIR CULTIVATION AND TREATMENT

BOTH ON A LARGE SCALE AND IN

FERN CASES.

BY CONTRIBUTORS TO THE JOURNAL OF HORTICULTURE.

Illustrated with Numerous Engravings.

LONDON:
JOURNAL OF HORTICULTURE & COTTAGE GARDENER
OFFICE,
162, FLEET STREET.

1863.

PREFACE.

IT has long been considered a desideratum to have a concise Manual of Garden Ferns. Of the British species there are many valuable handbooks; but, except in works of large extent and great cost, the English reader did not possess a book to which reference could be made for information on the Ferns grown in Stoves, Greenhouses, and Garden Ferneries. It is with the view of supplying this want that the present work is published.

Any merit that attaches to the excellent information found in the following pages is due to Mr. Thomas Appleby, long a skilful cultivator of this family of plants, and whose papers on the subject in the *Cottage Gardener* have been made available. To Mr. C. W. Croker also, a successful cultivator and a respectable pteridological botanist, a great portion of this work is due. Much of the cultural information has also been

PREFACE.

supplied by Mr. George Abbey and numerous other writers in the *Journal of Horticulture and Cottage Gardener;* and it is believed, now that the experience of these practical men is thus combined, that it will form the best Manual that has yet been produced on the subject.

INTRODUCTION.

It is hoped that the following pages will furnish our readers with plain and distinct directions for the cultivation of that most justly popular tribe of plants—the Ferns. We have attempted to give all the information which may be required for their successful management, with notes upon all the best Ferns which are easily attainable. The lists are not complete; for to have mentioned every species which is now to be found in our British stoves and greenhouses would have increased the book to too great a size. Besides, many of them are represented in this country by only one or two examples; and to propagate these to a sufficient extent for them to become popular plants will be a work of years. Others have been omitted from the large genera, or their names only given because it was thought that those enumerated would be found sufficient. We have used the names by which the plants are most generally known, not burdening our pages with long lists of synonymes, which may be obtained elsewhere; but in case a plant is well known by two names we have given them. To those who would study this interesting family scientifically we would recommend the many works upon the subject published by Sir W. Hooker, the Director of the Royal Gardens at Kew, Mr. Smith's Catalogue of Ferns, and the "Index Filicum" of Mr. Moore, of the Botanic Garden at Chelsea. We have endeavoured in these pages to steer as clear of technicalities as possible, employing but a few terms which are now in common use among Fern-growers.

The subject will be treated under the three heads of Stove, Greenhouse, and Hardy Ferns.

THE FERN-HOUSE.

With regard to the house best fitted for the cultivation of these plants, we shall quote the description of one given by Mr. George Abbey, gardener to E. Hailstone, Esq., Horton Hall, Bradford, which was originally published in the *Journal of Horticulture*. It will be too large to suit many of our readers, no doubt, but it will be easy to reduce the size without losing sight of the principle. There are many such houses already built, as, for instance, that of Mr. Backhouse, of York; and the plants look remarkably well planted-out upon the rockwork, and trailing about in a natural way over the rocks and stones. At present, however, we much more commonly see them grown in pots.

"The house that we intend to describe is of the following dimensions:—Length, 100 feet; breadth, 25 feet; and estimated cost, £250. It may be constructed as follows:— First dig out for footings of walls until a solid foundation is reached; and should any difficulty be found in obtaining a solid bottom, throw in concrete composed of one-eighth slaked lime, three-eighths good sharp sand, and one-half coarse gravel or broken stone rubbish.

"Build the walls of good-faced bricks, a brick and a half thick, or of stone, whichever can be obtained the cheapest. Six feet above the ground-level lay a layer of flagstones 8 inches wider than the thickness of the walls. The above said flagstones to be 3 inches thick, to face even with the exterior, but to project 8 inches into the interior of the house at both ends and both sides (the door excepted), on which two hot-water pipes—*i.e.*, a flow and return, are to be fixed hereafter. Build another foot more wall upon the flagstones, which raises the walls to rather more than 7 feet, the height desired.

"The ground plan given is merely to point out to those who have not seen anything of the kind, or have not the eye to draw from certain given details any correct idea of the effect intended to be produced by the carrying-out of the description.

"It is presumed that the site for the house is situated so as to be low enough for the water that supplies the fountain, &c., to be conveyed in iron pipes without having to make a reservoir especially for the purpose. The reservoir should not be less than 10 feet above the ground-level of the house. [For the details of the plan see the following page.]

"We will now proceed with the construction of the rock-work. The material throughout should consist of massive fragments of freestone rock that have been exposed to the weather for a considerable length of time, and, if possible, out of a wood, or where the sun's rays have been but faint. We prefer such from experience, of which we have had a little. Old, shaded stones are frequently covered with Mosses when they are brought from the woods, &c., and on some that we got about a year ago out of the woods in this locality, are thousands of seedling Ferns of no less than

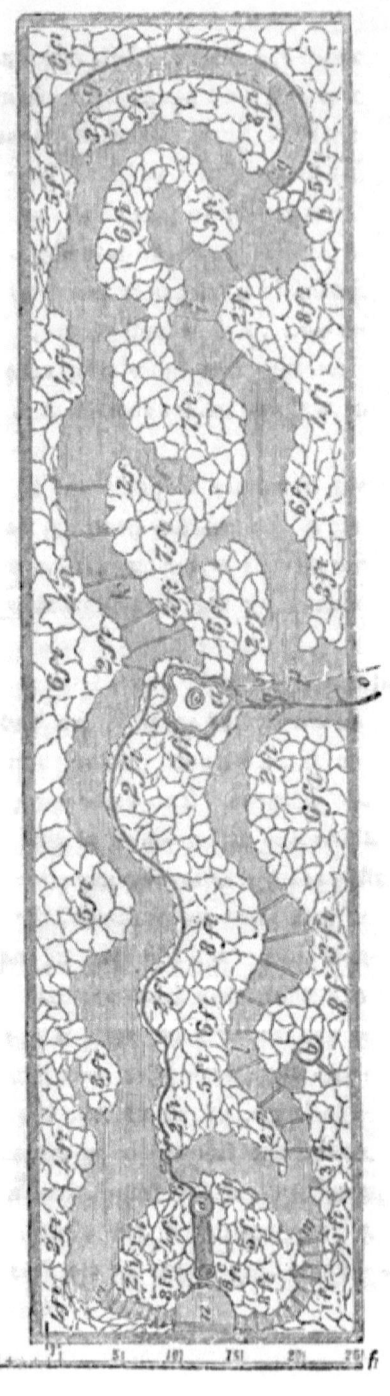

a Fountain (i.e., jet quarter-inch diameter, or less, according to the supply of water).
b Well of water—that is, fed by filtration from the top of same.
c Waterfall, height of the same about 6 feet, one-inch-bore supply-pipe, or less.
d Cistern that receives the water from the waterfall c.
e Open drain formed of stones, with the joists cemented 1 foot wide (stone-ridge coping stones are, with the joints cemented, capital materials for the purpose).
f Cave, with stone seat.
g Subterraneous passage.
h Dropping well.
i Walk, sunk here about 2 feet below its ordinary level, not making any steps, but allowing the flagstones to slope irregularly.

k Ditto to about 5 feet.
l Ditto to about 4 feet.
m n Steps leading to n, where there may be placed a rustic iron chair. The most attractive view of the house when completed will be from this point.
n Place for seat and platform from which to view the house.
o Doorway 5 feet wide.
p Drain that conveys the waste water.
q Water-pipe that supplies the a b c h.
r Point of entrance of the hot-water pipe.

The figures 1, 2, 3, &c., show the height of the rockwork in feet where the figure is fixed, that height being reckoned from the path, whether the same be level or sunk.

eight species, besides thirty species of Moss and Lichens galore, that impart an appearance of age to some rockwork here, which stones from the quarry could not have had for some years.

"We deprecate wood (tree stumps, &c.) for such work under glass, although some people say they are first-rate materials for the purpose, but we have not found them to be such. They may be very well where a collection of Fungi is desired, or to suit the fancy of those who like to do a thing one day and to alter it the next. Wood rots, and the stones that are above or on it fall, and the work has to be done over again at a time when the plants are about their best. Moreover, the plants do not thrive on them as they will do without them, which no doubt is owing to the venomous threads of the various Fungi that harbour there destroying their roots—the very mouth and existence of all plants, terrestrial or epiphytes.

"Commence the formation of the rock at the ends, so that it will be completed at the door. About 200 tons of rock will be required. They can be brought on carts or waggons to the door, thence on a small truck to the place required, and finally placed in position by the aid of a three-legs and blocks. The stones should be laid firm, by no means otherwise. Back stones are a good material for that purpose; soil lowers too much unless rammed down, which it should not. The soil used under the stones should be of a porous nature. Fix every stone firm, and lay them so as to leave some good-sized openings for soil (some large and some small), and fix the water-pipes as the work proceeds, laying them in such a position as to be examined in case of an accident, and so go on until the whole of the rockwork is completed.

"The flagstones should be laid so soon as the rock is completed, and the waterworks should be tried to see that they work satisfactorily. The flagstones should be undressed, and if one side be rougher and uglier than the other, we would lay that side uppermost. We would fix the heating apparatus next. A boiler would be wanted—a twenty-four-inch wrought-iron Monro's cannon boiler will shoot out ample boiling water into the 500 feet of four-inch pipe we would attach to it. This done, we certainly would try it to see that it worked well, of which we have no doubt. The roof should now be put on. The rafters should be 15 feet long, 7 inches by 3 in thickness (that is one sort); but we would have another 15 feet long, 4 inches by $2\frac{1}{2}$. Both these should be ploughed three-quarters of an inch deep by half an inch wide for the glass to rest on, on one of the narrow surfaces, which side, of course, would be placed upwards. The ridge-tree should be 8 inches by $2\frac{1}{2}$, and should be grooved its entire length for the glass to fit into, for we would use no cappings. The wall-plates 12 inches by $2\frac{1}{2}$ in thickness; and we would have a groove in these on the under side, half an inch from the outside edge, to prevent from following the wood the water from the roof that should fall into the spouts: if not grooved, the water follows the wall-plates and runs down the walls. The wall-plates should project exteriorly $1\frac{1}{2}$ inch. The south end should be sashed for glass, the other end should be walled-up of brick or stone. At both ends let there be a ventilator 4 feet by 3, fixed as near the top as possible, one of glass, the other of wood, and have them to work on a swivel.

"There should be double the quantity of rafters of the smaller size to what there is of the other or larger kind.

All the wood to be sound, well-seasoned red deal, dressed, and have a neat moulding on the under side of the rafters and ridge-tree. All the timber employed should have two good coats of lead paint before fixing. This done, commence fixing the roof. Fix a seven-inch rafter first, then two four-inch rafters, then a seven, and so on to the other end, placing them 18 inches asunder, jointing them at the top, and letting them into the wall-plates at bottom to the depth of half an inch. At the top they should enter the ridge-tree not less than three-quarters of an inch. Lay all the joints in white-lead paint and fasten them well, using screws for that purpose. Four cross-tie beams of inch-wrought-iron will be required to prevent the roof (wall-plates) from jutting out at the foot, each 25 feet long, four screw-holes at each end, let them into the wall-plates and screw them fast, one at each end, the other about 33 feet apart. The rafters should also have half-inch iron rods from large rafter to ditto, with a screw-hole opposite the centre of each small rafter. Fix these halfway up the rafters and screw them fast; that will keep the several rafters in their proper line—a point of some consequence to the glazier. Glaze throughout with Hartley's one-eighth-of-an-inch rough plate glass, the squares 1 foot 6 inches wide by 2 feet long, nailing them in with inch copper nails, and puttying the laps, which need not be more than a quarter of an inch. Give two coats of white-lead paint inside and outside, and then a coat of varnish. Our architect work is now at an end, and we are right glad, for we do not feel altogether at home. Perhaps we shall be there presently.

"Soil wherein Ferns are to be grown should be of a porous nature, and that is not liable to become adhesive by frequent and copious supplies of water. One-half turfy peat such as Orchid-growers use, and that which is a light colour, with pieces of decayed moss, and rather sandy, is the best; one-fourth turfy loam, and that which is called yellow or hazel loam is to be preferred; one-eighth pieces of greenstone broken to about the size of a Walnut; one-eighth silver sand; incorporate the above well together, chopping the peat with the spade, but do not pass any of the compost through a riddle. In the above compost they thrive amazingly. They are not benefited by the application of manure, or manure water of any description; and in some species it is so detrimental as to cause death. This applies chiefly to the lesser and fine-rooted kinds. The compost should be worked into the hollows and crevices of the rockwork with a pointed piece of wood or some such like implement. Plants of the small-growing sorts should be planted where the soil is shallow, and the openings between the stones the least. Those that have creeping stems, such as *Davallias*, &c., may be planted where their roots will have the chance of creeping on an overhanging rock: in such a position they are beautiful in the extreme. But as we shall give a list of such kinds as are suited for a greenhouse temperature hereafter, in order to save space we will not deal with that subject at present, except that some Ferns look considerably more to advantage when viewed in certain positions than when they are planted indiscriminately. If the plants have been grown in pots, which they generally are, they may be planted at any season of the year; if not, they should not be disturbed when growing, but rather wait until they are at rest (not growing). March and April are the best months, but we have planted them at all times of the year without failures of any consequence. The roof must be shaded. Tiffany (Shaw's) No. 3 is what most people use, and it answers the purpose admirably. It should be sewed together and nailed on with small tacks (nails) driven through a piece of leather or list about the size of a shilling. It should remain on permanently, and will last three years.

"*Watering.*—Some people imagine that Ferns are aquatics; at all events, they get generally too much of that they are fond of—viz., a moist atmosphere, sufficient water at the root as to prevent the fronds from flagging, and, when growing, an abundance of it—that is, when they are in want of water, give them a good drink, and not deal out to them half-allowances. Cold, dry currents of air are to be avoided, for it dries them up like cut grass under a July's sun. At all times the stones (rock) should be kept moist; and during the hotter summer months a light sprinkling overhead from the syringe every day at even is very beneficial."

SOIL.

To grow Ferns satisfactorily the right soil is an important point. Growing, as they generally do, in the thickets or jungles, in hot climates, where the soil is principally formed of decayed leaves, small branches of trees, their roots small and fibrous, in a close moist atmosphere, we have only to imitate such circumstances, and success will attend our efforts. In this country we must have houses artificially heated to the requisite degree, and the proper soil or compost procured. The materials for this compost, that we have used with perfect success, can be easily procured in most parts of Britain. They consist of vegetable mould, formed of decayed leaves, peat soil or, as it is generally termed, heath mould, silver sand, and sphagnum or bog moss. We mix these in the following proportions—

vegetable or leaf mould, one or two years old, one-third; fibrous peat, one-third; bog moss, finely chopped, one-third; and as much silver sand as will give it a whitish-silvery appearance. For very small plants we put this compost through a rather fine sieve; but for large plants we do not sift it at all, only pulling the peat in pieces, and taking out the very roughest pieces, stones, or other extraneous matters, mixing it thoroughly with the other materials, and using it in a state of moderate dryness and warmth. When mixed it has a considerable resemblance to the compost we use for most of the Orchid tribe.

In this rich, light, open compost the roots of the Ferns run freely, and the plants riot in health and luxuriance, due care being given to supply them with the proper heat and moisture; of which, more anon.

POTTING.

Ferns are, in this point, something like Heaths; they will not thrive luxuriantly if pot-bound, and therefore should be frequently repotted. Young plants from the seed-pan should be potted three times during the summer—the first time in March, the second in June, and the third in September. Larger plants will do well if potted in March and August.

In potting, the first thing to attend to is the drainage; for, though these plants love moisture, they will not thrive in stagnant water retained in the pots. The best material for drainage is broken potsherds, covered with a thin layer of moss. Place a large piece over the hole at the bottom of the pot, some smaller pieces over that, and a layer of some still smaller upon them; then a covering of moss, and upon it a small quantity of the rough fibres of the peat.

In shifting very large specimens it is sometimes advisable to reverse a small pot over the hole at the bottom before putting in the draining materials. Examine the balls attached to the roots; if they are very dry, soak them thoroughly in tepid water, and let them have time to drain off the superfluous moisture. If potted in a dry state, it is almost impossible ever to wet the old ball thoroughly, and the plant, consequently, languishes and turns sickly for a long time. If the ball is in a proper state of moisture it may be potted at once.

These plants will bear a large shift in such a light, open compost. Small plants may be allowed a full inch between the old ball and the sides of the new pot; and larger plants may have from $1\frac{1}{2}$ to 2 inches. Fill in the pot as much soil over the drainage as will raise the ball nearly level with the rim, then place the plant upon it, and fill the compost round it, pressing it down pretty firmly as the soil is put in. When quite full, give the pot a smart stroke or two upon the bench, to settle the soil equally in every part, and be careful to leave sufficient room between the top of the pot and the soil to hold water sufficient to wet the whole thoroughly every time water is applied. This space, as a matter of course, must be small for small plants, and so on in proportion to the size. Very large plants will require a full inch to hold water enough to wet such large balls.

The reader may here exclaim, "But how shall I know when the soil in the pots is thoroughly wetted?" In all the operations of gardening there is none that requires more judgment and experience than that of watering. Many a fine Fern, and Heath, too, have perished by improper treatment in watering, and that, in a great measure, has arisen from injudicious potting. If the space between the soil and the rim of the pot is too scanty, the water given will only wet 2 or 3 inches below the surface, the remainder will be as dry as the deserts of Arabia, and the roots miserably perish. The only sure way to find this out is to turn out the ball an hour or two after watering it, and it will soon be seen whether the water has penetrated to the bottom. The ball may also be so hard that the water runs down the sides of the pot without entering it. In such a case we thrust a sharp-pointed stick or iron rod into the ball, making numerous holes to allow the water to penetrate to the centre. In very severe cases, we have sometimes recovered a plant dying for want of water in the centre of the ball, by placing it in water long enough to soak it thoroughly; but such extreme cases will seldom, if ever, occur, if due attention is paid at the time of potting to leave space enough below the rim of the pot to hold water. The cultivator may soon, by experience, learn when the ball of earth in the pots is in a proper condition of moisture by sound—that is, by striking the side of the pot with his knuckles; if the sound be dull or heavy the soil is moist, but if the sound be clear and sharp the plant needs water.

PROPAGATION.

By Spores.—In our moist stoves, and more especially the Orchid-house, the more common kinds spring up from spores so much and so freely as to become troublesome. We remember a wall on the north side of an Orchid-house, at Pine Apple Place, which, partly from its situation, and partly from being syringed every day to moisten blocks of wood on which Orchids grew, was kept constantly moist. On this wall the common *Pteris serrulata* grew so thickly from spores as completely to cover it; so much so, that it became necessary to pull them away, and whitewash the wall, to prevent the Ferns from growing so much. And in Messrs. Loddige's Orchid-house there were growing on the walls quantities of the *Adiantum capillus-Veneris*, chiefly seedling plants. These facts point out forcibly how we ought to propagate Ferns from spores.

We have raised great numbers of choice species by placing a slightly moss-covered brick under a hand-light, in a moist heat, or shady part of an Orchid-house, or even common stove. On these bricks we scattered the spores, and soon had the pleasure to observe them growing; the only care bestowed was surrounding the bricks with common green moss, and keeping it moist by frequent sprinklings of tepid water. We were careful, of course, to sow spores, and not dust; for the capsules or spore-cases soon burst, the spores fly off, and leave nothing but their cases behind. The best way to be certain of real spores is to frequently brush off on the brick the real spores before they fly off from the fronds. The spores themselves have much the appearance of dust, and require a strong magnifier to distinguish them. If the desired species sown upon these bricks do not vegetate, the operator may be sure that no spores have been sown. Some kinds will not vegetate by this method, but may be raised under a bell-glass. To effect this, fill a pot with the compost described for potting Ferns in, sift a portion through a very fine sieve, and place it about half-an-inch thick upon the compost; then give it a good watering, so as thoroughly to wet the whole of the soil. Fit a bell-glass to the pot, lift it off again, and sow the spores upon the moist soil. The best way to sow the spores is first to cut off two or three fronds, and brush off the spores on to a white sheet of paper, then, with the finger and thumb, sow the spores evenly all over the surface of the moist earth. Place upon it a bell-glass, and set the pot in a shady part of the stove or Orchid-house. The sun must never be allowed to shine upon the bell-glass.

Fern-spores will keep for an extraordinary length of time. The late Mr. Shepherd, Curator of the Botanic Garden at Liverpool, obtained a crop of many kinds of stove Ferns by sowing them in pots filled with peat earth, covering each pot with a flat piece of common glass, and where the cultivator has no bell-glass he might adopt the same method. To prevent drip from the condensed water on the under side of the flat glass, all that he would have to do would be to turn the glass over when the vapour had condensed; the air of the house would take it off the glass. If bell-glasses are used (and we greatly prefer them) they will require wiping dry occasionally. The bell-glass should be a little smaller than the pot, so that water could be poured gently upon it to wet the surface of the soil whenever it appears dry. The spores are so minute, and so easily perish, that the finest rose-pot would infallibly destroy them, but by applying the water over the bell-glass, the soil, by capillary attraction, becomes gradually moistened, and thus the delicate spores are preserved uninjured. If all goes on favourably the plants will soon make their appearance, probably mixed with several common species. Some recommend baking the soil to prevent these from growing; but we always find seedlings of the desired species did not come up so freely, if at all, in soil so prepared. The experienced eye will soon detect the kinds wanted to grow, and the rest may be weeded out as soon as they are distinguished from the species expected. When these have attained their second or third fronds they should be pricked-out, as it is technically termed, thinly over the surface of fresh pots, in fresh compost, at about an inch apart. In this position they may be allowed to grow till the fronds touch each other, then pot them off singly into thumb-pots, place them in a shady place till they are fairly established, and then subject them to the same management as the larger established plants.

By Division.—Many kinds of Ferns can be propagated successfully by division. Some send out stolones or creeping rootshoots—the *Adiantum assimile* is a notable example—and these can be easily detached from the parent plant, potted and shaded for a few days, and then soon make good plants. These suckers, as they may be termed, are most conveniently detached at the time of potting; or a pot well filled with them may be taken to the potting-bench, the soil shaken off, and the plant divided into as many divisions as it will make, then potted separately, and shaded till established. Others that do not send out these side shoots or suckers may be divided into several plants, care being taken that each division has a good lot of roots to it. The *Adiantum cuneatum*, and several others, may be divided into several pieces or plants in this manner. One point we must not forget to mention, and that is, *young plants are most certain to grow when thus divided*. Old plants we have divided into apparently well-rooted divisions, and such we have often found to fail nearly entirely. Divisions of two-year-old plants, that have several crowns, succeed almost every one; but from plants three or four years old they almost as generally fail to grow.

INSECTS.

The brown scale is, perhaps, the most troublesome of all

the insect pests to which these plants are subject. They must be kept down by hand; and this should be done while they are young and light-coloured, otherwise their eggs are scattered, and the mischief is only increased. Mealy bug, with its tufts of white woolly substance, is not often seen among Ferns. Thrips are more frequently found; but generally speaking, as we have elsewhere shown, they are often a sign that the plant is grown in too much heat. They should be kept down, taking the plant as soon as they are noticed, laying it upon its side on the turf or on a mat, and syringing it off. Smoking with tobacco will also destroy them, as well as the green fly, which will make its appearance in spring when the plants are throwing up their new fronds.

FERN PILLARS.

Mr. J. Tyerman, the present Curator of the Liverpool Botanic Gardens, pointed out a very ornamental way of growing Ferns, a few years ago, in the pages of the *Cottage Gardener*. The annexed woodcut will give an idea of the effect which may thus be produced in the conservatory. Its construction will be understood by Mr. Tyerman's description. He says:—

"I am very desirous of calling your attention to a Fern-brick, the invention of Dr. Watson, a medical gentleman of this city. I have enclosed a few pencil sketches, showing the adaptability of them to various purposes of ornamental Fern-growing. The original intention of the inventor was to form a temporary wall or pier with square bricks, so that they might be taken out and replaced at pleasure; but I consider their greatest merit is to adapt them for ornamental conservatory or greenhouse decoration. A few explanations will give you my meaning.

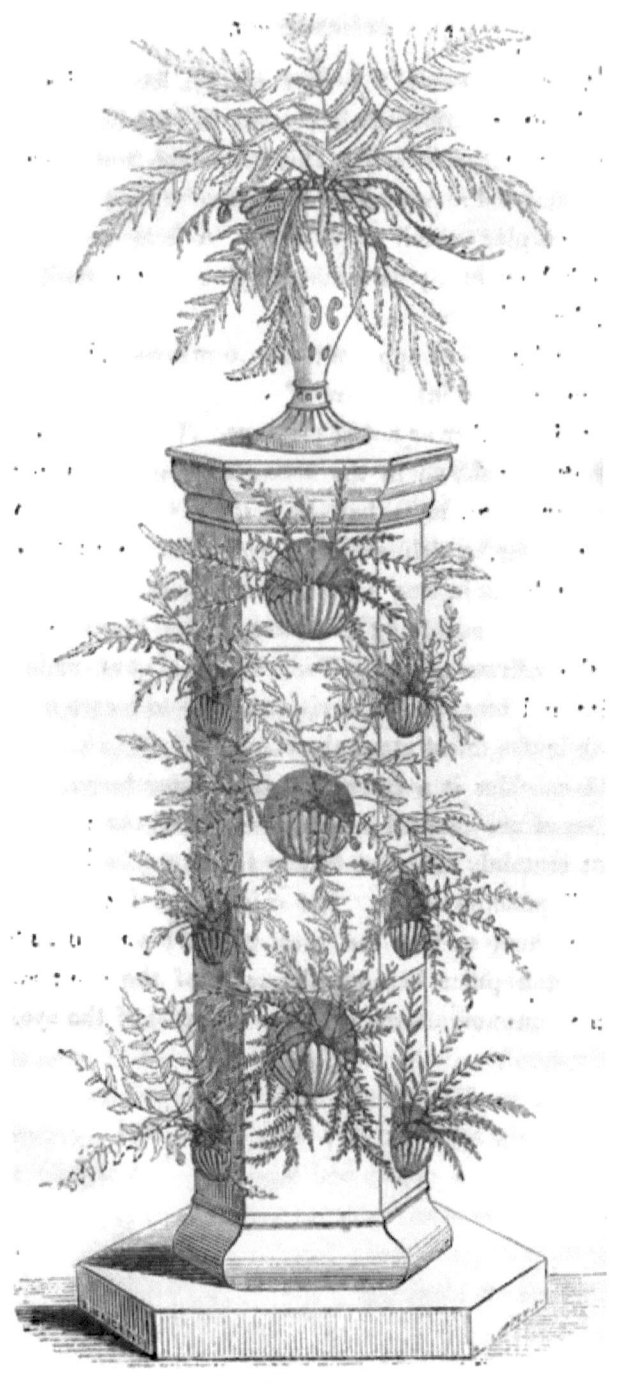

"A square brick, 9 inches by 4½, having its centre scooped out, a scollop-shell pattern is modelled to fit the lower part of the hollow. This forms the front, and has a very ornamental appearance. They can be built one over the other for a pier or wall at pleasure. A hole in the bottom of the hollow cavity is made, sloping to the back of the brick, for drainage.

"The invention appears to me to possess the most merit when constructed into pillars of any convenient height, and cemented together or not at pleasure. The hollow space in the centre, as shown in the accompanying sketch, could be filled with damp moss, hay, &c.; the vase on the top containing water, which could be contrived so as to slowly percolate by adjusting a cork to the hole in the bottom; and the water, supplying the roots of the Ferns by passing into the centre of the pillar, would always maintain a regular and an abundant moisture, so as to insure a healthy growth in the driest atmosphere.

"I consider it a matter of small importance which of the Ferns are planted north or south in the sides of the pillar; certainly the most fragile fronds would be benefited with all possible shade. The chief point I consider is to arrange them so that the erect-growing ones occupy the part of the pillar beneath the level of the eye; and the drooping ones on a level, or above the level of the eye."

STOVE FERNS.

In giving a list of Stove Ferns, we shall confine ourselves to such as can be readily procured, easily cultivated, and are of considerable beauty—three points of great importance to cultivators generally. The task is rather a heavy one, because there have been lately great alterations made in the names of Ferns by various writers upon this family. We shall, however, use the names commonly adopted, and arrange them alphabetically, as being more easy of reference, adding occasional hints of such peculiar cultivation as each species may require.

ACROPHORUS. See *Leucostegia*.

ACROSTICHUM.

ACROSTICHUM AUREUM, *Fig.* 1.—A Fern of considerable size, growing from 8 to 10 feet high, and sometimes making a stem 3 feet high, consequently requiring a large stove to grow it in. The fertile fronds are erect. Two or three of the lower pinnæ on the fronds are often barren. The barren leaves, or fronds, are 6 feet long, bending downwards, with thin, light green, side leaflets, or pinnæ. The fronds stand upon the top of an erect stem. To grow it well, pot it in turfy loam and sand kept very moist, and give a heat in summer of 80°. It is a noble species, native of morasses in the tropics both of the eastern and western hemispheres.

ADIANTUM.

The *Adiantums* are a large family of the most ornamental, and best known, perhaps, of any genus of Ferns. We shall find them growing in the stove, the greenhouse, and the open air; though they will all bear the stove, and flourish well in it, providing the more hardy ones have a short season of rest. They may generally be known by their black stalks and delicate foliage.

ADIANTUM BRASILIENSE (Brazilian).—A beautiful Brazilian Fern, growing a foot or more high. The fronds are twice-pinnated—that is, the midrib sends out side leaflets, and these again send out lesser side leaflets : hence they are termed bipinnate. The stalks are slightly hairy. Requires stove heat, and soil of an open texture. It is evergreen.

A. CARDIOCHLŒNA (Heart-shaped, referring to form of indusium).—A na-

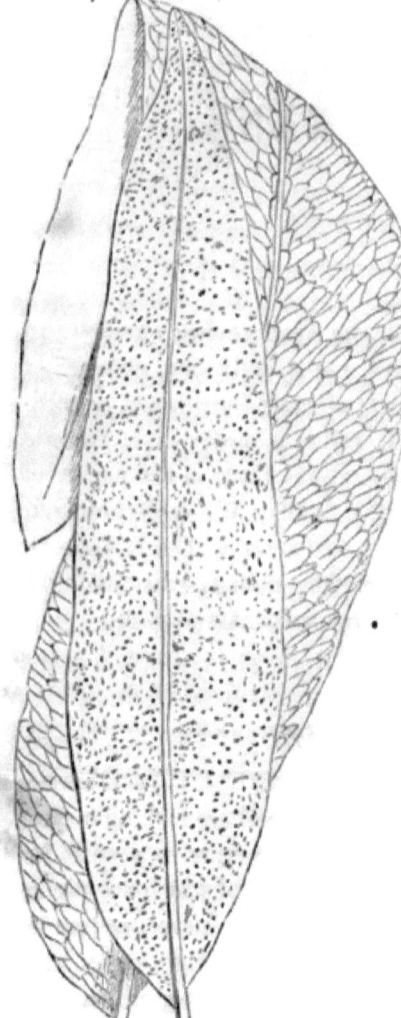

Fig. 1. Acrostichum aureum.

tive of tropical America. One of the largest-growing and most beautiful species in the whole genus. When well grown it will attain a height of 3 feet. It was introduced by M. Linden, of Brussels. This is sometimes called *A. polyphyllum.*

A. CAUDATUM (Tailed).—A very neat East-Indian Fern, with a long process at the end of the frond, which forms a kind of minute bulb, and roots readily when it touches the soil. It is a pinnated Fern, each frond growing a foot or more long. Is very ornamental when grown in a small ornamental basket.

A. CRISTATUM (Crested).—A native of Jamaica. Fronds bipinnate, each frond growing nearly a foot long. Sometimes called *A. villosum.* A very pretty and distinct species, with erect fronds and pinnules overlapping each other.

A. CURVATUM (Curved-leaved).—From Brazil. The fronds are pedate—that is, have the appearance of a bird's foot, each pinnated leaflet spreading out in that form from a common centre. A very elegant well-known Fern, growing sometimes 2 feet high; requires plenty of pot room, and a free open compost to grow in. It is evergreen.

A. CUNEATUM (Wedge-shaped).—Native of Brazil. May be readily known by its wedge-shaped pinnæ. Very beautiful and plentiful, and easily increased by division. This Fern is much used in Covent Garden for bouquets, to mix with and set off, by its lively green fronds and delicate black-polished stalks, the brightly-coloured flowers.

A. CONCINNUM (Neat).—From the West Indies and tropical America. This affords an example of a twice-pinnated frond, the lower pinnules covering the axil of the pinna. They bend gracefully downwards, and grow, when well cultivated, 2 feet long. We have grown this Fern in a pot 10 inches in diameter, in light compost, 2 feet through, and nearly 3 feet high. It is very elegant, and easily increased by division.

A. FOVEANUM (Mr. Foy's).—Native of Brazil. Sometimes called *A. intermedium.* It may be known by the fertile or spore-bearing fronds growing erect, and the barren ones drooping or bending downwards. When young the fronds have a reddish-brown appearance. They are bipinnate, growing, with good culture, 2 feet high. The stalks are hairy.

A. FORMOSUM (The Handsome).—From New Holland. Though this very handsome Fern will exist in a greenhouse, yet it grows so much finer in a moderately-heated stove, that we have introduced it here as a stove Fern. It is three times pinnated. It is a splendid Fern. We have had it 3 feet high, and several of the fronds 2 feet across. The stalks are black, and rather woolly at the base or rootstock.

A. LUNULATUM (Crescent-leaved).—An East-Indian deciduous Fern—that is, it dies down to the root in winter. The fronds droop downwards, rooting at the end in the same way as *A. caudatum*. From these end-rooting fronds it may be propagated. Each rooted end should be cut off, potted, and kept in a close heat till fresh fronds are formed; it will then be a separate good plant. The fronds are crescent-shaped, and thinly placed on the stalk. It is a truly elegant Fern, suitable for basket-culture on account of its pendulous habit. Very apt to perish whilst in a dormant state in winter if kept too wet or too dry.

A. MACROPHYLLUM (Broad-leaved).—This Jamaica Fern is the broadest-leaved of all the *Adiantums;* and, when well-grown, truly handsome. It requires, however, the warmest part of the stove to bring it to perfection. It is of an erect habit, and the young fronds are of a reddish colour. The fronds are twice-pinnate, and grow from 1 to 1½ foot in height. An open light compost suits it best.

A. PENTADACTYLON (Five-fingered).—A Brazilian species allied to *A. curvatum*, of which it is probably only a variety. It is a handsome Fern, lately introduced from the continental nurseries. Messrs. A. Henderson & Co. had it from Mr. Van Houtte, of the Ghent Nursery. We had fronds of it 18 inches high and a foot in diameter. The difference between it and *curvatum* appears to consist in the more regular length of each pinnated frond, and their disposition into five pinnæ in the pedate form. It requires a warm stove.

A. RENIFORME (Kidney-shape-leaved).—An elegant, dwarf, evergreen Fern, from Madeira, with simple fronds growing on stalks from 3 to 6 inches long. It will exist in a good greenhouse, but we have always found it difficult to keep alive and in health there. The fronds are uncommonly beautiful, of a bright shining green. The spore-masses are placed close to the edge of the reniform fronds, and nearly touch each other. Every collection ought to have a specimen of this charming little Fern.

A. ASARIFOLIUM (Asarum-leaved).—A native of Mauritius and Bourbon is now generally looked upon as a variety of the preceding species. It differs only in being larger, more coriaceous or leathery, and the two lobes at the base of the frond being developed, so as to meet or even to overlap.

A. SETULOSUM (Bristly).—This species is from Norfolk Island. Frond bipinnate or twice-winged. It may be known at once by the black bristle-like hairs of the upper surface of the fronds. A free-growing species, easily increased by division.

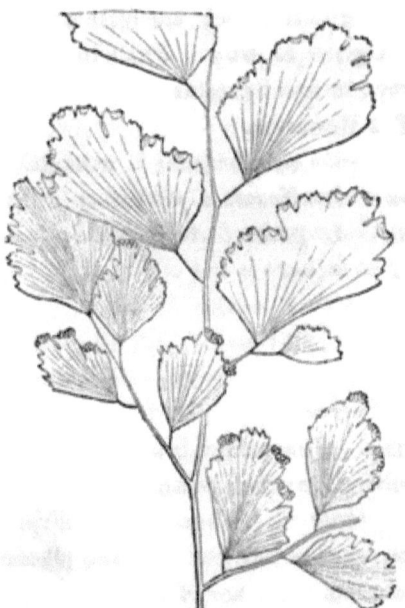

Fig. 2. Adiantum tenerum. (Natural size.)

A. TENERUM (Tender), *Fig.* 2.—From the West Indies. Is a 'very beautiful Fern, easily propagated by dividing the creeping rhizome or rootstock. It is evergreen, glabrous, growing 2 feet high, with the fronds four times pinnated or branched; each leaflet is rhomboidal, and a beautiful bright green.

A. TRAPEZIFORME (Trapezium-leaved).—A native of the West Indies. When this Fern is well grown we know of none more ornamental. To effect this it should be frequently potted; and if some small charcoal is mixed with the compost it will thrive much better. It may be increased by division as well as by spores. Its fronds are large, and the spore-masses are beautifully arranged on the edges. Stalks black and shining. It ought to be in every collection however small.

A. WILSONI (Wilson's).—A native of Jamaica. Fronds ternate or pinnate, with five pinnæ, which are leathery and dark green. It is a difficult plant to grow. From the veins being somewhat anastomosed, it has by some botanists been placed in another genus called Hewardia.

There are several other species of Adiantum in cultivation besides those enumerated, as *A. betulinum, A. flexuosum* (called also *A. Feei*), *A. obliquum, A. patens, A. pulverulentum, A. Wilesianum*, and others; and there is not one of them but is well deserving of cultivation.

ALSOPHILA.

A genus of large tree Ferns. Where there is plenty of room they are well worthy of cultivation; but in small collections their culture should not be attempted. They may be distinguished by their sori or spore-masses being round, and placed regularly about halfway between the edge of the pinnæ and the midrib, generally, but not always, at the end of the veins which branch out at regular intervals from the midrib. In cultivation they require plenty of pot room, and must never become dry.

There is great confusion among the names of tree Ferns,

more so than in any other division of the family. In no two gardens can you find a plant called by the same name. This may, perhaps, be accounted for by the fact that they are seldom seen in this country of a size sufficient to develope their true characters.

ALSOPHILA ARTICULATA (Jointed), *Fig. 3.*—A noble evergreen Fern from Jamaica, growing 5 feet high, with fronds 6 or 8 feet long. They are bipinnate, jointed or articulated with a rachis or stalk, which is covered with spines and scales.

A. FEROX (Rough or Prickly).—A West-Indian Fern. This may be known at once by the thorny prickles on the main stalk, as well as on those of the pinnæ. It is a large-growing species. The fronds are terminal on a stout stem, 5 feet high in this country, though it, of course, grows much higher in its shady native localities.

A. PRUINATA (Frosted-leaved).—From Brazil and West India Islands. This is a singular-looking species; the fronds and stalks are covered with soft woolly-looking hairs, giving the plant an appearance like hoar frost: hence its specific name. It is thrice and sometimes four times pinnated, with the fronds from 4 to 6 feet long. This plant is often called *Lophosoria pruinata.*

A. VILLOSA (Shaggy).—An evergreen Fern from Columbia. Distinguished from the preceding species by the stalks and fronds being covered all over with long, shaggy, hair-like processes. The fronds

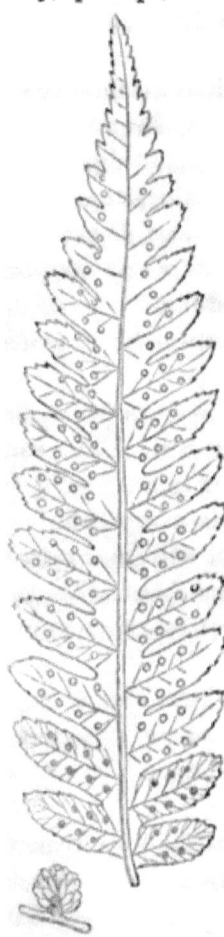

Fig. 3. Alsophila articulata; leaflet full size, with sorus rather magnified, and divided vertically to show the elevated receptacle.

also are somewhat longer, being often 7 feet in length, though the main stalk that supports them is low.

ANEMIA.

The name of this group of Ferns is derived from *aneimon*, a word meaning naked, in allusion to the two spikes which bear the spore-masses, and which in the fertile fronds always start from the lower leafy portion of the frond. All the species are easily raised from spores; and, as most of them do not make a creeping rhizome, this is the only way in which they can be increased. They are most of them small-growing plants, and are, consequently, well adapted for cultivation in glazed cases.

ANEMIA ADIANTIFOLIA (Adiantum-like).—A native of the warm parts of America. A very pretty little Fern, with fronds triangular in outline, 9 inches long and about 3 in width, twice-divided. This plant must not be overpotted.

A. COLLINA (Hill).—A West-Indian Fern with hairy pinnate (once-divided) fronds. The fronds are about a foot in length; and the pinnæ, or divisions, are ovate in form, tapering towards the top.

A. DREGEANA (Dreg's).—This beautiful little Fern is somewhat rare yet. It is like the last species in general appearance, but smaller, of a darker green colour, and smooth instead of being very hairy.

A. VILLOSA (Hairy).—This Fern also comes from tropical America. It is rather a small grower, with triangular fronds not more than a foot in length, including the hairy stipes. The fronds have a greyish colour. It is also called *A. flexuosa*, and *A. tomentosa*.

ANEMIDICTYON.

This genus, in habit and general appearance, closely resembles the last, and differs from it only in having netted instead of free veins. This peculiarity is pointed out by the name.

ANEMIDICTYON PHYLLITIDIS (Phyllis-like).—A well-known and common Fern, originally imported from America. The pinnate fronds are about 18 inches in height. There are several distinct varieties of this plant, as *A. fraxinifolium*, with narrow pinnæ and more erect fronds, and *A. hirtum* with more hairy fronds.

ANETIUM.

ANETIUM CITRIFOLIUM (Citron-leaved), *Fig.* 4.—A genus of West-Indian Ferns approaching *Acrostichum*, from which it may be distinguished at once by the spore-masses being irregularly scattered all over the under surface of the fronds. There is only one species in cultivation. Its fronds are simple—that is, not divided, and the rootstock creeping. By this it may be increased.

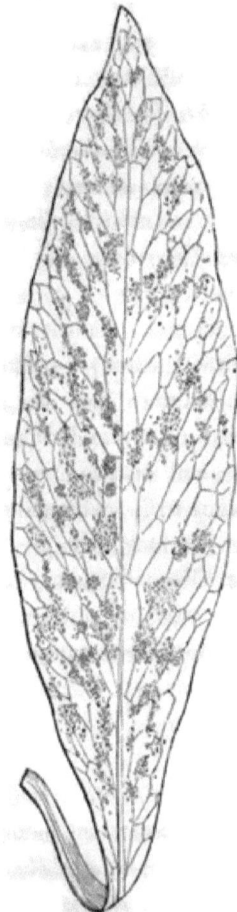

Fig. 4. Anetium citrifolium.
(Entire frond medium size.)

ANTROPHYUM.

ANTROPHYUM LANCEOLATUM (Spear-head-leaved), *Fig.* 5.—A West-Indian, dwarf, simple-fronded Fern; curious from the fact that the spore-masses are growing in channels, as it were, sunk in the frond. The fronds grow a foot long, and are of a narrow lance-shape, and thickly set on a short rootstock or rhizome. It is a very curious, interesting, dwarf, evergreen Fern, and worthy of general cultivation.

ARTHROPTERIS.

A genus very nearly allied to *Lastrea*. It was named by Mr. J. Smith, of Kew, one of the best authorities upon Ferns. The name is derived from *arthron*, a joint, and *pteris* a Fern; and refers to the articulation about halfway up the stalks of the fronds.

ARTHROPTERIS ALBO-PUNCTATA (White-dotted). — The fronds are about a foot high, lanceolate in form, twice-divided, deep green, and with the upper surface dotted with small white spots near the margin. It is a native of West Africa. It should be grown in a wire basket; the creeping rhizomes can then make their way out in every direction, and will soon cause it to be a mass of fronds.

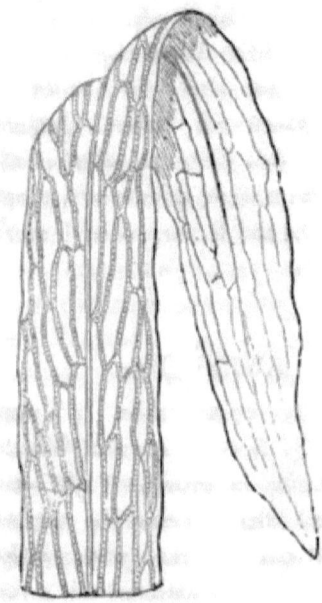

Fig. 5. Antrophyum lanceolatum.
(Top of frond natural size.)

ASPIDIUM.

From *aspidion*, a little shield, the spore-masses being covered with a shield or protecting skin. The genus *Aspidium* was formerly a very large one, but modern botanists have reduced the number of species considerably; the rest are divided into at least ten genera. This genus is very subject to the attacks of the brown scale; indeed it is very difficult to keep the Aspidiums clean.

ASPIDIUM TRIFOLIATUM (Three-leaved), *Fig. 6.*—A somewhat dwarf, West-Indian species. The spore-masses are regularly distributed over the middle part of the fertile fronds, and are exceedingly beautiful. The fronds are not always trifoliate, for there are generally two pairs of pinnæ besides the terminal one. On account of its being dwarf, having fine, large, evergreen pinnæ, and elegant veining, with its beautiful shield-like sori or spore-masses, this species is very desirable.

A. MACROPHYLLUM (Broad-leaved).—A West-Indian, evergreen, noble, strong-growing Fern, with pinnated fronds nearly 3 feet long. Spore-masses kidney-shaped, and very regularly distributed on each side of the midrib of the pinnæ. The fronds are large and of a pale green.

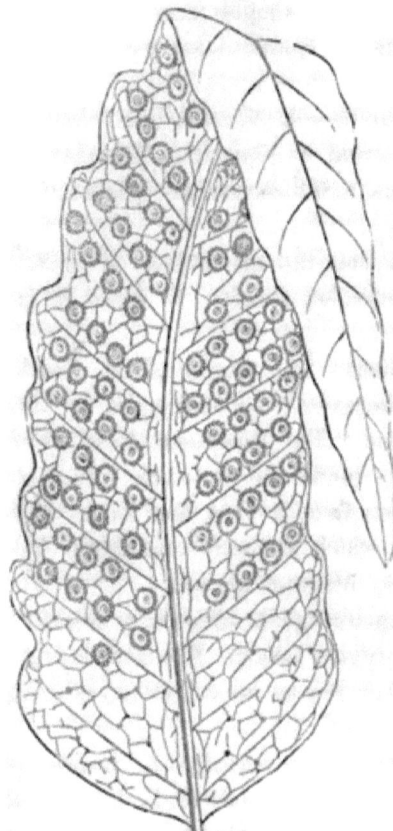

Fig. 6. Aspidium trifoliatum. (Pinna natural size.)

The species above mentioned are those most worthy of cultivation; but there are several others to be found in gardens, as *A. apiifolium, A. cicutarium, A. coadunatum, A. ebenum,* &c.

ASPLENIUM.

A large assemblage of beautiful Ferns are arranged under this name. They may be known by examining the arrangement of the spore-masses. These are placed on the upper side of the veins, running in lines from the midrib of each leaflet. The fronds are various, from a simple form to pinnate, bipinnate, and tripinnate, but the spore-masses are uniformly long, narrow, and simple.

Asplenium auritum (Eared).—A West-Indian pinnated Fern, with the pinnæ twice-parted or bipartite. The plant is easily propagated by division, as its crowns are produced in clusters.

A. bifidum (Forked).—A beautiful species from Mauritius, with somewhat erect finely-divided fronds. It must be increased by spores.

A. brasiliensis (Brazilian).—The fronds of this South-American Asplenium are simple—a rare occurrence in this genus. It is sometimes called "*The Bird's-nest Fern*," from its fronds being set circularly round the rootstock. They are frequently in cultivation seen from 3 to 4 feet long. This is a variety of *A. serratum*, which it nearly resembles. The same name is applied to a very different species.

A. brachypteron (Channel-winged).—This is a beautiful, low-growing, rare Fern from Sierra Leone. The fronds spread horizontally, much in the same way as an Adiantum, growing only 8 or 9 inches high.

A. cicutarium (Water-Hemlock-leaved).—A native of tropical America. The fronds are thrice-divided; it is one of the prettiest species of the family. Increased by spores.

A. Dalhousianum (Lord Dalhousie's).—This is also called *A. alternans*. It is a native of the Himalayan Mountains. The form of the fronds is very like that of the Ceterach, but it is without the scales which distinguish that Fern. It was introduced recently by Mr. R. Sim, Nurseryman, of Foot's Cray.

A. diversifolium (Various-leaved).—Called also *A. dimorphum*. It is a native of Norfolk Island. Though this singular Fern will exist in a greenhouse, yet it thrives much better in a moderately-heated stove. The fronds vary much—some are narrow and fertile, others are broader and barren; whilst others are partly fertile and partly barren. We once had a plant with a rather long rhizome, and at each of the joints of the rootstock there sprung up a plant, evidently a sucker. We allowed them to grow till they produced roots, and then carefully detached them from the parent plant, potted them in small pots, and placed them under a hand-light, where they soon made fresh roots and growth, thus giving us a good stock of this rather rare elegantly-curious Fern.

A. FALCATUM (Sickle-leaved).—An East-Indian, beautiful, evergreen Fern, with stout leathery fronds deeply cut at the edges. The fronds frequently, when well grown, reach 2 feet high. It seldom can be propagated by division, but grows freely from seed.

A. FORMOSUM (Handsome).—A native of the West Indies and the tropical parts of America. The fronds are pinnate (once-divided), with deeply-cut pinnæ. The fronds radiate from a crown, and droop gracefully on every side. This very beautiful Fern was extremely rare until recently, but it is now becoming more plentiful.

A. LASERPITIIFOLIUM.—This long name means having leaves like those of an umbelliferous plant called *Laserpitium*. It is a native of Java, and was introduced a few years ago by Messrs. Rollisson. When full grown the fronds are $2\frac{1}{2}$ feet long, and four or five times divided. It is a very graceful species; but there is no other means of increasing it except from spores, and it is still somewhat scarce.

A. LÆTUM (Gay).—One of the tropical forms of *A. marinum*. A bright green, erect-growing, pinnated Fern from the West Indies, of great beauty, growing 2 feet high. The rootstock is erect, and sometimes branching, by which it may be increased. It loves light, open, rich soil, and liberal pot room.

A. MONANTHEMUM (One-flowered, in reference to there being but one sorus upon each division of the frond).—It has been found in the warmer parts of America, in South Africa, and in Madeira. It is a very neat little plant, well suited for Wardian cases. The fronds are 4 or 5 inches long, only once-divided, and these divisions so close together as sometimes almost to overlap.

A. OBLIQUUM (Oblique-leaved).—A native of the Polynesian Islands, and found by Mr. Allan Cunningham in the dense forests of Wangaroa, in the warm part of New Zealand. The dark green glossy fronds are once-divided; the divisions being lance-shaped, oblique at the base, and toothed along the margin.

A. OBTUSILOBUM (Blunt-lobed).—This Fern has been recently introduced by Mr. Veitch, of Chelsea, from the New Hebrides. A very pretty little Fern, having fronds about 3 or 4 inches high. It makes runners, which produce little plants at the points. In this way it may be readily propagated. It will be very suitable for growing in a suspended basket.

A. OLIGOPHYLLUM (Few-leaved).—A Brazilian Fern, with oblong lance-shaped leaflets, pinnated on the frond, which attains a foot in length; and, therefore, may be considered a dwarf Fern fit to grow in a small collection. The leaflets are thinly placed on the frond: hence its specific name. The rootstock creeps; and, therefore, may be increased by division.

A. PULCHELLUM (Fair).—A West-Indian, pinnated, dwarf Fern, with slender elegant fronds about 9 inches long. The leaves, or pinnæ, are lance-shaped, rather curved. The spore-masses are long and narrow, and of a bright brown colour, very beautiful. It is one of the most elegant Ferns of the genus that require stove culture; easily increased by division.

A. PUMILUM (Dwarf).—This is another West-Indian little gem, but is rather scarce in collections. It seldom grows more than a few inches high, and has been lately introduced from the Parisian gardens. The fronds are of triangular shape—a rare form in this genus. The stalks and fronds are downy, feeling like velvet to the touch. It generally loses its fronds in winter. As soon as this little gem is sufficiently increased it ought to be in every collection. The rootstock is creeping; and, therefore, it may readily be increased by division.

A. PLANICAULE (Smooth-stalked).—An East-Indian Fern, easily increased by its creeping rhizomes. It is, however, worthy of cultivation, on account of its beautiful lively green foliage. The stalks are dark-coloured; the fronds bipinnate, slender, and somewhat triangularly-formed, growing 1½ foot high, rather erect, and thickly set on the creeping rhizomes.

A. RADICANS (Rooting).—A Cuban Fern, grows 1½ foot long. This may be distinguished by the termination of the frond being devoid of pinnæ, and forming a tuft that produces roots first, and afterwards fronds, forming a plant if it touches the soil, and also by the black stalks.

A. RACHIRHIZON (Rachis-rooting).—The *Asplenium rhizophorum* of gardens. This is a beautiful dark green species, and worthy of general cultivation. Like the preceding species, it is easily increased by the rooting apex of full-grown fronds. All these rooting Ferns should have the end of the tuft-bearing frond pegged-down either in small separate pots set conveniently near the parent plant, or on the soil of the pot containing the plant. The first is the best method, because then the young plant, when established, will not require to be taken up and potted, but will have its roots undisturbed in its little pot till it needs more pot room.

A. SERRA (Saw-leaved).—A pinnated Brazilian Fern of great beauty. We have grown it in a ten-inch pot 3 feet high, and as much through, with twenty fronds in the pot. The fronds rise first erect, then gracefully curve downwards. The leaflets are of a beautiful light green, shining, and very regularly deep-cut at the edges like the teeth of a saw. The stalks are thickly covered with narrow brown scales, and stand upon a thick, scaly, creeping rootstock. Easily increased by division.

A. SERRATUM (Cut-leaved).—The fronds of this noble

Jamaican Fern are simple, 2 feet long and 4 inches wide in the broadest part, and cut at the edges. They form a circle on an erect rootstock, similar to the well-known Bird's-nest Fern. Slow of increase by division, but grows freely from spores.

A. VEITCHIANUM (Veitch's).—This Fern, which is almost as well known under the name of *A. Belangeri*, is a native of Java. Its fronds, produced in a cluster from the apex of the rhizome, are somewhat erect, lanceolate in form, and twice-divided; the ultimate divisions are narrow, and when fertile bearing only one sorus each. The fronds are viviparous, and the plant may be increased by pegging-down an old frond on the surface of the soil.

A. VIVIPARUM (Viviparous).—This is an elegant narrow-leaved, thrice-pinnated Fern, from Mauritius, of a lively green, growing not more than a foot high. It produces living plants at the end of each frond, by which it may be readily increased, in the same way as *A. rachirhizon*, described above.

A. UMBROSUM (Shady).—This is from Madeira, and is the *Allantodia umbrosa* of R. Brown, and *Asplenium Aitoni* of some gardens. It requires a moderate stove, though it will exist in a warm greenhouse; it is rather a large Fern, growing from 3 to 4 feet high. The fronds are thrice-pinnated. The leaflets are lance-shaped, and rounded at the top. The stalk has a few dark scales at the base; and the rootstock is short, thick, and creeps close to the soil.

There are a great many more stove Aspleniums; for it is, perhaps, the largest genus in all the family; but we have enumerated those which are most easily obtainable, and most worthy of cultivation. As almost every species has something to recommend it, we here add the names of others which want of space prevents our describing at length:—*A. alatum* (tropical America); *A. Ceylonense*, small, pretty (Ceylon); *A. dentatum*, frond 2 inches high (West Indies); *A. dispersum* (tropical America); *A. eburneum* (India); *A. fragrans*, sweet-smelling after it is dried (West Indies); *A. fœniculaceum*

(Mexico); *A. macilentum* (tropical America); *A. macrophyllum* (Mauritius); *A. mexicanum*, small, pretty (Mexico); *A. myriophyllum* (recently introduced from Mexico by Linden); *A. nitens* (Brazil); *A. nitidum* (East Indies); *A. præmorsum* (Tropics, east and west); *A. zamiæfolium* (Venezuela).

BLECHNUM.

The species belonging to this genus may easily be distinguished by the spore-vessels, or sori, being generally arranged in lines on each side of the midrib on the frond. Our common *Blechnum spicant* is now separated from the genus and transferred to *Lomaria*, because the fertile fronds of that genus are contracted, which is not the case with the true Blechnums. Most of the species in this genus, as now constituted, are natives of the tropical parts of the world; and, consequently, require a warm moist stove. They are easily cultivated, not being liable to perish through mismanagement, unless neglected in watering for a long period.

BLECHNUM AUSTRALE (Southern).—A pinnated Fern, from the Cape of Good Hope, of considerable beauty, easily increased by division. The fronds are about a foot long, pinnated; the leaflets are sessile—that is, have no footstalk, slightly sickle-shaped, running out into a lance-shape. The end one is entire, and lengthened-out like a tail. It is a good Fern, worthy of general cultivation, and by no means scarce. This is now more commonly called *B. cognatum*.

B. BRASILIENSE (Brazilian).—We once had a large crop of this fine Fern, from spores sown on a rough sandstone, placed under a hand-light amongst moss. It seldom produces offsets to increase by division. The fronds frequently attain 4 feet or more in length; they are pinnate, or winged, and each wing, or leaflet, is from 7 to 8 inches long. The caudex, or stem, on which the fronds are placed circularly, is, when fully grown, 2 feet high. By this description it will be perceived that this is a large, noble Fern, requiring a tolerably large stove to show it off to the greatest advantage. Give plenty of pot room, moisture, and heat, and a young plant will, in three years, attain fronds the size mentioned.

B. COGNATUM. See *B. australe*.

B. CORCOVADENSE (A native of the Corcovado Mountain) — This is the name given to a variety of *B. brasiliense*, known by the young fronds being bright pink.

B. GLANDULOSUM (Gland-bearing).—A Brazilian Fern. Comparatively, this is a dwarf species, the fronds reaching only a foot in length. They are pinnate, with very narrow pinnæ, sharp at the end, and of a pale green. The fronds are set upon a creeping rhizome, or rootstock, by which it may be increased, if divided with a portion of roots to each division.

B. GRACILE (Graceful), *Fig. 7*.—A Brazilian evergreen Fern. Fronds about a foot long, pinnate, glabrous. Stalks reddish, rather scaly at the base, of a crimson colour while young, but becoming dark green as they arrive at maturity.

B. INTERMEDIUM (Intermediate).—A pretty dwarf Brazilian Fern, easily cultivated, and suitable for small houses. It only attains 6 or 8 inches in height even when well grown. The fronds are very variable in form, sometimes being entire, at others trifoliate, and sometimes they are pinnate, but only have two pair of pinnæ; the end one is about 4 inches long. The stalks are slightly coloured with red, which adds greatly to their beauty. It is known also by the names *B. trifoliatum*, and *B. longifolium* in some gardens.

B. LANCEOLA (Small Lance-headed).—This is also a Brazilian dwarf Fern, growing only 6 inches long. The fronds are simple—that is, with only one entire leaf of a deep dark green. It has, also, the peculiarity of having all the fronds, when fully grown, spore-bearing or fertile. It is easily grown and increased by division.

B. OCCIDENTALE (Western).—From the West Indies and Brazil. It is pinnated, and the pinnæ are usually opposite.

The fronds are nearly a foot long. Easily increased by its creeping rhizome.

B. ORIENTALE (Eastern).—A native of the East Indian Islands. The thick, leathery, once-divided fronds are, when full grown, 3 or even 4 feet in length. It is a noble Fern, but as yet somewhat scarce.

B. POLYPODIOIDES (Polypodium-like).—A native of the

Fig. 7. Blechnum gracile. (Top of frond natural size.)

tropical parts of America, like so many of the others. The fronds are about 18 inches in length, once-divided, and narrow tapering towards the point.

B. SERRULATUM (Saw-leaved).—Native of tropical America, Australia, and some of the East Indian Islands. A rather tall species. The fronds grow 2 feet long; they are pinnate, with a fleshy saw-like margin to each leaflet or pinna, the pinnæ being jointed where they are attached to the rachis. In this it differs from all the other species. The rhizome is peculiarly lengthened-out, and by dividing it the plant may be increased easily. It is a very elegant Fern, but rather scarce.

The Blechnums above mentioned are those most worthy of cultivation; but there are others which deserve mention. *B. cartilagineum*, a large-growing kind from the warm parts of Australia, rare; *B. hastatum*, from the west coast of South America; *B. punctulatum*, a distinct species, but rare at present; *B. attenuatum*, recently introduced from the continental nurseries, we have never yet seen the fertile fronds.

BRAINEA.

BRAINEA INSIGNIS (Remarkable).—This plant was originally introduced from Hong Kong about ten years ago (1852), and there were only a few specimens in the country until just recently, when some of the continental nurserymen succeeded in raising a stock of it from spores. The fronds are pinnate, about 2 feet in length, and thrown out from the apex of a short, thick stem, which is densely covered with dark brown, or black chaffy scales. It presents the appearance of a Cycad if seen from a little distance; it is extremely distinct and striking.

CALLIPTERIS.

Derived from *kalos*, beautiful, and *pteris*, a Fern. A small genus, separated from *Diplazium*; its small veins, or venules, being regularly pinnated, or branched-off from the large vein or midrib like a herring-bone. It is one of Mr. J. Smith's new genera.

CALLIPTERIS PROLIFERA (Proliferous).—This ornamental Ceylon Fern was introduced in 1845, and is a strong-growing species, the fronds attaining from 3 to 4 feet long; they are twice-pinnated, and the pinnæ or leaflets are lance-shaped, with a deeply-cut margin. The frond-stalks are thorny, placed upon a thick creeping rootstock. It is increased by division, or the young plants produced on the fronds, and requires plenty of pot room, and to be frequently syringed overhead.

C. MALABARICA (Malabar), *Fig.* 8.—Native of various parts of the East Indies. This is, amongst Fern-cultivators, the well-known *Diplazium Serampurense*. It may be readily distinguished from the preceding species by the fronds being pubescent, or covered with a woolly substance, and by the stalks of the fronds being deeply channelled. It is a large free-growing Fern, easily increased by spores coming up spontaneously on the soil of other plants, as well as its own, in a moist hot stove. This used to be known formerly as *Diplazium esculentum*.

CAMPTERIA.

CAMPTERIA BIAURITA (Twice-eared), *Fig.* 9.—A West-Indian genus and species, formed by Mr. J. Smith from *Pteris*, because of its peculiar form of spore-vessels and its solitary looped veins. The fronds are of a long triangular form, often reaching 4 feet long. They are pinnate and the pinnæ are without

Fig. 8. Callipteris malabarica. (Small part of frond near the top natural size.)

footstalks, clothing the midrib completely. They are deeply cut in a comb-like manner; or, as it is termed, pectinate, or pinnatifid. The stalk of the frond is very long, almost extending to half its length. It is a handsome Fern, requiring a rather large stove to show it to advantage. The rhizome is erect and branched, and by cutting off a branch and placing it under a hand-light, or bell-glass, roots will soon be produced, and a separate plant made. It is often called *Litobrochia biaurita*.

CAMPYLONEURON. See *Cyrtophlebium*.

Fig. 9. Campteria biaurita. (Part of a pinna medium size.)

CASSEBEERA.

A commemorative name in honour of a German botanist, J. H. Cassebeer. A genus of beautiful Ferns, allied to *Pteris* and *Cheilanthes*. Its principal character is founded upon the spore-masses being placed upon the top of four veins, and having each a marginal edge protecting it. Every species is very beautiful, and of a rather dwarf habit, rendering them suitable for small collections. Many species mentioned under the name of *Cassebeera* are as frequently seen in gardens under the names of *Cheilanthes* or *Pellæa*. The almost infinite multiplication of synonymes among Ferns is one of the greatest difficulties that the lover of these plants has to contend against.

CASSEBEERA CUNEATA (Wedge-shaped). — A tripinnated Mexican Fern of a neat habit; may be grown in a greenhouse, but thrives much better in a moderate stove. The fronds grow 10 inches high, and are of a light pleasing green. It is easily known by its barren fronds being wedge-shaped, and its spore-bearing or fertile pinnæ being of a comb-shape, and narrower towards the stems. Easily increased by division.

C. DEALBATA (Powdered).—A very neat small-growing species, dusted over with white powder; nearly related to *C. farinosa*, and almost as pretty. It is a native of Mexico. It is sometimes called *C. pulveracea*.

C. FARINOSA (Mealy), *Fig.* 10.—Native of Nepaul. This is perhaps the handsomest Fern in cultivation. The fronds are beautifully green on the upper surface; and, when turned upwards, may be seen to be of a pure white or powdery appearance. The fronds in shape are triangular, with black stems. They are bipinnated, or twice-divided, about a foot long, adhering to a short erect rhizome. Some cultivators of Ferns are very successful in raising this truly beautiful Fern from spores. It does not increase easily by division. As it is a moderate-sized Fern it ought to be in every collection.

Fig. 10. Cassebeera farinosa. (Pinnæ full size.)

C. INTRAMARGINALIS (Within the margin, referring to the sori).—A beautiful Mexican Fern, nearly hardy enough for the greenhouse, only it loves a moist heat, which the greenhouse when well managed never affords. It thrives much better in a close moist heat in a stove. Easily distinguished from its fellows by its slender continuous spore-masses, which are just within the margin of the frond. It is a beautiful Fern, but rather delicate. The fronds grow a foot long, and are bipinnate and tripinnate towards the base. The pinnæ are saw-toothed on the edges. The stems are slender and dark brown.

C. PEDATA (Bird's-footed).—A West-Indian of dwarf habit, and very beautiful. The fronds are divided into five parts, something in the way of the claws of a bird. Each division is pinnated, and droops gracefully downwards. It is rather a delicate species, and thrives better if a little charcoal be mixed with the soil. It grows about 8 or 10 inches in height.

CERATODACTYLIS.

This name is derived from two words which signify "leathery-fingered," and refers to the form and appearance of the fertile portions of the fronds. There is only one species known; it is a native of Mexico, and was introduced a few years ago by M. Linden, of Brussels.

CERATODACTYLIS OSMUNDOIDES (Royal-Fern-like).—The lower portions of the frond are in form very like those of the Osmunda, but of a grey green colour. The upper portions of the fronds are fertile, and contracted, with the margins rolled-in. The stipes are covered with scales of a silvery colour. We have never yet seen the fronds more than 2 feet in length; but older plants may attain a larger size. It is one of the most beautiful Ferns in cultivation; it is also called *Llavea cordifolia*.

CERATOPTERIS.

Keras, a horn, and *pteris*, a Fern—that is, a Fern bearing a horn. A stag's horn we suppose is meant, because the fertile fronds are divided and twisted, something like the branching horns of an old stag. These fertile fronds are very curious. The spore-masses are distributed, at regular distances, on the under side, and the edges of the pinnæ are reflexed, or turned inwards, on the under side partially covering the spore-cases.

The sterile or barren fronds are beautifully veined, thrice-pinnated, also reflexed at the edges. In the hollow of the segments of the fronds there are little knobs which throw out roots, and will, in consequence, form plants if properly managed.

CERATOPTERIS THALICTRIOIDES (Thalictrum-like), *Fig.* 11.—An annual aquatic stove Fern, common in ponds in hot countries.

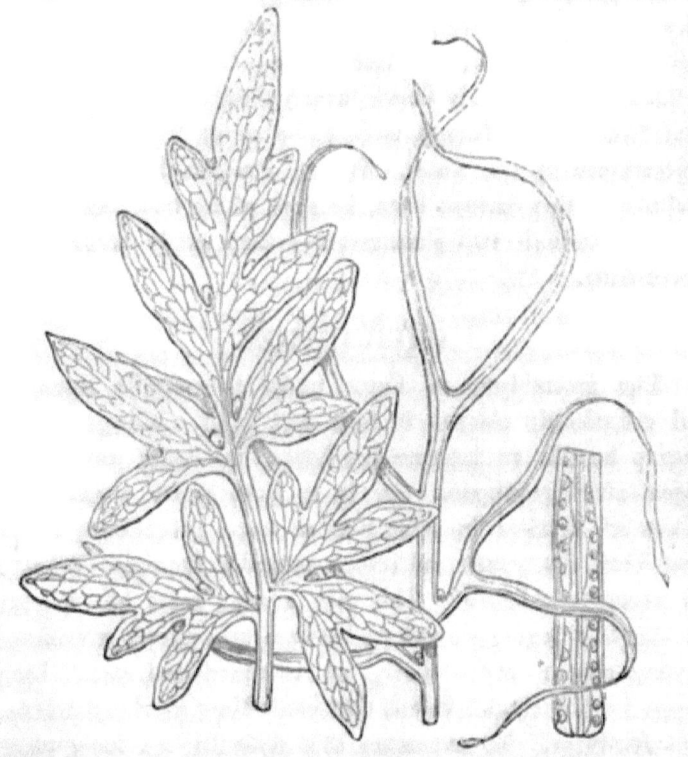

Fig. 11. Ceratopteris thalictrioides. (Parts of barren and fertile fronds; piece of fertile one magnified.)

We have grown this Fern in large pots, just set overhead in a cistern, in the Orchid-house, fully 3 feet high, with both kinds of fronds in high perfection. The plants, being only annual, die in the winter; but if young plants are raised, either from spores or by the little knobs, late in the autumn, they will survive the winter, and make finer plants the following summer. Sow the spores in a shallow pan filled with light compost, and keep it nearly full of water. To be quite safe sow some in autumn and some in spring. The plants will soon come up, covering the soil at first with flat seed-leaves, which soon send up from the base small fronds; then is the time to pot them off into thumb-pots, which should be immersed in the water, leaving the young frond above the surface. As they advance in growth give more pot room; the last shift need not exceed six-inch pots. Attend to this point—never allow the surface of the soil, even in the largest pots, to be above 2 inches beneath the surface of the water. We have rather dwelt upon the culture of this curious Fern, because of its being an aquatic, and an annual—two circumstances that rarely occur in the Fern tribe.

CHEILANTHES.

The assemblage of Ferns under this family name are all exceedingly elegant in form and habit. Many of them thrive best in an intermediate-house, not doing well in any open airy greenhouse, nor in a close moist warm stove. They are marked in some lists as warm greenhouse Ferns; but then the young cultivator naturally inquires, What is a warm greenhouse? The only answer must be, A house heated to a degree somewhere between an ordinary greenhouse and a stove: consequently, an intermediate-house. Large must be the establishment that can afford so many different temperatures. To overcome this difficulty we have placed the more delicate species on a shelf near to the front of the ordinary stove, where the air-apertures were placed. These species requiring such a situation are indicated by an asterisk (*). All such should have a large portion of silver sand in the compost, and be sparingly watered, even when freely growing, and the foliage should never be syringed.

Several species included under this genus are known in some gardens by the name of *Myriopteris*.

CHEILANTHES ALABAMENSIS (From Alabama).—This is one of the prettiest of the genus in which every species is pretty. It is a native of the warmer parts of the United States of America. The fronds, supported by dark brown stalks, do not often grow more than 6 inches high; they are finely divided, and of a glaucous green colour. It must be raised from spores.

C. ARGENTEA (Silvery).—A Fern from central Asia and Siberia of the greatest beauty, growing only about 6 inches high. Fronds bipinnate, the lowest pinnæ spreading out the longest, and gradually shortening to the apex, covered with a silvery-white powder. Stalks, both of the pinnæ and fronds, shining black. Increased slowly by division.

* C. HIRTA (Hairy).—An African Fern of great beauty. The fronds grow a foot long, and are covered with gland-bearing hairs; they are thrice-pinnated, the pinnæ are delicately small, and the stalks are brown. A very elegant Fern.

C. HIRTA *var.* ELLISIANA (Rev. W. Ellis's variety).—This beautiful Fern was introduced from Madagascar a few years ago by the reverend gentleman whose name it bears, and to whom we are also indebted for many other new and interesting plants. It is similar to the parent species, but is nearly twice as large. The fronds are produced from a central crown. It does not make offshoots, but may be readily increased by spores.

C. LENDIGERA (Maggot-bearing).—A decided stove Fern from tropical America. We have always found it thrive best in the Orchid-house. A more beautiful elegant Fern is not in cultivation. It is not possible to say too much of its loveliness. The fronds are thrice cut or pinnated, growing a foot long, and of a most delicate green; the pinnæ, or small divisions, are long and narrow, and the pinnules are thickly placed on them, and exceedingly small also. The spore-masses are few on each pinnule, and are partially concealed by the margin reflexing half over them. It is not difficult to grow; and increasing pretty freely by spores, if sown under a bell-glass, on small pieces of porous sandstone; or young plants may be increased by division.

C. MICROPHYLLA (Small-leaved).—A West-Indian Fern, with beautiful small pinnules, covered moderately with gland-bearing hairs. It is this pubescence that renders the species so clothed so impatient of being wetted over the foliage. The fronds are delicately slender, twice-pinnated, growing 18 inches long, and gracefully waving with the least breath of air. The pinnules are rather broad at the base, and the spore-masses are continued round the edge of the leaves. It is very beautiful.

C. PROFUSA (Profuse).—A very pretty little species. The fronds are not more than 3 inches high, twice-divided, covered with hairs. The plant soon spreads so as to cover the entire surface of the soil. It may be easily increased by division; indeed, it is necessary frequently to divide it when repotted.

C. RADIATA (Rayed).—A South-American, delicate, lovely Fern, almost equal to *C. lendigera.* Fronds a foot high. The branches are spread-out, or rayed like the spokes of a wheel; each branch is pinnated. The fronds have rather long footstalks, jointed on the base, with the margins scolloped-out or crenated. The spore-masses are distinct, not continuous, but spread often all round the frond. Stalks black, set upon a bundled rootstock. May be raised easily from seed in the same way as *C. lendigera.*

C. SPECTABILIS (Showy).—This is a rather diffuse Brazilian Fern, attaining a considerable size. The fronds are thrice-pinnated, growing 3 feet long, and of a beautiful light green. It is of a straggling habit, the fronds being so slender that they often break down with their own weight. It is, however, a fine Fern if a little care is taken to support the fronds. The fronds are terminal, placed upon a bundled rootstock, or rhizome.

* C. TENUIFOLIA (Slender-leaved).—A native of the East Indies and Australia. It is rather difficult to manage in

winter. It, as well as some others of the kind, should then only receive enough water to keep it alive. The frond is thrice-pinnated, about a foot long. The pinnules are long and sharp-pointed, slightly turned upwards at the edges. The stalks are brown and scaly—a rare circumstance in this genus. Increases readily by division of the creeping rhizome.

C. VISCOSA (Clammy), *Fig.* 12.—This Fern is a native of Mexico. Fronds about a foot high, light green, covered with clammy glandulous hairs. The accompanying woodcut, natural size, is a small piece of a frond.

Fig. 12. Cheilanthes viscosa.

For C. CUNEATA, C. FARINOSA, C. INTRAMARGINALIS, C. PEDATA, C. RADIATA, and other species, see *Cassebeera*.

There are several other kinds, but it would occupy too much space to describe them all at length. They are all worth growing where there is room enough; where space is limited it would be as well to select from those above mentioned. They all require the same care in watering, and the same general treatment; and they have all finely-divided and elegant fronds:—*C. elegans*, *C. frigida*, *C. glauca hirsuta*, *C. microphylla*, *C. multifida*, *C. myriophylla*, *C. Preissiana*, *C. Sieberi*, *C. squamosa*. Some other species are enumerated under the greenhouse Ferns.

CIBOTIUM.

One of the many genera taken from *Aspidium*, and so named from *Kebotion*, a little box or chest, the form of the seed-vessel.

CIBOTIUM BAROMETZ (The Scythian Lamb Fern), *Fig*. 13.—A strong-growing Cochin-China Fern, the rootstock of which is short and thick, and covered with long brownish hairs, giving it an animal-like appearance: hence its fabulous name. The fronds are bipinnate. The lowest pinnæ are long, and gradually shorten upwards. They grow erect, and often reach 10 feet in length. Each has a stem, and the spore-masses are seated near the base. It is a handsome Fern; but to grow it well requires a large stove. Easily increased by division.

C. SCHIEDEI (Schiede's).—A Mexican Fern of great beauty, easily distinguished from the preceding species by the stalks, as well as the rhizome being covered with the long woolly brown hairs, and by the tree-like rhizome, which in cultivation has reached 3 feet high. Upon this rootstock the fronds are placed, and are 6 or 8 feet long, rather drooping, bipinnate. The spore-masses are produced on the lower part of the pinnæ, and number from three to six on the margins of the leaves so situated. It must be propagated by spores, as the rhizome does not creep.

Two new species of this genus have been recently introduced by M. Linden, of Brussels, under the names of *C. Cummingi*, and *C. princeps*. All

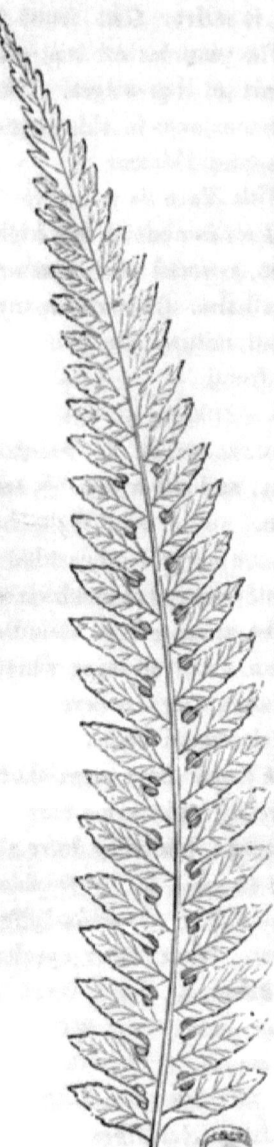

Fig. 13. Cibotium Barometz. (Pinnule natural size. Indusium magnified.)

the plants already in the country are comparatively small; but from the rapidity with which they grow they would seem to rival those before named in the size to which they will ultimately attain. They appear to be quite distinct and noble-looking plants.

CINCINALIS.

Under this name we sometimes find three plants cultivated in gardens which are here enumerated under the names of *Nothochlæna flavens*, *N. nivea*, and *N. tenera*, by which they are more generally known.

COLYSIS.

A genus containing only one species in cultivation. It was formerly included under *Drynaria*, but was divided from that group by Mr. J. Smith, of Kew.

COLYSIS MEMBRANACEA (Membranous).—This, which is also sometimes called *Pleopeltis membranacea*, is a native of the East Indies. The fronds are about 18 inches in length and undivided. They are also thinner than in almost all Ferns; and, therefore, exhibit the arrangement of the veins very beautifully. It has a creeping rhizome, and may, therefore, be increased by division.

CONIOGRAMMA JAVANICA. See *Gymnogramma javanica*.

CYATHEA.

A tall-growing genus of Ferns, allied to *Dicksonia*. In their native habitats some of this species become trees 50 feet high, with a head of fronds at the top, giving them a Palm-like appearance. The species in cultivation have been lately introduced into British gardens, and consequently are rare.

CYATHEA ARBOREA (Tree-like).—In Jamaica, its native

place, this species is truly a tree Fern. The fronds are tripinnate, from 6 to 8 feet long, standing on an erect caudex or stem. They are very stiff, and of a dull green, with scales on the underside of the leaves. The stalks are almost black, and have thorns on them. The spore-masses are cup-shaped, with the spores standing above the edge, looking, when magnified, very like an acorn enclosed in its cup. It must be increased by spores. Being such a large Fern, its culture should not be attempted except where there is plenty of room.

C. DEALBATA (Powdered). —A New Zealand tree Fern of great beauty. A friend of ours sent us some years ago a quantity of spores of this fine Fern; but whether they had perished on the voyage, or been shaken out of the cases and lost, we could never get one to make its appearance. We have seen dead stems of it nearly as thick as a man's body, and upwards of 10 feet high. It is said, in our wars with the natives, these Fern-stems served the savages as skulking-places, from whence many a deadly arrow has been shot at the unsuspecting Briton. The fronds are very beautiful, of a bluish-green on the upper surface, and richly powdered with white underneath. They are 6 or 7 feet long, jointed, and placed on the top of

Fig. 14. Cyathea elegans. (Pinnule natural size, and segment showing position of veins and sori, and a sorus magnified.)

the upright caudex. Stems covered with scales. Requires a roomy stove or warm conservatory, and is increased by spores.

C. ELEGANS (Elegant), *Fig.* 14.—A tree Fern from Jamaica, and perhaps the handsomest in cultivation. The Kew plant is 8 feet high in the stem, with some fronds 10 feet long. They are thrice-pinnated, the lowest pinnæ spreading considerably, and gradually growing less upwards. The frondstalks are densely covered with almost white scales, which add greatly to its beauty. Requires plenty of space to show itself, and can only be increased by spores.

C. MEDULLARIS (Pithy).—One of the most magnificent of tree Ferns. A native of the warmer parts of New Zealand, the Fiji Islands, &c. Full grown the fronds are 14 or 15 feet in length; the stipes of a beautiful purple colour. This plant grows very rapidly, and is only fit for cultivation where there is plenty of room. There are some magnificent specimens in the Royal Botanic Gardens at Kew.

C. PATENS (Spreading).—A Jamaica Fern of great attractions. The fronds are slender, gracefully spreading out and drooping. They are, like the whole genus, thrice-cut or pinnated, and are of a beautiful yellowish-green. The stem is somewhat slender, and 3 or 4 feet high. Upon it the fronds are placed, spreading out to 6 or 8 feet long. The stalks are light brown, covered with prickly scales. This fine Fern is well worthy of cultivation where there is room for it to expand. There are several other species of this fine tribe of Ferns described.

CYCLOPELTIS.

This name is derived from the Greek *kyklos*, a circle, and *pelte*, a shield, referring to the round indusium. The genus is represented by one species only. It was formerly included in the genus Lastrea. The new name was given it by Mr. J. Smith, of Kew, a gentleman possessing an extraordinary knowledge of the family of Ferns.

CYCLOPELTIS SEMICORDATA (Half-heart-shaped), *Fig.* 15.—Native of West India Islands. Fronds bright shining green, about 2½ feet high, pinnate. Pinnæ smooth, sessile, about 4 inches long. Base irregularly cordate or auriculate, and articulated with the rachis, which is downy. Sori round This Fern seems to be more rare than it was a few years ago; perhaps because there is no other way of increasing it except by spores.

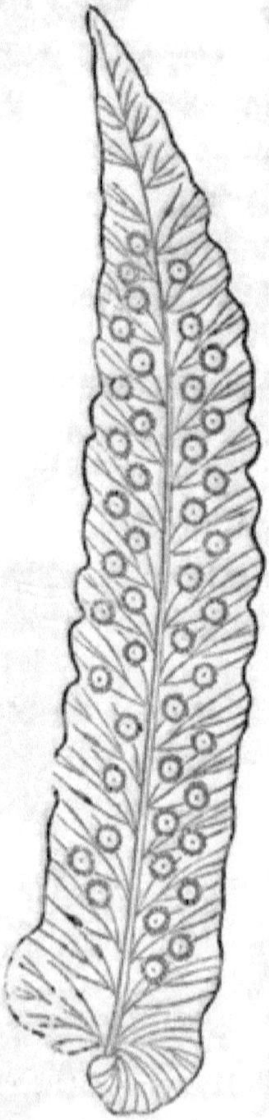

CYRTOGONIUM.

From *kyrtos*, curved, and *gonu*. A genus of Ferns separated by Mr. Smith, of Kew, from *Acrostichum*. The small veins on the fronds are singularly and suddenly bent or angled like the knee of the human frame. These are often known by the name *Pœcilopteris*.

CYRTOGONIUM CRISPATULUM (Spreading-crested).—A handsome Fern from Ceylon. Fronds pinnate, inclining to be erect, crenate or cut at the margin, of the deepest green. There are barren and fertile, or spore-bearing leaflets, the latter shorter and more contracted than the former. On the barren fronds there is, in the hollow of the scollops, a short thorny substance. The stems have some scales, and the rhizome creeps: hence it is easily increased by division. The whole plant seldom exceeds 2 feet in height, and it may be grown in a moderate-sized stove.

Fig. 15. Cyclopeltis semicordata. (Pinna full size.)

C. FLAGELLIFERUM (Whip-bearing), *Fig.* 16.—An East-Indian Fern of the easiest culture. We have cultivated it for years, in

CYRTOGONIUM—CYRTOMIUM. 35

small pots, in the deepest shade of the stove. It is easily known by the frond having two pinnæ at the base, the end one becoming narrower towards the end, in the same way as the whip, but more suddenly, and by its producing at the end a knob or knot, which, if not taken off, will soon send out leaves, and finally roots; by these it may be readily increased. It is very subject to the attacks of the brown scale, more so than most Ferns.

CYRTOMIUM.

Most of the species of Cyrtomium are greenhouse plants, but there is one kind which requires a stove for its cultivation, that is

CYRTOMIUM CARYOTIDEUM (Caryota-like). — This very beautiful Fern was raised from spores, sent from India by W. Wilson Saunders, Esq., of Reigate. It has pinnate fronds about 2 feet in length, of a dull green colour. The pinnæ have sometimes a pointed lobe near the base, and the upper leaflet is divided into three pointed lobes, somewhat like that of the Wine-Palm (*Caryota urens*).

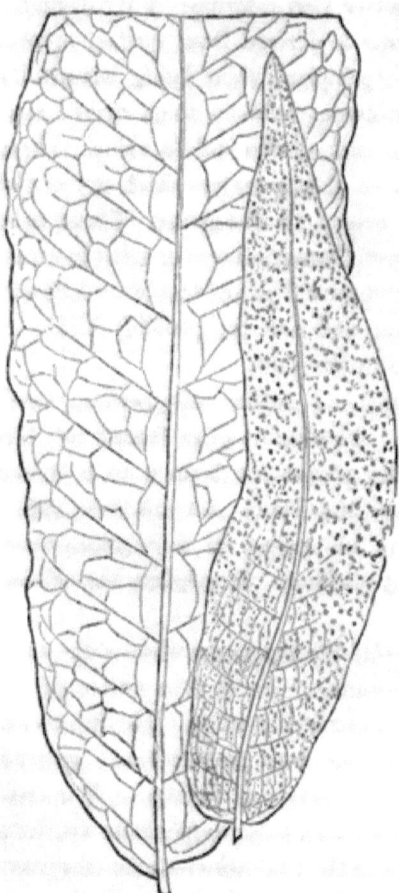

Fig. 16. Cyrtogonium flagelliferum. (Pinnæ of barren and fertile fronds natural size.)

CYRTOPHLEBIUM.

A well-defined genus of stove Ferns, formed by Mr. J. Smith from *Polypodium*. The name is derived from *kyrtos*, curved, and *phlebs*, a vein; all the principal veins being beautifully curved upwards, and the midveins between them curved also. There are two seed-cases on each of the middle veins. These may be considered the peculiar characters by which any of the species may be known to belong to the genus. These have recently been called by name of *Campyloneuron* in some gardens.

CYRTOPHLEBIUM ANGUSTIFOLIUM (Narrow-leaved).—A South-American Fern. Fronds long and narrow, growing thickly on a short rhizome. Increased by division.

C. DECURRENS (Decurrent).—A rather tall-growing, handsome Fern from the Brazils. The fronds grow from 2 to 3 feet high, and are pinnated; the pinnæ are from 6 to 8 inches long, according to the size of the frond. As this Fern grows erect and compact, it may be grown in a moderate-sized stove. Readily increased by division. It exhibits the veining beautifully.

C. NITIDUM (Shining).—Of all the genus this is the most upright and stiff-growing species. As it is a native of the West Indies it requires the heat of the stove. The fronds are often 2 feet long, and of a shining deep green colour; growing on a short, blunt, scaly, and creeping rhizome. We have grown this Fern very successfully in a deep shade far from the roof, where it served to hide the naked stems of several tall plants of *Ficus elastica*. The peculiar form of the veins is the least seen in this species. Increased slowly by division.

C. PHYLLITIDIS (Hart's-tongue).—A West-Indian Fern with simple fronds. Similar to the last-named species, but the leaves are narrower, rather longer, and undulate, or wavy, paler green, and more leathery, and it attains a larger magnitude. Requires frequently repotting, or it will become potbound. We have had a plant fill a pot densely with its feathery roots in a month's time. If kept too long in the same pot it then requires so much water to keep it from flagging that the earth becomes sodden, and the fine roots perish; the plant becomes sickly, and the fronds lose their bright green, becoming of a yellowish hue. This is, indeed, the case with most Ferns, but more especially with the species belonging to this genus.

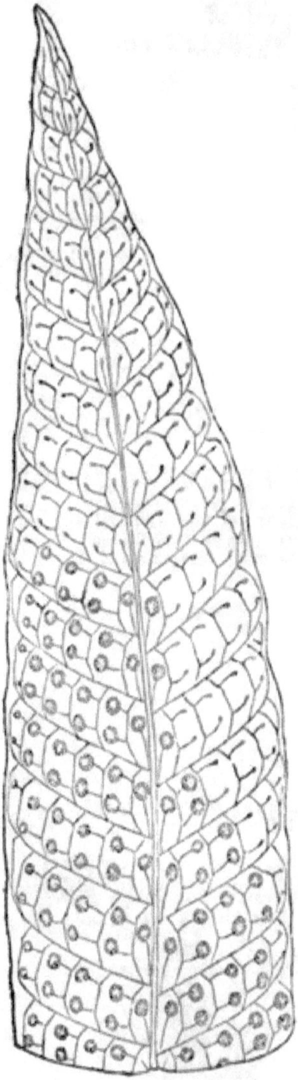

C. REPENS (Creeping), *Fig.* 17.—A West-Indian Fern with a creeping rhizome running to a considerable distance. The fronds are simple—that is, not cut or pinnated; and in this species recline, whereas in all the others they stand erect. In addition to this ample specific distinction, the upper side of the frond is covered with white scales. It is a proper plant to ornament rockwork, or to plant on a rustic block of wood, or even to place in a rustic basket. Increased very plentifully by its creeping rhizome.

There are a few other species in cultivation, as *C. cæspitosum, C. ensifolium, C. rigidum, &c.*; but all resemble each other in having undivided fronds, and a creeping rhizome.

Fig. 17. Cyrtophlebium repens. (Top of frond natural size.)

DAVALLIA.

This is one of the most beautiful genera in the whole family of Ferns, and from the Hare's-foot Fern giving a good type of it, it is also well known. All the species are characterised by having finely-divided fronds, very graceful and elegant; and creeping rhizomes, which are thick in some kinds, but in others fine as the quill of a pen. They are usually covered with brown scales. They are readily increased by division. As these characters are common to all the species, except where otherwise mentioned, we need not repeat them under every name.

DAVALLIA BULLATA (Studded).—An East-Indian Fern, rather small-growing compared with some of the other kinds. Fronds dark green and shining, about 6 inches high. It generally loses its fronds in winter.

D. DECORA (Graceful).—A very pretty species, also from the East. The fronds do not grow to more than a foot in length. The scales covering the rhizomes are of a delicate light brown colour.

D. DISSECTA (Dissected).—Fronds attain a height of 18 inches or 2 feet. This, as well as many other of the Davallias, looks very beautiful grown in a wire basket and suspended from the roof.

D. ELATA (Tall).—Fronds nearly a yard high, but drooping over gracefully. When mature the fronds are green, but while young they have a rosy tint. It is a very good plan in potting this and other species of the family to use very rough peat, and to pile it into a cone above the pot, keeping the pieces of turf together with pegs. The rhizomes of most kinds do not like to be buried.

D. ELEGANS (Elegant).—Another of the small-growing kinds imported from Ceylon. The fronds are about 18 inches long. It is not so attractive a Fern as some of the others.

D. PENTAPHYLLA (Five-leaved).—First introduced by Mr. Rollisson, of Tooting, from the Malayan Archipelago, among Orchids. It is a very distinct and useful Fern, well adapted either for growing in a basket, or for covering a damp wall in the stove. The fronds are only a few inches long, and instead of being finely cut, consist of only five narrow divisions. They are of a very dark shining green. The rhizomes are thin, and lengthen very quickly; they often hang down several feet in length.

D. POLYANTHA (Many-flowered, referring to the sori).—This is one of the large-growing kinds. The fronds will grow to a length of a yard, or even more in old plants, including the crimson stipes. The fronds while young are of a beautiful rosy colour.

There are several other kinds to be found in collections of stove Ferns, but those above mentioned are the best and most distinct.

DICTYOGLOSSUM.

Divided from *Acrostichum* by Mr. Smith. The distinguishing characteristic of the genus consists in the spore-masses being densely scattered over the under surface of the fertile fronds, excepting on the margin, which is clear of them. The name is derived from *diktyon*, a net, and *glossa*, a tongue, alluding to the veins crossing and recrossing each other, and the tongue-like shape of the fertile fronds. There is only one species—namely,

DICTYOGLOSSUM CRINITUM (Hairy), *Fig.* 18.—A curious hairy Fern from that rich island of Ferns, Jamaica. The fertile fronds are very distinct from the barren ones; besides being spore-bearing, they have a stem, or stipes, 6 or 8 inches high, which, as well as the upper side of the frond, is covered with narrow black hairs. The frond itself is oval, tapering to the point, whereas the barren frond is more broadly lanceolate. Both grow about a foot long, and 8 inches broad at the widest part, but the sterile is usually larger. The fronds are placed upon a stout creeping rhizome, by which it may be increased, though but slowly, by division. Though a broad-leaved Fern, it grows within a small compass and, therefore, is suitable for a moderate-sized stove. Known also as *Hymenodium crinitum*. It is very difficult to rear from spores.

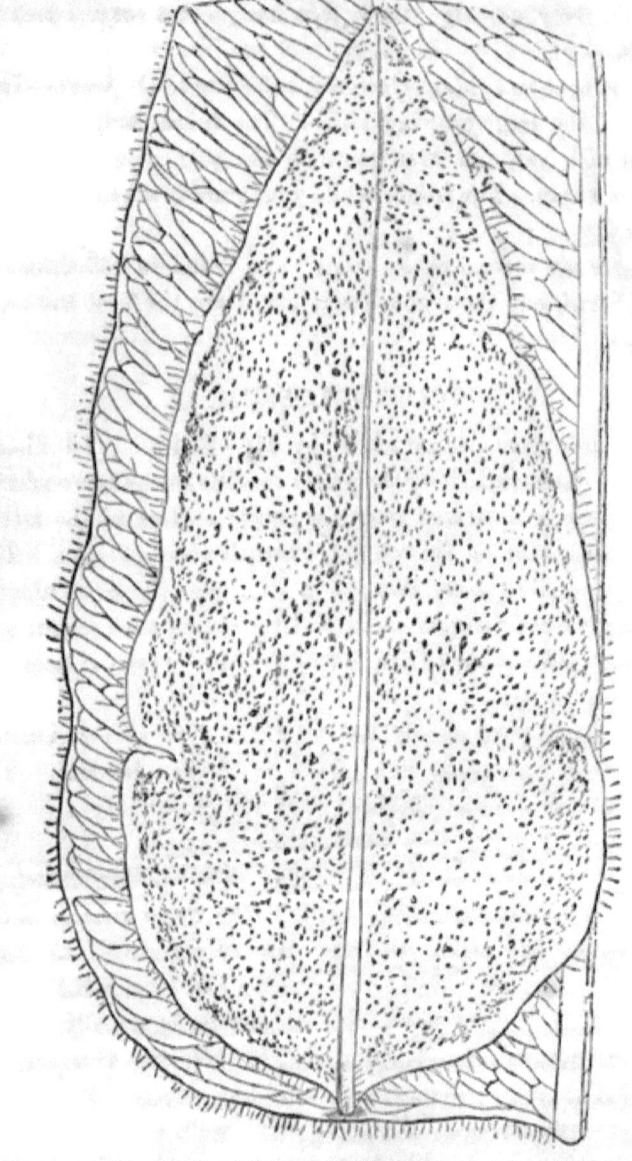

Fig. 18. Dictyoglossum crinitum. (Fertile frond and part of sterile half natural size.)

DICTYOXIPHIUM.

Derived from the Greek *diktyon*, a net, and *xiphos*, a sword, referring to the shape and net-like venation of the fronds. Nearly allied to Lindsæa. There is only one species in cultivation.

DICTYOXIPHIUM PANAMENSE (Panama), *Fig.* 19.— Originally found at Panama, but since then in other parts of South America. Fronds 2 feet high, bright green, smooth, erect-growing, entire, sword-shaped, leathery. It can only be increased by spores, or very rarely and slowly by division. It is by no means a striking or very beautiful plant.

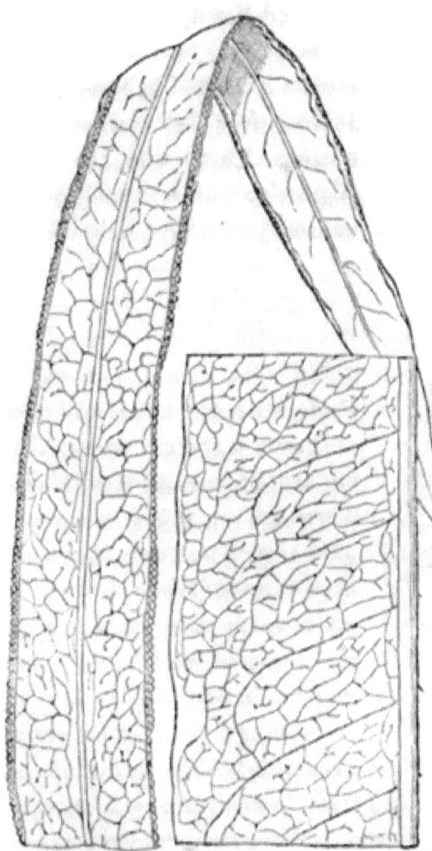

Fig. 19. Dictyoxiphium panamense. (Top of fertile frond, and section from barren frond, natural size.)

DIDYMOCHLÆNA.

This generic name is derived from *didymos*, double, and *chlaina*, a cloak, alluding to the double indusium. There is only one known species, and even that is rather rarely met with.

DIDYMOCHLÆNA TRUNCATULA (Rather truncate), *Fig.* 20.— Native of West Indian and Philippine Islands. Fronds bright green, elegant, about 4 feet high, broadly lanceolate, bipinnate;

pinnæ about 9 inches long, sessile. Pinnules overlapping and leathery, rather truncate at base; margin slightly crenulate.

Fig. 20. Didymochlæna truncatula. (Top of pinna full size.)

Stipes, rachis, and midrib covered densely with reddish-brown-coloured down and scales. It is very apt to throw off its leaflets if allowed to become dry. It can only be increased by spores. Those who have seen it growing wild say that it grows naturally in a light rich soil.

DIPLAZIUM.

In this genus, formed by Professor Swartz, the cultivator of Ferns will find several that he has known as *Aspleniums*. They are separated on account of the spore-masses being placed in pairs, with each back opposite, on a single small vein: hence its characteristic name, from *diplazo*, to double.

DIPLAZIUM ACUMINATUM (Tapering).—The spores of this very distinct species were sent from Ceylon to a gentleman on the Continent a few years ago. He was very fortunate in raising them, and the species has now become pretty plentiful. The fronds are quite smooth, almost shining, pinnate, and about 18 inches in length.

D. ALTERNIFOLIUM (Alternate-leaved).—This species is sometimes called also *D. integrifolium*, because, while young, the fronds are undivided. As they attain maturity they produce two pairs of side pinnæ, and one larger terminal one. The fronds are dark green, and very thick and leathery. It was introduced from Java.

D. ARBORESCENS (Tree-like).—A tall Fern from St. Helena, nearly hardy enough for the greenhouse. It grows beautifully planted out in a shady part of a conservatory. Fronds bipinnate; the lower pinnæ spread out, the upper ones gradually shortening-in. They grow 3 feet long, and are of a pleasing light green. The leaves are cut at the edges. The stems are scaly, and the rootstock is erect. It must be increased by spores.

D. COARCTATUM (Close-pressed).—A handsome Brazilian Fern, reaching 1½ foot in height. The fronds are pinnate; the pinnæ with a footstalk to each. The leaflets are cut at the edges, and thickly set, or close-pressed on the stalk. The rootstock is erect: consequently cannot be divided, and, therefore, the species must be increased by seeds.

D. DECUSSATUM (Crossed).—This is the *Asplenium decussatum* of Wallich. It is an East-Indian species, rather coarse in habit, but a free grower. Fronds pinnate, and covered with woolly-like hairs. It grows 3 feet high, and is easily increased by its creeping rhizome.

D. JUGLANDIFOLIUM (Walnut-leaved).—This is a well-known South-American Fern. A specimen formerly grown in the garden of Mrs. Lawrence, Ealing Park, was 5 feet high, and as much through. In general it does not grow more than 2 feet high. The fronds are pinnate, and of a bright green. Leaflets large and slightly cut. Rootstock bundled—that is, many heads of fronds set upon it. One or more of these taken off close to the base, and placed in pots under a hand-light in heat, soon emit roots, and form a good plant.

D. PLANTAGINEUM (Plantain-leaved), *Fig.* 21.—The only one of the genus with simple fronds. It is from the West Indies, and is of a dwarf habit, producing young plants from the base of the frond. The fronds are nearly all fertile. On account of its dwarf habit it is suitable for small collections.

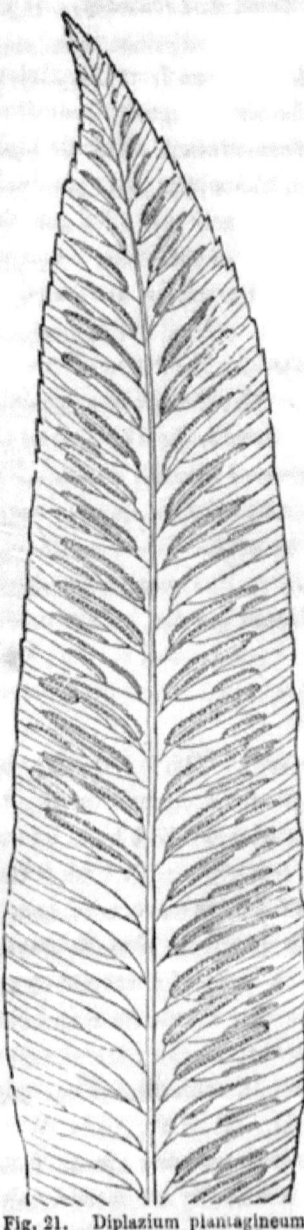

Fig. 21. Diplazium plantagineum (Frond medium size.)

Increased in the same way as *D. juglandifolium*, or by its buds at the base of the fronds.

D. SHEPHERDI (Shepherd's).—A beautiful Jamaica Fern, named in honour of the late Mr. Shepherd, of the Liverpool Botanic Gardens, a most successful cultivator of the tribe. Fronds pinnate, growing a foot or more in height. Spore-masses very regularly and beautifully arranged. It is a lovely Fern, and may be increased by division.

D. STRIATUM (Striated).—A Jamaica Fern of considerable magnitude. The fronds are twice-pinnated, and grow frequently 5 feet long, and each wing, or pinna, a foot long. The stalks and ribs of the leaves are covered with fine hairs. The rootstock is erect, not creeping, and, therefore, the plant must be increased by spores.

D. SUBALATUM (Half-winged). —This is a rare Fern in cultivation. Native of the warmest parts of South America. The fronds are thrice-pinnated at the base, and twice-pinnated above, growing 4 feet high; and the rootstock is a single stem

2 feet high. The stalks are channelled, or winged: hence the specific name. It is a remarkable, distinct, handsome Fern, requiring a large stove to grow it well. Increased by spores only.

D. SYLVATICUM (Wood).—A Fern from Ceylon of great beauty. The fronds are pinnate; the lower pinnæ being long and spreading, and gradually shorter as they approach the end of the frond; they grow from 2 to 3 feet long. Leaflets almost round, and cut at the edges. The stem is covered with dark brown scales, and the rhizome has several heads of fronds upon it. By these it may be increased.

D. THWAITESI (Thwaites').—This is a native of Ceylon. whence the spores were sent to this country by the gentleman whose name it bears. It is hardly so desirable a species as most of the others, because the fronds being covered with hairs, they are very liable to become dirty. The once-divided fronds grow about 6 inches in height. Its creeping rhizomes increase rapidly. It is also called *D. lasiopteris*.

DOODIA.

A commemorative name in honour of Mr. S. Doody, an early student of Ferns and Mosses. It is a genus of small-growing Ferns, with the fronds very rough to the touch. Allied to *Woodwardia*.

DOODIA ASPERA (File-like, or Rough).—A very neat, handsome Fern from New Holland. It will live in a good greenhouse, but thrives much better in a moderate stove. The fronds grow upright, very rigid, from 8 to 10 inches high, and are of a dark green. Leaflets sickle-shaped, the edge sharply cut, so as almost to be like spines. A suitable species for small collections, and easily increased by division.

D. CAUDATA (Tailed).—This plant needs no description, it is the commonest Fern in cultivation: perhaps it is not too much to say that there is not a fernery in the country where it is not to be seen. Its spores vegetate so freely that it comes up as a weed everywhere. It was originally introduced from Australia.

D. BLECHNOIDES (Blechnum-like), *Fig.* 22.—An Australian Fern, very similar to the last species, but may be distinguished from it by its greater size, and having its stems densely covered with black scales. May be increased by its bundled rhizome.

D. LUNULATA (Crescent-shaped).—Introduced some years ago from New Zealand. It is a graceful, elegant Fern, and very remarkable by its fronds being red when young. They are, when full grown, 1½ foot long, very slender, and drooping gracefully. The leaflets are crescent-shaped, and spiny at the edges. The stipes purplish-red. Rootstock creeping. Increased by division.

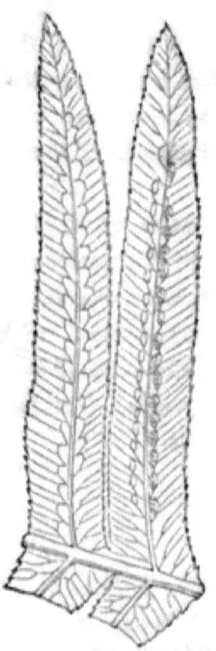

Fig. 22. Doodia blechnoides. (Part of frond natural size.)

There is a very beautiful little tasselled *Doodia*, which is by some said to be a variety of *D. caudata*, others think it a sport from *D. lunulata*. It is known by the names of *D. monstrosa* and *D. corymbifera*. It is a perfect little gem in its way; there is a crest very dense and about an inch wide at the top of the frond, and all the other divisions are crested to a less extent.

DORYOPTERIS.

A small genus of Ferns, separated from *Pteris* by Mr. J. Smith. Derived from *dory*, a spear, and *pteris*, a Fern. One of the species has fronds in that form. The genus may be known by the spore-masses being narrow, placed on the margin, and in a continued line, and by the reticulation of the veins. The species are all of a dwarf habit, and are, therefore, proper to cultivate in small collections.

DORYOPTERIS COLLINA (Hill).—A Brazilian Fern, growing not more than 10 inches high, with leathery, palmate, bright green fronds. The sterile ones are sometimes thrice, and sometimes five times parted; the fertile ones are always five-parted, or spread out in five divisions like a man's hand. It is an elegant species, and somewhat rare.

D. PALMATA (Hand-shaped).—Differs from the preceding species by being taller, and by the lobes of each frond having more divisions, so as to be almost pinnated. The sterile fronds also are almost simple when young. It is very beautiful, easily grown, and increased by division.

D. SAGITTIFOLIA (Arrow-headed), *Fig.*23.—A Brazilian Fern of great beauty. The fronds are simple, acute, nearly a foot high, almost all spore-bearing stems black and smooth. Increases readily by division. This species is very distinct, very elegant, and ought to be in every collection however small.

DRYMOGLOSSUM.

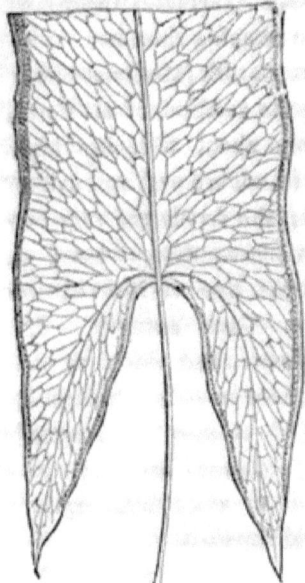

Fig. 23. Doryopteris sagittifolia. (Part of medium-sized frond.)

A genus of low, creeping, curious Ferns, established by M. Presl. The essential characters by which it may be known are an irregular compound of the veins, and the position of the spore-masses, which are placed on each margin in a continuous line on the upper part of the fertile fronds.

STOVE FERNS.

DRYMOGLOSSUM LANCEOLATUM (Lance-shaped), *Fig.* 24.—A Jamaica Fern of considerable beauty. Fronds from 10 inches to a foot long, simple, and narrower towards the end, where the contraction takes place. The spore-masses commence and are continued nearly to the apex, or end, in a continuous line, very near the edge, but not quite close to it. The irregularly-running veins are imbedded inside the frond. Increases readily by dividing the creeping rhizome.

D. PILOSELLOIDES (Mouse-ear-like).—Probably the smallest of all Ferns, growing only about 2 inches high. The sterile fronds are oval and narrow at the base; the fertile are very narrow, and, in consequence of being so, the continuous line of spore-masses almost cover them entirely. The fronds are simple, and placed on each side of a slender creeping rhizome, by dividing which it may be increased. This small Fern grows best on a moss-covered block of wood, hung up in a shady part of the stove.

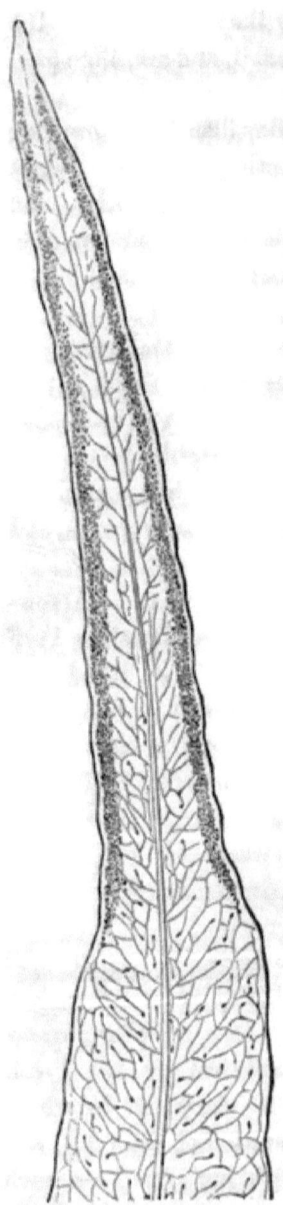

Fig. 24. Drymoglossum lanceolatum. (Top of frond natural size.)

DRYNARIA.

A rather large genus. Name derived from *dryinos*, the oak, in allusion to the form of the leaf of the species upon which the genus was formed. Distinguished generally by having two distinct forms of frond, and by the spore-masses being naked—that is, without any indusium or covering, and the compound crooked lines of veins.

DRYNARIA CORONANS (Crowning).—This is another East-Indian Fern, and a noble specimen it makes. The fronds are sessile—that is, stalkless, erect, somewhat rigid, pinnatifid or deeply-lobed on each side nearly down to the midrib. These fronds are 3 feet or even more in height. The rhizome, covered with amber-coloured scales, creeps, and has always a tendency to turn in a spiral direction. This is also the case with *D. morbillosa*; and both in their native countries grow round the stems of old trees, which may, perhaps, account for it.

D. DIVERSIFOLIA (Variously-shaped-leaved).—A very beautiful East-Indian Fern, with once-divided fertile fronds about 2 feet in length. These are of a delicate light green colour, and as they droop very gracefully the plant is very suitable for cultivation in a suspended basket. The old fronds turn yellow in August, but there is always a crop of new ones ready to succeed them at once. It makes also sterile fronds, shaped somewhat like the leaf of the oak; these should be left on the plant even after they are brown and dry, for they contrast beautifully with the other fronds. It may easily be increased by division.

D. IRIOIDES (Iris-like). See *Microsorum*.

D. MORBILLOSA (——— ?).—This noble Fern was introduced from the Malayan Archipelago. It closely resembles *D. coronans* in appearance and habit, and, indeed, is often confounded with that species. It has the same kind of rigid, erect, stemless fronds, but is broader, more coarse-looking, and not so elegant as that plant.

D. MUSÆFOLIA (Musa-leaved).—A rigid, entire-fronded Fern from the East Indies. The fronds are stalkless, and rise at once from the creeping rhizome; they are of a pale green, and show the arrangement of the veins beautifully, looking like a piece of elaborate lacework. Like the other species of this family, it can be increased by division without much trouble.

D. PROPINQUA (Allied).—This Fern, which, like many of its allies, comes from the East Indies, is deciduous—that is, it loses its fronds in winter. The dark green fronds, some 18 inches high, are divided nearly to the midrib into tapering segments. It also produces the oak-like sterile fronds along its creeping rhizome.

D. QUERCIFOLIA (Oak-leaved).—This fine Fern has a wide geographical distribution. It is found in all the hottest parts of the East. This species, like several others, has both sterile and fertile fronds on the same plant. The sterile fronds have no stalk, are heart-shaped, and jagged or waved at the edges; in form like the leaf of the oak, whence the name. The fertile fronds have a short stalk, are pinnate with narrow segments, each segment having a thick binding or edge. The spore-masses are circular, and are placed in groups over the under surface of the leaves. It is well worthy of cultivation. We have grown the species on a low shelf, far from the light, with the pots plunged in moss, into which the roots ran freely, and by this moist steady treatment they grew very satisfactorily. We found it easy to increase by division.

ELAPHOGLOSSUM.

A genus formed from *Acrostichum*. Distinguished from that and other allied genera by its simple fronds, with forked distinct veins.

ELAPHOGLOSSUM CALLÆFOLIUM (Calla-leaved). — An undivided-leaved Fern from Java. It has barren and fertile fronds, the former rather broadly acuminate, or sharp-pointed, shining deep green, with wavy edges; the stalks are of dark colour underneath. The fertile fronds are narrower and more erect. Both fronds grow about a foot high, and are jointed at the base.

The rootstock creeps: hence it is easily increased by division. A desirable species for any collection.

E. CRASSINERVE (Thick-nerved).—This West-Indian Fern may be distinguished from the last by its stouter fronds and thicker veins, and by the height of the barren fronds. These attain, frequently, 2 feet in height, whilst the fertile fronds seldom exceed 1 foot. The barren fronds are also undulated, and of a dull green. Easily increased by dividing its short creeping rootstock.

E. CONFORME (Conformed), *Fig.* 25.—A species nearly hardy enough for the greenhouse, but thrives better in a cool stove through the winter. It is from the Cape of Good Hope, where it is found growing on shady rocks. The sterile fronds are very beautifully veined with almost perfect regularity, and of a long oval form, narrow at the base, and terminating in a sharp point; growing about a foot high. The fertile fronds are much smaller, and covered throughout with spore-masses The

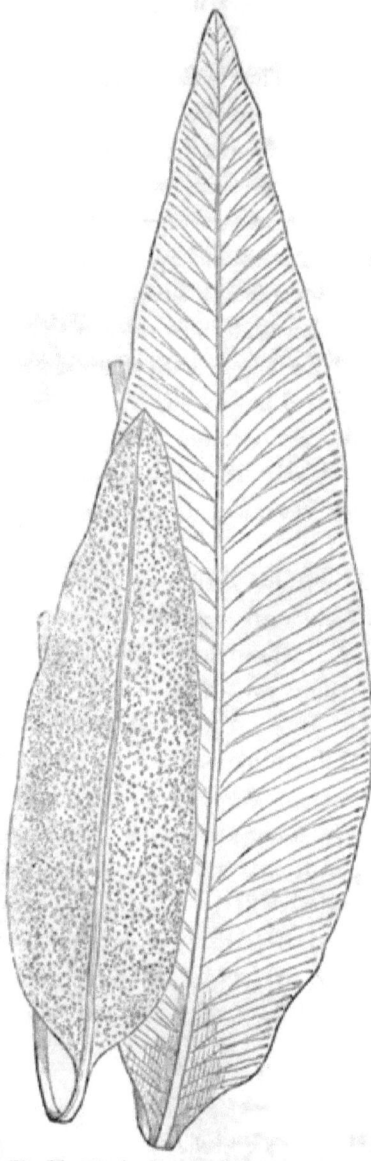

Fig. 25. Elaphoglossum conforme. (Barren and fertile fronds medium size.)

rootstock creeps, and is covered with scales. Increased by division. It is a pretty, neat species, and worthy of general cultivation.

E. LONGIFOLIUM (Long-leaved).—This is the tallest species of the whole genus, growing in its native country (West Indies), fully 2 feet high. Sterile fronds long-lance-shape, narrow at the base, and sharp at the extreme point, and rather wavy at the edges. Fertile fronds erect, and the same form. Rhizome creeping, and easily increased by division.

E. SCOLOPENDRIIFOLIUM (Scolopendrium-leaved).—A Brazilian Fern of great beauty. The barren fronds are more than a foot long, pale green, wavy at the edges, and of an oblong lance-shape. The stalks are about 6 inches long; and these, with the margins of the fronds, are covered with hair-like scales. Fertile fronds upright, nearly 18 inches high, upon a stalk of 8 inches. Rootstock creeping, short, and scaly. Increased by division.

E. VILLOSUM (Shaggy).—A curious handsome Fern from the West Indies. The barren fronds are remarkable by being covered with long shaggy hairs. These hairs are beautiful objects under the microscope; they are of an oblong lance-shape, sharp-pointed, and a foot long. Fertile fronds narrow and short. Increased by its creeping rootstock.

There are several other species of *Elaphoglossum* in cultivation, but they are all similar to those mentioned, in having undivided somewhat strap-shaped fronds more or less pointed at each end. As those enumerated will be enough for any ordinary collection, we merely mention the names of a few others; they are, *E. apodum*, *E. frigidum* (or *perelegans*), *E. latifolium*, *E. lepidotum*, *E. microlepis*, *E. muscosum*. They are all natives of tropical America.

EUPODIUM.

This genus is very nearly related to *Marattia*, from which

it differs only in having the many-celled spore-mass supported upon a stalk instead of being flat upon the frond. There is only one species in cultivation, and even it is at present rare.

EUPODIUM KAULFUSSII (Kaulfuss's). — The erect, spreading, three-times-divided fronds rise from between the leathery scales forming the crown of the plant. The ultimate divisions of the frond are small, toothed, and of a light green colour. It appears to be a rather difficult plant to manage; if once allowed to become dry the segments of the fronds at once drop off. It is a native of Brazil. There seems to be no other means of increasing it except by spores.

FADYENIA.

A genus named in honour of Dr. McFadyen, who spent several years of his life in Jamaica. There is only one species known, and a very curious little Fern it is. We have cultivated it for several years, and found it to grow best if the pot containing

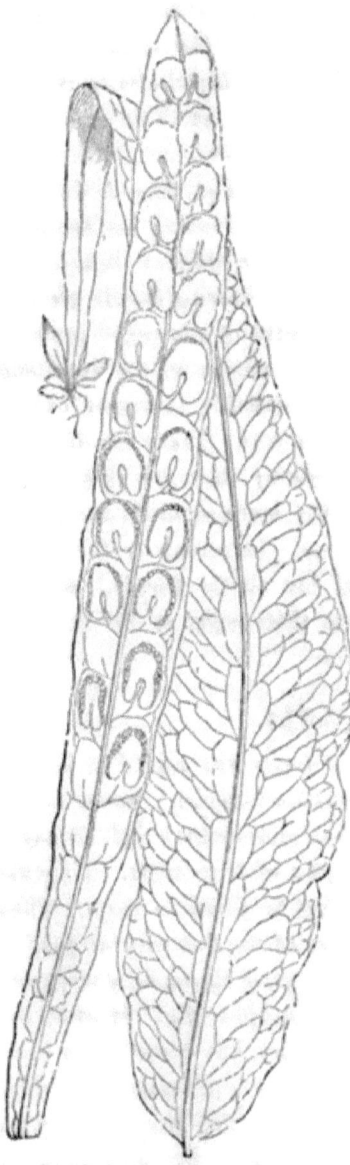

Fig. 26. Fadyenia prolifera. (Barren and fertile fronds natural size.)

the plant were placed in a shallow pan of water in the Orchid-house. Very little water was given to the soil in the pot. The plants grew strong and spread over the surface of the earth, completely covering it with their broad sterile fronds, which frequently produced young plants at their ends. It cannot be kept too hot in any ordinary stove.

FADYENIA PROLIFERA (Proliferous), *Fig.* 26.—A Jamaica Fern. The sterile fronds are simple, spreading horizontally, and frequently producing plants at the points: hence it is called Proliferous. The fertile or spore-bearing fronds are also simple, but stand upright in the centre of the plant, growing about 5 inches high, lance-shaped, narrower at the base, and blunt at the apex. The most remarkable character of the species is the indusium covering the sori. These are disposed alternately on each side of the midrib; they are very nearly the shape of a horseshoe, with the margins thick and hairy, and are very large and conspicuous. Increased by the young plants produced at the ends of the sterile fronds. A very curious, interesting, small Fern, that ought to be in every collection.

GLEICHENIA.

This favourite and remarkable genus was named in honour of Baron P. Von Gleichen, a German botanist. Every collection of Ferns shown at our great metropolitan exhibitions is sure to contain one or two examples of Gleichenia. They are well deserving the importance that is given to them. They are expensive plants to buy because of the difficulty of parting them; for, although they have creeping rhizomes, yet, parted with the utmost care, they are very liable to die. Most of the species will succeed in the greenhouse, but those below mentioned are from tropical countries, and require a stove for their cultivation. A few Gleichenias have recently been raised from spores. If our nurserymen can succeed in propagating them in this way they will soon become more plentiful.

GLEICHENIA DICHOTOMA (Branching into equal divisions).—This Fern is a native of Ceylon, and was first introduced into Prussia, whence it has since found its way all over Europe. It is rather a dwarf-growing kind with glaucous fronds. It is rather a delicate plant, and should not be overpotted; indeed, shallow boxes or pans are best for all the Gleichenias.

G. FURCATA (Forked).—Rather a scarce West-Indian Fern. The fronds are 18 inches or 2 feet long, dark green, and somewhat downy. The stems are brown and wiry, as in all the members of the family.

G. GLAUCESCENS (Somewhat of a bluish-green colour).—A magnificent strong-growing Fern, originally imported from the West Indies to the Royal Botanic Gardens at Kew. It is still somewhat rare. The stems will attain the height of 3 feet or more, and are generally well clothed with delicately-coloured fronds.

GONIOPHLEBIUM.

A genus of Ferns formed out of Polypodium by Presl, and so named from *gonia*, an angle, and *phlebia*, a vein, the veins forming angles on the under side of the fronds. The distinguishing characters of the genus consist in the angular position of the veins, the sori being round, and placed at the end of the veinlets.

GONIOPHLEBIUM CATHERINÆ (St. Catherine's).—A Brazilian Fern of great beauty. Fronds almost triangular, pinnate; the leaflets blunt and oblong. Rootstock creeping, and covered with scales wrapping over each other. Spore-masses in one series, and only on the upper part of the frond. Another elegant Fern, increased by dividing the rootstock.

G. CUSPIDATUM (Sharp-pointed).—A very beautiful and rare Fern from Java. Fronds pinnate with lance-shaped leaflets. Increased by dividing the scaly rootstocks. The fronds are about 3 feet high.

G. HARPEODES (Scimitar-like).— A tall-growing, rather

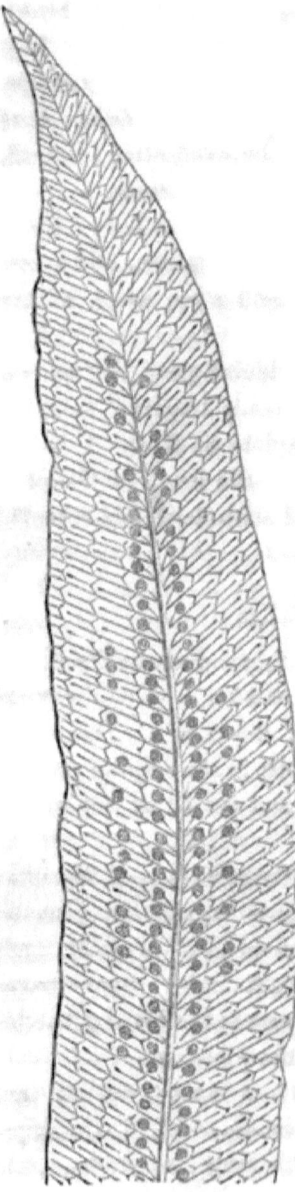

Fig. 27. Goniophlebium menisciifolium. (Pinna natural size.)

coarse Brazilian Fern. Fronds pinnate; the leaflets curved in a scimitar-like form. The fronds stand nearly erect upon a stalk a foot or more long, and often the frond itself reaches the height of 3 or 4 feet: hence it should only be grown where there is plenty of room. Spore-masses large, and in one series. Increased easily by dividing the thick, scaly, creeping rootstock.

G. INCANUM (Hoary).—A West-Indian Fern of dwarf habit. Fronds deeply divided, about 9 inches long, densely covered with hoary scales. Sori in one series. Veins indistinct. Rootstock creeping and scaly. It may be increased by division. This species is known also as *Lepicystis incana*.

G. LATIPES (Broad-footed).—A Brazilian Fern of a neat habit. Fronds pinnated, slender, and drooping, growing 18 inches high; leaflets long and narrow, undulated and spreading. Spore-masses small, and in two ranks. Increased by dividing the curiously-spotted creeping rootstock.

G. MENISCIIFOLIUM (Meniscium-leaved), *Fig.* 27.—A tall-growing Brazilian Fern of great beauty, arising from the beautiful arrangement of the angulated veins.

Fronds pinnate, growing 3 feet high; the leaflets are 6 inches, sharp, lance-shaped, undulated or wavy, and of a shining, bright green colour. Spore-masses large, often in two rows, and of a yellowish colour. Stalk bright green, and jointed on the creeping, scaly rootstock. Increased by division. A truly elegant Fern, but requires plenty of room to show off its beauty to advantage.

G. NERIIFOLIUM (Oleander-leaved).—A very fine species, with fronds about a yard high. They are pinnate, the side divisions being lance-shaped, about 6 inches long, and about three-quarters of an inch wide. The terminal leaflet is larger. Rhizome scaly and creeping.

G. PILOSELLOIDES (Pilosella-like).—A West-Indian, low-growing, creeping Fern, suitable for rustic baskets to suspend in the stove. Fronds simple, sterile, covered with light-coloured hairs, oval-shaped, and only 2 inches high; fertile, hairy, narrower than the barren fronds, and grows nearly double the height. Spore-masses in one series, and each surrounded with narrow scales. Rootstock slender and creeping. Increased very readily by division. This species is sometimes called *Lopholepis*.

G. SUBAURICULATUM (Half-eared).—From the Isle of Luzon. The most beautiful Fern in the genus. Fronds pinnate, growing 4 feet long; leaflets long and narrow, bright green, and subauriculate at the base. The fronds being long and slender, they are pendulous: hence it is a grand plant for a basket. There is a plant of it at Kew so growing that it has nearly twenty full-grown fronds, some of which are nearly 8 feet long. This is a noble elegant plant, and this is the way the plant ought to be grown to show its beauty. Increased by spores or by division, but it does not increase so rapidly in this way as some other species. It is the plant formerly called *Polypodium Reinwardtii*.

G. SEPULTUM (Covered).—A very remarkable South-American Fern of great beauty, and very rare. The fronds are lance-shaped and pinnate, and, when well grown, a foot or more in length. This deserves its designation of a very remarkable Fern from the fact that the pinnæ, or leaflets, are covered thickly with narrow fringed scales of a light hoary colour. These feathery scales give the plant a very distinct and beautiful appearance, so much so that anybody may distinguish it amongst a numerous collection many yards off. It will bear a lower temperature than most other stove Ferns. The *Adiantum macrophyllum* was quite killed in the same house in which this same *Goniophlebium* is quite healthy and uninjured. This is a remarkable fact, that some plants from hot regions bear more cold than others; and so, no doubt, many Ferns from warm climates have a constitution more hardy than we are aware of. This Fern we have increased, though slowly, by dividing the white slow-creeping rootstock. This is known in many gardens as *Lepicystis*.

G. VACCINIIFOLIUM (Bilberry-leaved).—This is another of those very small-fronded creeping kinds, which show themselves to most advantage when creeping over an old stem. It is a native of the forests of tropical America. The sterile fronds are oval, not more than an inch in length; but the fertile fronds, which are rather rarely developed, are a little longer and narrower.

G. VERRUCOSUM (Warted).—This Fern was imported from Malacca, and is rather scarce. Its fronds are pinnate with lanceolate pinnæ. They are often 7 or even 8 feet in length, and being too weak to support themselves they droop downwards at once. The plant should, therefore, be grown either at the top of a piece of rockwork, or, better still, in a suspended basket. There is a swelling on the upper side of the frond corresponding with the sorus below, whence the name.

Those above mentioned are the most distinct and striking kinds of *Goniophlebium;* but there are some few other kinds which should not be passed over without mention, as *G. colpodes, G. dissimile, G. fraxinifolium, G. glaucum, G. lætum,*

G. Owariense (another of the very small creeping kinds), *G. rhagadiolepis* (*Lepicystis*), &c.

GONIOPTERIS.

This is a well-defined genus, formed out of Polypodium by Presl. The name alludes to the lesser veins running in angles (*gonia*), and *pteris*, a Fern; or, in simple English, the Angular Fern. The species of this genus are not numerous, and grow only to a medium size, never exceeding 3 feet, and generally not more than 1 foot in height. The most interesting are—

GONIOPTERIS CRENATA (Scolloped-edged), *Fig.* 28.—A native of the West Indies, and very handsome. Fronds rather under 2 feet high, pinnate; pinnæ crenate, downy, pale green. Sori medial—that is, between the veins.

Under the name of *G. Ghiesbrechtii* M. Linden introduced a Fern which appears to be a variety of that above mentioned; it is more downy, and has but little to recommend it. It was named in honour of the botanical collector who discovered it.

G. FRAXINIFOLIA (Ash-

Fig. 28. Goniopteris crenata.

leaved).—A Brazilian Fern, with fronds 2 feet long; they are pinnate, and the pinnæ, or leaflets, are smooth, shining, and of a dark green. Many of these pinnæ form little buds at the end, which, in a damp stove, soon put out roots; and, if these are carefully cut off and planted shallow in a pot, under a bell-glass, they soon make good plants.

G. PENNIGERA (Feathered).—Though this elegant Fern is a native of New Zealand, it requires the stove to grow it to its greatest beauty. The barren fronds grow 1½ foot long, are spread open, and pinnate; the pinnæ are covered thinly with short hairs, and are of a long, narrow shape, like feathers. The fertile fronds grow more erect than the others. The spore-masses are placed in the middle, between the main ribs on the angle of the smaller veins. Increased by dividing the creeping rhizome. A very beautiful medium-sized Fern, worthy of general cultivation.

G. PROLIFERA (Proliferous).—This is a most curious and interesting East-Indian Fern. The fronds are once-divided, with lanceolate divisions. The peculiarity about the plant is that it will make a frond 3 or 4 feet long, which, if allowed to touch the soil, will make roots at the point, and then start on again in the same direction, so that it will soon get from one end of the house to the other.

G. REPTANS (Creeping).—A pretty little creeping Fern from Jamaica. The once-divided fronds lie almost flat upon the soil, and, rooting at the points, soon produce a numerous progeny of young plants. The fronds are about 9 inches long. It has a neat habit, and is well worthy of cultivation, though it is not often seen in gardens.

This genus is not generally a favourite one with Fern-growers. We have, therefore, described enough, probably, and may content ourselves with adding the names of a few others which are in cultivation:—*G. aspenoides*, *G. gracilis*, *G. megalodes* (or *obliterata*), *G. serrulata*, and *G. tetragona*. All from the West Indies and tropical America.

GYMNOGRAMMA.

This genus is one of the most interesting and most beautiful in cultivation, containing the elegant Gold and Silver Ferns. The name is derived from *gymnos*, naked, and *gramma*, writing, because the sori have no cover. With a moderate magnifier the spore-cases may be seen scattered over the lower surface of the frond without any covering. All growers of Ferns ought to have a tolerably good microscope to observe their wonderful conformation. Without such an instrument the greatest beauties of the tribe are lost to the unassisted eye. No *Gymnogramma* should ever be watered overhead, or syringed; for otherwise the white or yellow powder is washed off, and the beauty of the plant destroyed.

GYMNOGRAMMA CHRYSOPHYLLA (Golden-leaved).—Emphatically said to be "one of the most beautiful exotics in cultivation." Grows plentifully in the West Indies and South America, on stumps of trees and in crevices of shaded rocks. The fronds seldom exceed a foot in height, excepting under high cultivation, in a moist high temperature. They are bipinnate, or twice-divided, and the pinnæ are of an oval shape, slightly cut at the edges. The great beauty of this Fern consists in the under side being covered with a bright golden-coloured powder. Who has not been delighted, on seeing this Fern for the first time, at the bright yellow colour on the under side of the leaves? The upper surface, being of the usual green colour, has nothing remarkable about it; but, on turning the plant upside down, then the glorious golden yellow always calls forth exclamations of wonder and delight. Its culture is easy; the only point that must not be neglected is water. This element must be regularly supplied. It seeds freely; and, in favourable circumstances, the spores vegetate as freely. These circumstances are a constantly moist atmosphere with a high temperature. We have had them come up, as it were, spontaneously in the shady parts of the Orchid-house; but the more sure way is to scatter the spores on some sandstones, laid on a bed of moss, kept moist, and covered with a hand-light, or large bell-glass. The very young fronds of great numbers of Gymnogramma are beautifully cut into linear strips, and form almost a circle. By these they may be known from weedy common Ferns. When they have made the third leaf they should be transplanted into very small pots, replaced under the glass, and remain there till fresh roots are emitted. After that, place them in a shady place, and treat them like their congeners.

G. JAVANICA (From Java).—This strong-growing Fern is hardly worth cultivating except in large collections. Its fronds are supported upon long bare stems, sometimes 3 feet long; the upper part is twice or three times divided, the ultimate divisions being light green in colour, and lanceolate in form. It is also known as *Coniogramma*.

G. PERUVIANA ARGYROPHYLLA (Silver-leaved variety of the Peruvian).—This is the best Silver Fern in cultivation. The fronds, which are about a foot in length, are completely covered with pure white powder on the lower side; the upper surface is also powdered, but not to such an extent.

G. PULCHELLA (Pretty).—Like all the rest of the *Gymnogrammæ*, this is a native of tropical America. The fronds rise to about 1½ foot above the soil; they are very finely divided, and usually covered with white powder below, though the waxy dust is sometimes of a pale sulphur colour. The fronds of this Fern have a great tendency to divide into two equal parts, making it appear as if two fronds were joined together. A variety, in which this tendency to divide the stem is carried still further, has recently been sent out under the name of *G. pulchella ramosa*.

G. SULPHUREA (Sulphur-coloured).—This is one of the smallest, and, at the same time, the prettiest of the genus. The fronds seldom grow more than 6 or 8 inches long. The under side of the fronds and stems supporting them densely covered with clear sulphur-coloured powder. Like most of the others, it is easily raised from spores.

G. TARTAREA (Infernal).—So named, we suppose, because the stems are black as ink. As a contrast to the deep blackness of the stalks, the under side of the fronds is densely covered with a white powder: hence it has been called the Silver Fern. The fronds are broader at the base than the former species, often tripinnate; and the leaflets, or pinnæ, are oval, the lowest one divided into lobes. The grand distinguishing mark, however, is the white powder. Its culture is the same as for the preceding.

G. TOMENTOSA (Hairy), *Fig.* 29.—Native of Brazil and West Indies. It is very beautiful and tender. Fronds bipinnate, hairy, varying from 1 to 2 feet in height. Sori medial, obliquely forked. Stalk black.

G. TRIFOLIATA (Three-leaved).—This curious species has recently been imported from the West Indies. It is perfectly distinct in its appearance from any other Fern in cultivation. The fronds, which, it must be recollected, are rather brittle, grow quite upright; and, when full grown, they will probably attain a height of 4 feet. They produce clusters of pinnæ in threes all the way up the stem; they are shaped like long and narrow willow leaves. They are slightly dusted with yellow powder. There seem to be two varieties of this Fern imported, one with stems smooth, the other covered with brown scales.

Fig. 29. Gymnogramma tomentosa. (Pinna medium size.)

There are many other species of *Gymnogramma* to be found

in our gardens, as, for instance, two which are annuals and spring up as weeds wherever they have been grown—*G. chærophylla* and *G. leptophylla*. Three kinds, which are more or less hairy or downy, and not possessed of the coloured powder which we most of us look upon as characteristic of the genus—*G. lanata*, *G. tomentosa*, and *G. rufa*. There are also a few more powdered ones well worth growing—*G. calomelanos*, *G. L'Herminieri*, *G. Martensii*, *G. speciosa*, *G. Geardtii*, and others. The first-mentioned and *speciosa* are white, the others are Golden Ferns.

There are now several beautiful tufted and tasselled forms of Golden and Silver Ferns, but they seldom produce spores; and, therefore, we may naturally expect that they will continue rare for some time to come.

There are some others, but not particularly interesting; *G. ochracea* is quite a weed in the Orchid-house, and has some little of the golden powder on the stalks. It is often sold for the true Golden Fern.

GYMNOPTERIS.

From the Greek, *gymnos*, naked, and *pteris*, a Fern; alluding to the exposed fertile fronds. Sori partly or entirely covering the pinnæ. The species differ from each other most remarkably; the one first mentioned being a coarse-growing plant, while the next is remarkably neat.

Gymnopteris nicotianæfolia (Tobacco-leaved), *Fig*. 30.—Native of West Indies. Fertile frond about 18 inches high, erect, pinnate, or bipinnate below. Pinnæ large, oval. Stipes covered with narrow scales. Sterile frond about 2 feet high, smooth, pinnate, bright green, shining. This plant is not generally a favourite with cultivators; it is not only rather coarse in its habit, but is also very subject to the brown scale.

G. quercifolia (Oak-leaved).—A beautiful little gem, introduced from Ceylon a few years since. It looks like a cluster of oak leaves growing close to the soil, and covering the surface of the pot. It may readily be increased by division; care should be taken not to overpot it.

There is another species called *G. aliena*, which is still rather rare and not very striking.

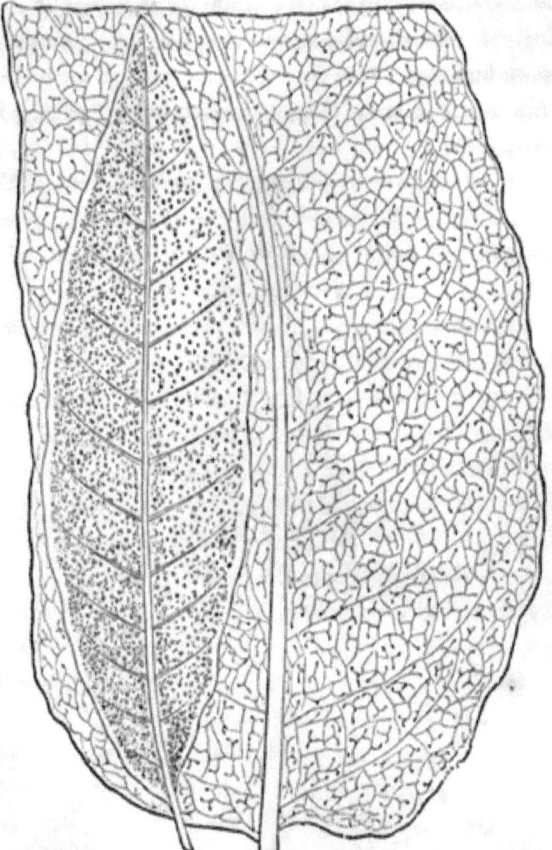

Fig. 30. Gymnopteris nicotianæfolia. (Part of sterile frond and pinna of fertile frond medium size.)

HEMIONITES.

A curious dwarf tribe of Ferns of considerable beauty. On account of their dwarf habit they are suitable for small collections, and their singular beauty recommends them even to the largest. The name is a very ancient one. It was first used by that ancient writer Dioscorides, and is derived from *hemionos*, a mule, because the plant was supposed to be barren—an erroneous idea, for the plants not only produce spores, but are actually viviparous—that is, producing plants on the fronds. The principal generic character consists in the superficial netted spore-masses.

HEMIONITES PALMATA (Hand-shaped), *Fig.* 31.—A West-

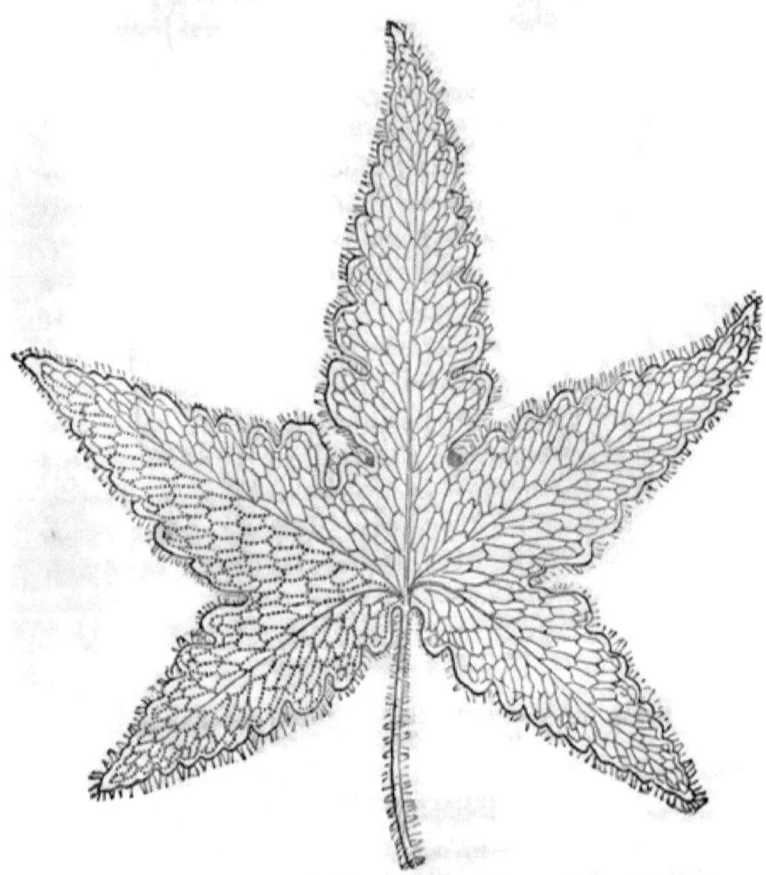

Fig. 31. Hemionites palmata. (Frond medium size.)

Indian Fern of great beauty. The fronds are of two kinds, barren and fertile. The fertile grow erect, about a foot high, with the spore-masses standing out above the surface, and covering it with network. The sterile fronds grow horizontally, or nearly so. Both are hand-shaped, or palmate, with five deeply-cut divisions, hairy, and producing at the bottom of each finger-like division a knob or bud. These, in time, will form a plant, if taken off and potted when roots are beginning to appear, and placed under a bell-glass, in a close moist heat. We have grown this species exceedingly large and fine in the Orchid-house. It requires a high moist temperature to grow it to perfection. Cultivators that have no Orchid-house should place this plant among moss kept moist, and a large bell-glass or hand-light over it.

There are two other species of this genus in our gardens— *H. cordata* (heart-shaped), and *H. pedata* (shaped like a bird's foot). In both of these the fronds are smooth instead of hairy, as in the above-named plant, but they are also like it in being very subject to the attacks of thrips. These insects always make their appearance first upon these and one or two other plants mentioned, but if not at once looked to and destroyed they soon spread to other plants; and when attacked by these little pests they soon lose the bright green colour which is their great charm. *H. cordata* is a native of the East-Indian Islands, and *H. pedata* comes from Mexico. Both are small-growing, beautiful plants, but they have the drawback above mentioned.

HEMITELIA.

Under this name are arranged some of the most beautiful of the tree Ferns. The name is derived from *hemi*, half, and *telia*, perfect; the indusium containing the spore-cases having the appearance of a cup of regular form. To see their beauty properly they should be examined with a pocket-lens; the cups piled-up with spore-cases will then be plainly seen.

HEMITELIA SPECIOSA (Showy), *Fig.* 32.—A South American Fern of large dimensions. The veins of this species are pinnate, the lowest pair running up from the midrib to the edge of the leaf. The next pair are placed above them, running parallel, and also to the margin; and at the end of each vein may be seen the beautiful cup with its tiny pyramid of spore-cases. The fronds are pinnate, 4 to 6 feet high, and each pinna is more than a foot long, and nearly 2 inches broad. These fronds are placed upon a tree-like stem, which in their native home is often 20 feet high.

The other species known in Britain are *H. grandifolia* (Trinidad); *H. Hostmanii* (Guiana); and *H. horrida.* This last is covered with aculeate or prickly scales, very formidable things to encounter in passing through the forests of Jamaica. The whole genus must be increased by spores, though sometimes a young plant is produced at the base of an old leaf amongst the scales; when that happens, tie a little moss just under the sprouting young plant, and as soon as roots are produced cut

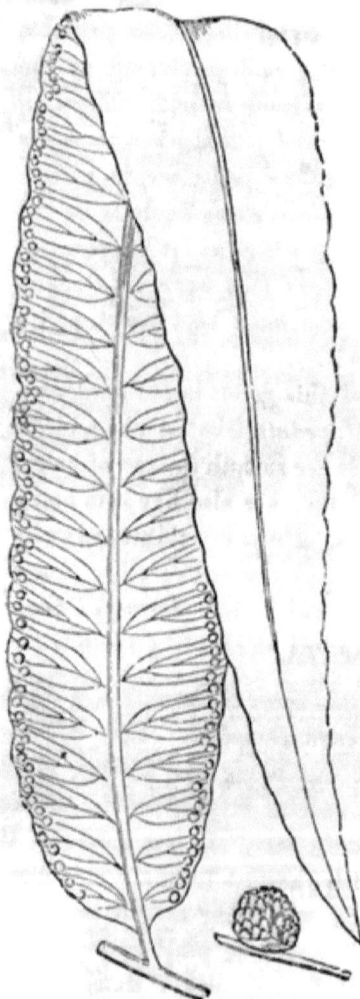

Fig. 32. Hemitelia speciosa. (Pinna medium size; a sorus magnified.)

it off and plant it in a small pot placed under a bell-glass till fairly established.

HEMIDICTYUM.

The genus was formed by Presl, the name being derived from *hemi*, half, and *diktyon*, a net; from the veins being netted only halfway across the pinnules. There is only one species in cultivation, and it was formerly called *Asplenium* (or *Diplazium*) *marginatum*.

HEMIDICTYUM MARGINATUM (Margined).—A native of tropical America. The fronds of this noble Fern rise to the height of 5 or 6 feet. They are pinnate, the pairs of pinnæ being each a foot long and 2 or 3 inches wide. The fronds, as well as the stalks supporting them, are quite smooth, and of a pale green colour. The fronds are very thin, and rapidly turn brown at the edges if the sun be allowed to shine upon them.

HEWARDIA. See *Adiantum Wilsonii*.

HUMATA.

The plants arranged under this name of Cavanilles' formerly formed a part of the large genus *Davallia*. The cups containing the spore-cases stand out along the margin of the fronds. There are only two species in cultivation, and one of these, *H. pedata*, is extremely rare. It is a native of the East Indies, and produced little divided fronds, triangular in outline, and of a dark green colour. They are not more than 3 inches in length. The soil should be piled up into a cone above the rim of the pot, and the creeping rhizomes pegged to it.

HUMATA HETEROPHYLLA (Variously-formed leaved).—The sterile fronds of this Fern are lance-shaped and undivided, but the fruit-bearing ones are deeply cut along the margin.

It makes long creeping rhizomes, which grow very fast: consequently it looks well grown in a suspended wire basket. It is also a native of the East.

HYMENODIUM. See *Dyctyoglossum*.

HYMENOPYLLUM.

Of this beautiful and interesting genus there are several species which require a stove temperature. The mode of treatment under which they succeed best is the same as that of the *Trichomanes*, to which genus we refer our readers for further information on this point. Messrs. Backhouse and Son, of York, have devoted much attention to this genus and the allied one, *Trichomanes*. They have introduced a great number of species; and the collection has been further increased by Mr. R. Sim, who has imported some very lovely New-Zealand forms.

HYMENOPHYLLUM ABRUPTUM (Abrupt or blunt).—A pretty little West-Indian Fern, with broad, once-divided, smooth, semi-transparent fronds, which are 2 inches long, and rather blunt at the apex, whence its name is derived.

H. CILIATUM (With hairs, like eye-lashes, round the margins).—Introduced several years ago from Jamaica. It forms dense clusters of its delicate little fronds. When once established it rapidly increases. The other stove kinds we mention by name, but they are, and will be for some time, very rare. *H. asplenioides* (asplenium-like), *H. cruentum* (crimson), *H. hirsutum* (hairy), *H. nudum* (naked), *H. Plumieri* (Plumier's), and *H. sericeum* (silky).

HYPODERRIS.

Derived from the Greek *hypo*, under, and *derris*, skin; from the indusium being attached partly under the sori. There is only one representative of this genus in cultivation.

It has creeping rhizomes, and may easily be increased by division.

HYPODERRIS BROWNII (Brown's), *Fig.* 33.—Native of Trinidad. Fronds about 18 inches high, light green, simple,

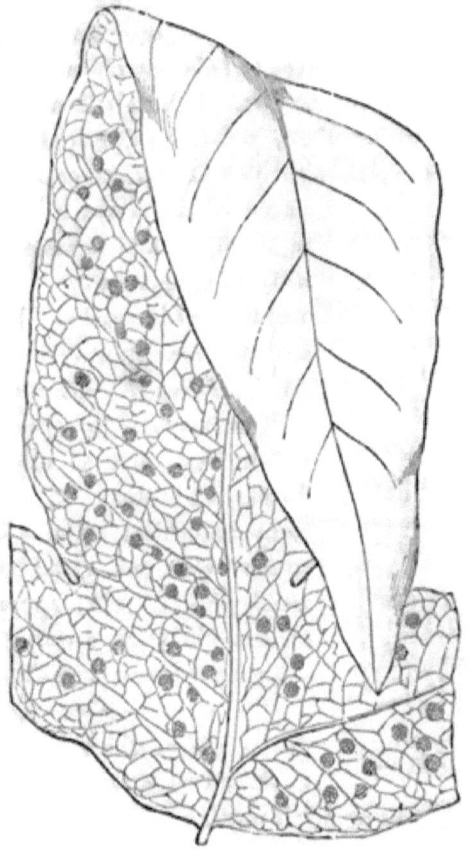

Fig. 33. Hypoderris Brownii. (Part of a frond medium size.)

or trilobate; lateral lobes small; middle one very large, undulated, rather membranous. Stipes and rachis thickly sprinkled with small pale scales. The fronds of this plant are very liable to turn brown in winter; they should not therefore be wetted overhead at that season.

HYPOLEPIS.

The name of this genus is derived from *hypo*, under, and *lepis*, a scale, the seeds being under or concealed by a scaly covering.

HYPOLEPIS REPENS (Creeping), *Fig.* 34.—A strong-growing Fern from the West Indies. In large stoves, where plants of dense foliage are wanted to hide any object in shady places, no Fern is so useful as this. Although it may be regarded as a coarse-growing Fern, yet the soft-coloured light green foliage is very pleasing. We have cultivated it under the stages of the stove to hide the hot-water pipes, and against naked walls with the best effect. There is a variety with curled leaves, more curious than beautiful; some authors call it *H. repens difforme*.

The fronds of the species grow 3 or 4 feet high, and of the form called decompound—that is, ramified into many branchlets. The whole plant is covered with soft, gland-bearing hairs, which give it a silky appearance. Increases freely by dividing the freely-creeping rhizome, and also by spores.

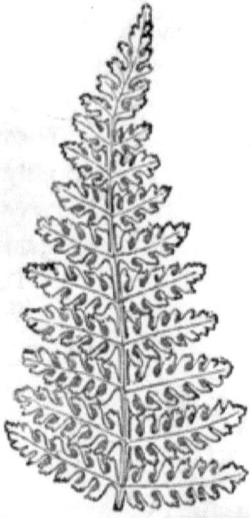

Fig. 34. Hypolepis repens. (Pinnule natural size.)

There is another species called *H. tenuifolia*, which has a very similar habit and appearance; in fact they are too much alike to render it worth while to grow both kinds.

LEPICYSTIS.

A name given by Mr. Smith, of Kew, one of the best authorities on Ferns, to those species of *Goniophlebium* which are densely covered with scales, as *G. incanum*, *G. sepultum*, &c., under which names they will be found in these pages.

LEPTOGRAMMA.

A lovely genus of Ferns, separated by Mr. Smith, of Kew, from *Gymnogramma*. Name derived from *leptos*, slender, and *gramma*, writing; the spore-masses being long and slender, like fine writing.

LEPTOGRAMMA VILLOSA (Hairy), *Fig.* 35.—A Brazilian Fern, of the neatest habit and most regular form, in respect of fronds, veins, and spore-masses, of any Fern known. Fronds hairy, twice-divided or bipinnated, growing 2 feet long; the pinnæ are regularly and oppositely disposed on each side of the stalk, and the veins are arranged on each side of the midrib, like the bones from the back-bone in a herring. Then the sori or spore-masses are regularly disposed on the veins towards the lower part of each pinna. Such an elegant Fern ought to be in every collection. It is the only species grown in this country, and is exceedingly rare, though it may be increased by dividing the creeping rhizome or rootstock.

Fig. 35. Leptogramma villosa. (Top of pinna medium size.)

LEUCOSTEGIA.

The plants known by this name were divided by Presl from the well-known genus *Davallia*. We have seen *L. immersa* do pretty well in a greenhouse, but as they certainly succeed better in the stove, it was thought advisable to introduce them here. They are very readily increased by division. They lose their fronds in winter, and the pots may then be turned on their sides, or placed on a shelf and kept dry until they begin to start. If they require potting, or it is thought advisable to part them, it should be done before they commence making their fronds in spring. They are sometimes known under the name of *Acrophorus*. The name *Leucostegia* is derived from *leucos*, white, and *stege*, a covering, alluding to the pale indusium.

LEUCOSTEGIA CHÆROPHYLLA (Chervil-leaved). — An East-Indian Fern, having light delicate green fronds, which are about a foot or 18 inches long; they are cut up into fine segments, and are somewhat erect.

L. IMMERSA (Imbedded, referring to the sori), *Fig.* 36.—The pale green fronds of this Fern hang somewhat horizontally, spreading out almost flat, with the points drooping. The fronds are repeatedly divided, but not into such fine segments as the last-named plant. There is a little pouch-like swelling above the spore-masses on the upper sides of the fronds.

There is a third species sometimes met with in gardens, and called *L. pulcher* (the beautiful).

Fig. 36. Leucostegia immersa. (Pinna full size; spore-mass magnified.)

LINDSÆA.

This name is commemorative of Mr. Lindsay, a cryptogamist. This is a very extensive tropical genus, most of the species of which are as elegant as the Maiden-hair Ferns. There seems, however, to be a difficulty in growing them, as many beautiful kinds have been introduced and afterwards lost again. *L. cultrata* was quite common eight or nine years ago, but we have not seen a plant of it for some time, and believe it to be extinct, or nearly so. Just recently several kinds have been again imported, but will be rare for some time to come.

LINDSÆA TRAPEZIFORME (Trapezium-shaped pinnæ), *Fig.* 37. —Native of East and West Indies. Fronds 18 inches high, smooth, bipinnate; divisions of the pinnæ overlapping as shown in the figure. It was introduced in 1845, but has lately been very rare. Like most of the others, it is very elegant, and we hope shortly to see a good many of them imported. There are a dozen or two of kinds in the tropics which would be well worth growing.

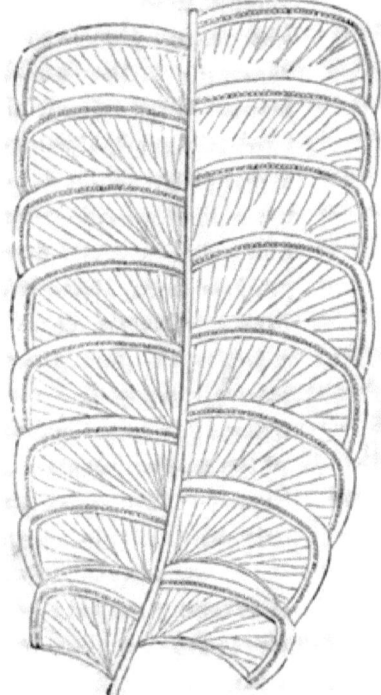

Fig. 37. Lindsæa trapeziforme. (Base of pinna full size.)

LITOBROCHIA.

The species in this genus were formerly arranged under *Pteris*. They are distinguished principally by their netted veins. The species are rather numerous, and are chiefly from the hotter regions of the world: hence they require a high temperature. We shall only particularly mention a few.

LITOBROCHIA DENTICULATA (Toothed), *Fig.* 38.—A Brazilian evergreen Fern. Fronds 12 to 18 inches high, glabrous; lower branches subpinnate; upper part pinnate, with lower segments divided. Barren pinnæ broad, oblong, acuminate, spiny, toothed at edge. Fertile fronds shape of barren. Sori continuous.

L. LEPTOPHYLLA (Slender-leaved).—We have grown this Brazilian Fern many years, but always found that to do it well it was necessary to keep it constantly in the Orchid-house. Sterile fronds almost triangular, bipinnate and tripinnate at the base; pinnæ light greyish-green, linear, and cut at the margin into thorny, teeth-like forms. Fertile fronds erect, with the spore-masses running in a continuous line on the margin of the narrow leaflets. A beautiful Fern, increased only, but freely, by spores.

L. VESPERTILIONIS (Bat's-wing-shaped.) — A strong-growing Fern, very common in tropical countries; and well adapted for filling a dark corner in the stove. It grows 3 or 4 feet high, and the fronds are several times divided. They are of a glaucous green colour. This plant is well suited for exhibition, but is too strong a grower for small collections. It has a creeping rhizome. The spores germinate very freely.

LLAVEA CORDIFOLIA. See *Ceratodactylus osmundoides*.

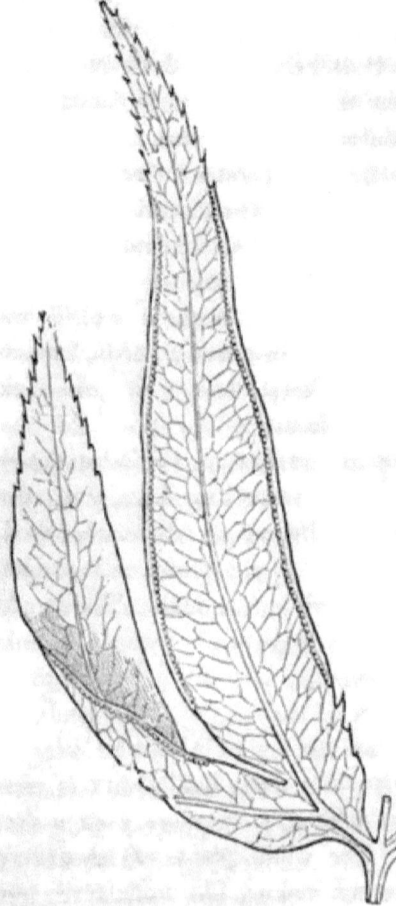

Fig. 38. Litobrochia denticulata. (Pinna medium size.)

LOMARIA.

A large genus of Ferns whose geographical distribution embraces almost every country and climate in the world. The well-known *Blechnum spicant* of this country, so common at the foot of rocks in Derbyshire, belongs to this genus, under the name of *Lomaria spicant*. Any person acquainted with this Fern may have a good idea of the whole genus. *Lomaria* is closely allied to *Blechnum*, differing from it in its contracted fertile fronds. It will be found that many species of *Lomaria* which are usually grown in a stove succeed much better, and keep cleaner, if cultivated in a cooler house.

LOMARIA ATTENUATA (Thin-leaved).— A pinnated, interesting Fern from the Mauritius. Barren fronds lance-shaped, with the edge of the pinnæ quite entire, growing about a foot high. The fronds have a pink tinge while young. Fertile fronds pinnate, growing a foot high in the centre of the others. Both kinds are placed on the top of a slender stem or caudex. We have had plants of this species with a stem more than a foot high. The whole plant was then very interesting, looking like a miniature tree Fern. Increased by offsets, which are often produced on the stem. A suitable Fern for small collections.

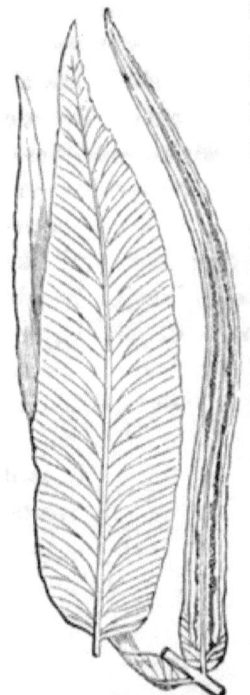

Fig. 39. Lomaria onocleoides. (Pinna of barren and piece of fertile frond natural size.)

L. FALCATA (Sickle-shaped).—This is also called *L. gigantea*. It comes from Natal. The dark-green glossy fronds are 2 feet in length. It is one of the most striking Ferns cultivated, and would tell with much effect upon the exhibition-stages. It has not so strong a tendency to produce fertile fronds as some of the others, and this may be looked upon as an advantage, as they soon turn brown and become unsightly.

L. ONOCLEOIDES (Onoclea-like), *Fig.* 39.—An interesting Fern, found in most of the West Indian Islands. Barren fronds oval, lance-shape, pinnate; the leaflets or pinnæ thick and leathery, wavy at the edges, and roundly cut at the margin towards the top. Fertile fronds pinnate, also the pinnæ are narrow and contracted. Stalk of the fronds scaly. The rootstock is creeping: hence it may be increased by division. The whole plant seldom exceeds a foot in height: therefore it is a desirable species for a small collection.

LONCHITIS.

From the Greek *lonche*, a lance, referring to the shape of the frond. Closely allied to *Litobrochia*.

LONCHITIS PUBESCENS (Hairy), *Fig.* 40. — Native of Mauritius. Arborescent. Fronds light green, about 4 feet long, hairy, bipinnate. Pinnæ lanceolate; pinnules oblong, pointed opposite, membranous, pinnatifid, segments rounded. Spore-masses seated in the sinuses of pinnules. It is rather rare. It is only now and then that a young plant can be parted off the old ones.

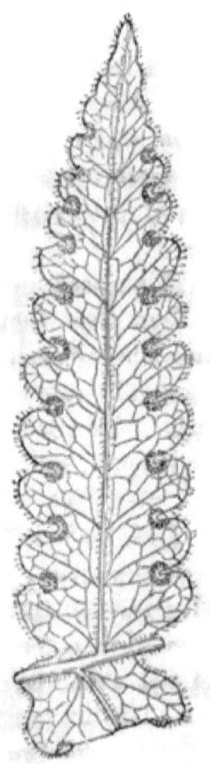

Fig. 40. Lonchitis pubescens. (Part of pinna medium size.)

LOPHOSORIA. See *Alsophila pruinata*.

LYGODICTYON.

This genus, containing only one plant, differs only from

Lygodium in having netted instead of free veins, as the name implies.

LYGODICTYON FORSTERI (Forster's).—A native of the South Sea Islands. It makes a dense dwarf bush, very pretty, and of a delicate light green colour. The stems, as in *Lygodium*, are wiry, and the plant can be propagated by division. The fronds are very small, and produced in pairs.

LYGODIUM.

This name is derived from *lygodes*, flexible, and was given in allusion to the twining habit of the plants arranged under this generic term. It is a very interesting group, and no collection of Ferns should be without a representative of it. When in fructification they are still more interesting than at other times, for the spores are produced in little spike-like processes, which give the fronds the appearance of being fringed. They are very variable in the form of their fronds, and consequently some confusion among the names.

LYGODIUM FLEXUOSUM (Climbing. *L. volubile* of some gardens).—One of the most striking plants of the group; originally imported from the East Indies. It succeeds very well, and produces a very pleasing appearance, if trained to one of the supports of the roof. The fronds are divided into five or six long narrow lobes.

L. JAPONICUM (Japanese).—Not so strong a grower as the last, and more dense in its habits. Like the others, it may be increased by division. It hardly requires a stove heat, perhaps; but with us it has always looked poor and stunted in the greenhouse.

L. PALMATUM (Palmate, or shaped like a hand).—This is a very distinct species. It scarcely attempts to climb at all, but its fronds make a dense cluster about a foot above the soil. It is a native of America.

L. POLYSTACHYUM (Many-shooted).—This Fern was imported from central India by Mr. Veitch. When first we saw it we thought it must be a kind of *Gleichenia;* but as the plant became older it put on the true character of this genus. The fronds are branched, like most of the family, and are downy on the upper surface.

There are several other *Lygodiums* in our gardens, but those above mentioned are the most distinct. The others are *L. scandens*, *L. venustum*, *L. articulatum*.

MARATTIA.

A genus allied to *Angiopteris*, and, like it, is of a half aquatic kind of habit—making thick fleshy roots, and delighting in plenty of water during summer. Though these plants do not attain so great a size as the *Angiopteris*, yet they are too large for any place where there is not an abundance of room in the stove. The name was given in honour of J. F. Maratti, an Italian botanist.

MARATTIA LAXA (Loose).—Fronds 3 or 4 feet high, thrice-divided, light green. This plant almost always looks flaccid, as though wanting water. It is by no means attractive.

M. PURPURASCENS (Purplish).—The dark green fronds rise with thick stems from a more massive-looking crown than that of the last species. Fronds of this will often be seen 4 feet long, and spreading out from the centre every way. It is somewhat brittle, or would otherwise form a noble exhibition plant.

MENISCIUM.

A genus of Ferns remarkable for their regular veining. So beautifully are those veins disposed, that they form numerous regularly-disposed rectilinear parallelograms, and the fructification is arranged in the form of a crescent: hence its name, from *meniskos*, a crescent. Upon this character the genus is founded.

MENISCIUM PALUSTRE (Marsh), *Fig.* 41.—A South-American Fern of great beauty, though rather a large one, requiring considerable space to grow it well. Fronds pinnate, growing 4 feet high; pinnæ 8 inches long. When of full size every frond is fertile. The spore-masses are regularly disposed between the veins in crescent-shape. There are sometimes small buds formed at the base of the pinnæ, and by these, as well as by dividing the creeping rhizome, the species may be increased. We have grown this Fern to even a larger size than indicated above, by potting it frequently—that is, every three months, in rough sandy peat and half-decayed leaves pressed close. It is a fine Fern, and worthy of being grown wherever there is room.

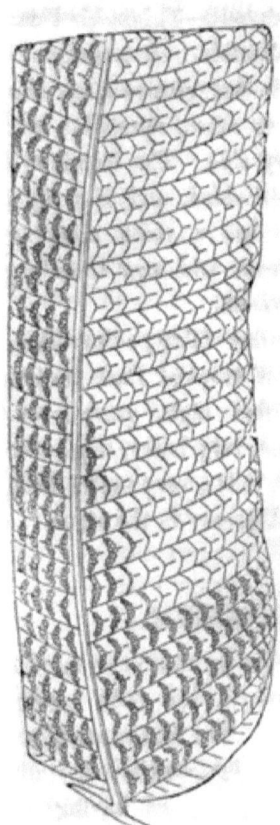

Fig. 41. Meniscium palustre. (Part of pinna natural size.)

M. SIMPLEX (Simple-fronded). —A rare dwarf Fern, from the warmer parts of China. Fronds simple, elliptical, or halbert-shaped in form, beautifully veined. The fertile fronds are more erect than the others, and have longer stalks. Increased by dividing its creeping rhizome. It should be in every collection, however small.

MICROLEPIA.

From the Greek, *mikros*, small, and *lepis*, a scale, alluding to the indusium. A large-growing set of Ferns, having creeping rhizomes, so that they can readily be increased by division. *M. platyphylla* is the best, and makes a noble specimen for exhibition.

MICROLEPIA PLATYPHYLLA (Broad-leaved).—This noble Fern was introduced from the East Indian Islands. It is a strong-growing plant, well adapted for exhibition purposes, as the fronds grow to the height of 4 feet or more, spreading out gracefully on every side. The fronds are bipinnate or twice-divided, and of a light green colour. It has a thick creeping rhizome or rootstock, and may therefore be increased by division.

M. POLYPODIOIDES (Polypodium-like), *Fig.* 42.—Native of tropical East Indies. Fronds about 4 feet high, grass-green, triangular in outline, very hairy, tripinnate or thrice-divided. It is a very useful Fern for filling up a dark corner in the stove.

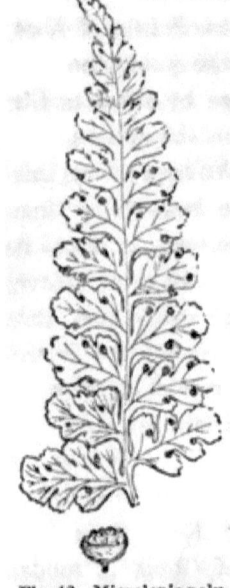

Fig. 42. Microlepia polypodioides. (Pinna medium size; sorus magnified.)

MICROSORUM.

This name refers to the very minute sori which distinguish the only species placed in the genus. The fronds are about 18 inches or 2 feet high, undivided, stalkless, thick and leathery, and having the little dots of spore-masses scattered thickly over the lower side. Rhizomes creeping. The plant has very little to recommend it, as the fronds are stiff and rigid, and without any of the elegance which generally characterises the family. It is a native of the tropics both in the East and the West. There is a curious variety of this plant, which is at present rather rare, in which the points of the fronds are developed into large tassels, like some of the forms of *Scolopendrium*.

There is a variety, which we first saw in the garden at

Wentworth House, with the points of the fronds repeatedly divided, like those of a crested *Scolopendrium*, and to such an extent was this tassel developed that it quite bent the fronds down.

MYRIOPTERIS. See *Cheilanthes*.

NEOTTOPTERIS.

A noble genus of Ferns, formed by Mr. Smith, of Kew, out of *Asplenium*, from which genus it differs by the continuous marginal vein running on the edge of every leaf or

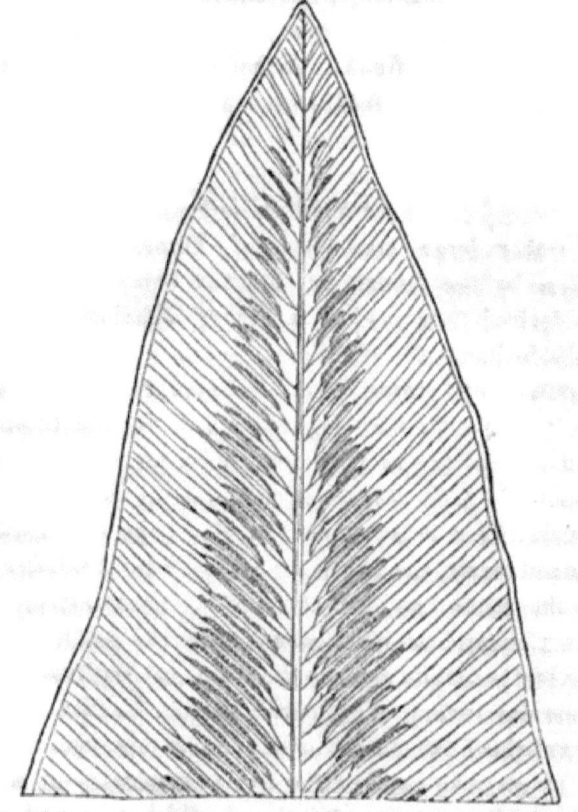

Fig. 43. Neottopteris vulgaris. (Top of frond natural size.)

frond, connecting or binding, as it were, all the cross veins at their extreme points. The name is derived from *neottia*, a bird's nest: hence it is commonly called "*The Bird's-nest Fern;*" the fronds being arranged circularly around the top of the tufted rootstock, giving it a fanciful similarity to a bird's nest.

NEOTTOPTERIS VULGARIS (Common), *Fig.* 43.— A Fern rather widely distributed, it having been found in India, the Mauritius, and the tropical parts of New Holland, besides on several islands in the Indian seas. Fronds simple, growing 3 or 4 feet high; midrib black, and triangular on the under side. Spore-masses large, placed in lines about halfway between the midrib and the margin, and filling only the upper part of the frond. A handsome Fern even when small, and increases freely by spores. It is also called *N. australasica*.

NEPHRODIUM.

A rather large assemblage of Ferns, separated from *Aspidium* by the foreign and learned botanist, Dr. Schott. Name derived from *nephros*, a kidney, alluding to the form of the indusium.

NEPHRODIUM MOLLE (Soft).— Every collector is almost certain to have this very common Fern. It used to be quite a weed with us in the Orchid-house, coming up from spores abundantly in almost every pot, and even on the walls between the bricks. Yet it is a very fine Fern; the fructification is so free and lovely, the fronds are covered with soft hair: hence its specific name; and the cover of the spore-masses is very hairy. The plant grows about 2 feet high.

A very beautiful and novel variety of *Nephrodium molle* was introduced from West Africa by Mr. R. Sim, the Fern-grower of the Foot's Cray Nursery, a few years ago, under the name of *corymbiferum*. The frond terminates in a dense crest, spreading to several inches in thickness; and all the divisions of the frond end in tassels or crests of the same kind, but smaller. The fronds often divide at the base into two. Altogether this is a most unique and curious plant.

N. MULTILINEATUM (Many-lined).—The arrangement of the veins of this beautiful Fern is extremely elegant, quite as much so as in *Meniscium*. Fronds pinnate, growing 2 feet high, and of a lively green colour; pinnæ or wings lance-shaped, and pointed with a deeply-notched margin. Spore-masses covered with a kidney-shaped shield or indusium. A beautiful Fern from Ceylon; and increases freely by dividing the creeping rhizome.

N. TERMINANS (Ending), *Fig.* 44.—An East-Indian Fern of considerable beauty. It is somewhat similar to the last species. The spore-masses are at the points of the veins: hence its specific name. Its fronds are about a foot in height, once-divided, and of a light green colour. It may be propagated by division of the rhizome, or by spores.

The rest of the species cultivated in Great Britain are *N. articulatum* (Jointed); *N. Hookerii* (Sir W. Hooker's), raised among some Orchids imported to the Botanic Garden, Sheffield; *N. unitum* (Joined); *N. patens* (Spreading), from Demerara; *N. truncatum* (Cut-off),

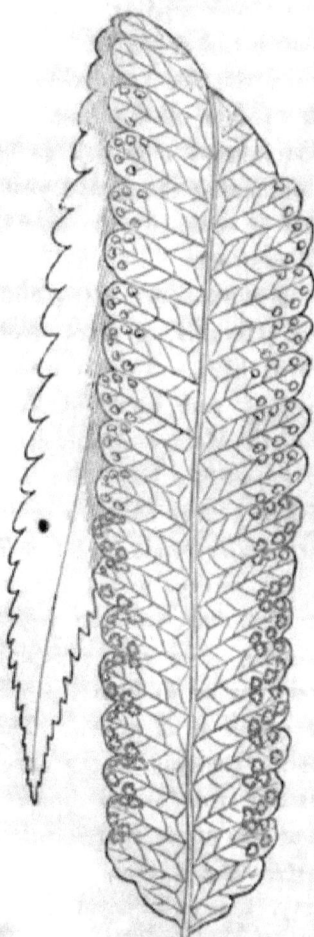

Fig. 44. Nephrodium terminans.
(Pinna natural size.)

a native of the South Sea Islands; and *N. venustum* (Beautiful), a Jamaica plant.

NEPHROLEPIS.

Generic name derived from the Greek *nephros*, a kidney, and *lepis*, a scale; the indusium being kidney-shaped. Many of the species in this genus have a singular peculiarity: if the points of the fronds be not injured they will go on lengthening the second year; this is especially the case in *N. exaltata*.

NEPHROLEPIS DAVALLIOIDES (Davallia, or Hare's-foot-Fern, like).—This is a very distinct and beautiful Fern from the Malayan Archipelago. It grows to a large size, and makes a very effective specimen. The fronds are 5 feet in length, or even more; upright at first, but with the points bending over and sweeping down so as to hide the pot in which it is grown. The sterile portions of the once-divided fronds are broader than the upper spore-bearing parts. Mr. R. Sim, of Foot's Cray, the well-known Fern-grower, has introduced a very distinct variety of this Fern, with the pinnæ more deeply divided and overlapping each other. It has been called *N. davallioides dissecta*.

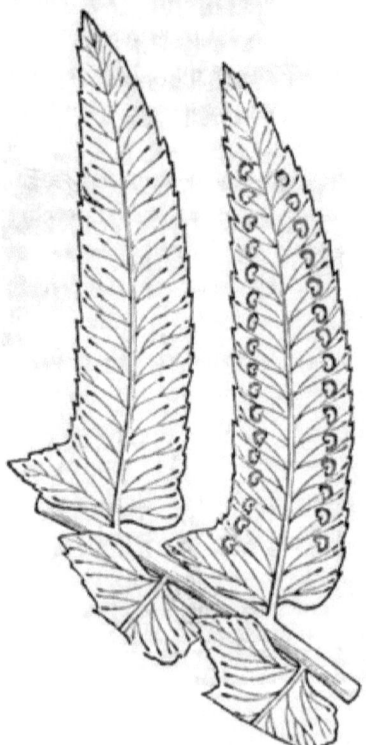

Fig. 45. Nephrolepis exaltata. (Part of frond full size.)

N. EXALTATA (Lofty), *Fig.* 45.—Native of South America,

West Indies, &c. Fronds from 3 to 6 feet high, and 2 or 3 inches broad, yellowish-green, pinnate, eared on the upper side of the base. Stem and stalks clothed with brown scales. Easily increased by division.

N. HIRSUTULA (The Small Hairy).—An East-Indian species, rather rare in gardens. Its once-divided fronds are about 2 feet in height, and stand almost upright. The stipes is covered with hairs of a reddish-brown colour.

N. PECTINATA (Comb-shaped).—A small-growing kind from the warmer parts of America. It has just the same habit as the other species, but upon a miniature scale. The fronds are not more than a foot high, and about $1\frac{1}{2}$ inch in width.

N. SPLENDENS (Splendid).—This, again, is one of the large-growing sorts, and not much unlike *N. davallioides*, except that the fertile pinnæ are not toothed as in that species; at least not to so great an extent. The fronds attain the length of 4 feet.

N. TUBEROSA (Tuberous-rooted).—An East-Indian species, producing little tubers among the roots about the size of nuts. It is said that these tubers have been occasionally collected and used as food by the natives. The fronds are about a yard in length, and 4 inches in width. It dies down in winter, and the pot must then be carefully placed on one side and kept somewhat dry.

There are a few other kinds to be met with in gardens— as *N. acuta* (sharp-pointed), *N. ensifolia* (sword-shaped), *N. undulata* (wavy); but those above mentioned are the most distinct.

NIPHOBOLUS.

A very pretty, dwarf, useful genus of Ferns. The name is derived from *nipholus*, covered with snow; the fronds being covered with white starry clusters of short hairs. We have used these Ferns much to ornament rustic rockwork

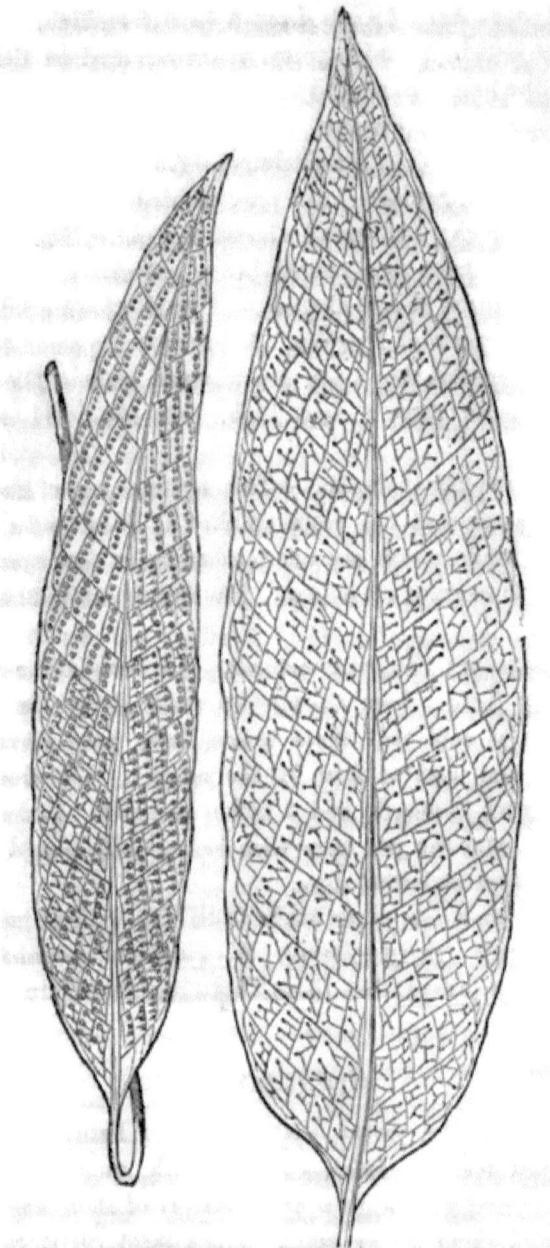

Fig. 46. Niphobolus lingua. (Fertile frond [smaller] and barren frond both natural size.)

in the stove, and grown them in rustic baskets, vases, &c., with the happiest effect. It is a very distinct genus, and may be known at once by its simple fronds and star-like clusters of short hairs.

NIPHOBOLUS ANGUSTATUS (Narrow).—This is the *N. sphærocephalus* of some gardens. Like the rest of the species of this genus, the fronds are entire or undivided. They are very thick and leathery. They are stalkless, and about a foot in length, having a width of about 1½ inch in the middle.

N. LINGUA (Tongue-shaped), *Fig.* 46.—An evergreen, pretty species, native of China and Japan. Barren fronds averaging 8 inches in height, dull green on upper surface, and whitish beneath. Fertile fronds narrower, but same size. Sori brownish-red, in parallel rows.

N. PERTUSUS (Bored). — An East-Indian dwarf Fern, creeping very fast on rockwork. Fronds simple, 6 inches long, very thick and leathery. Fertile fronds narrow. Spore-masses thickly placed on the upper half of the frond, giving it the appearance of a piece of new leather. The rest of the species are *N. Gardnerii* (Dr. Gardner's); *N. nummularifolius* (Nummularia-leaved), a very small Fern; *N. rupestris* (Rock); and *N. varius* (Variable).

NOTHOCHLÆNA.

We have now arrived at a genus of Ferns possessing as much delicate beauty as any already noticed. The only drawback on their general cultivation is the difficulty of keeping them in a state of health amongst other Ferns that require a moist atmosphere. The fronds of most of the species are covered with a fine down, or woolly scales. These retain moisture, and, in long-continued dark weather, in consequence of the wet being retained on the fronds, they perish, and the plants perish also. To guard against this evil, it is necessary to place the plants in the driest and least shady part of the house, and *never to wet the leaves, either with the watering-pot or the syringe.* With these few warning remarks on their culture, we shall briefly notice a few of the most interesting species, though every one of the genus is worthy of cultivation.

NOTHOCHLÆNA ECKLONIANA (Ecklon's).—Though from the Cape of Good Hope, this elegant Fern requires a moderate stove, but the conditions of culture mentioned above must be strictly complied with. Fronds tripinnate, growing a foot high; leaflets oblong and blunt at the extremities, deeply cut, and the edges rising. They are covered with narrow scales of a white colour, giving them a woolly character. A fine batch of seedlings of this elegant Fern may be got by sowing the spores on some pieces of rough peat, placing the pot containing them in a pan of water, and covering the whole with a large bell-glass. The moisture arising from the water keeps the soil moist enough for the spores to germinate, when, as soon as observed, prop-up the bell-glass with a small stone, gradually increasing the aperture till the plants make their third leaf; then the glass should be entirely removed, and after a few days the plants potted-off, placed in a shady spot, and inured by degrees to bear the full light. Most Ferns would grow (if the spores were good), treated in a similar manner. It may, however, be propagated by dividing the creeping rhizome.

N. FLAVENS (Yellow).—This beautiful little Fern, from the central parts of America, is sometimes known in gardens as *Cincinalis flavens.* The fronds are tripinnate, about 6 inches high, including the slender black stalks supporting them. The divisions of the fronds are bright green on the upper side, while the lower surface is covered with yellow powder.

N. MARANTÆ (Maranta's: he was an old botanist).—This plant is a native of the South of Europe, and extends eastward into Asia. The fronds are about a foot in length, and 2 inches in width, twice-divided, supported by short stalks covered with brownish scales.

N. NIVEA (Snowy).—This, as well as the following species, is sometimes included in the genus *Cincinalis*. It comes from the tropical parts of America. It has thrice-divided fronds, only about 4 inches in length; they are slightly dusted with white powder above, and densely covered with it on the under side. It is a perfect little gem.

N. SQUAMATA (Scaly).—A Mexican dwarf Fern of great beauty. Fronds pinnate, growing only about 6 inches high; leaflets dark green on the upper side, and white beneath.

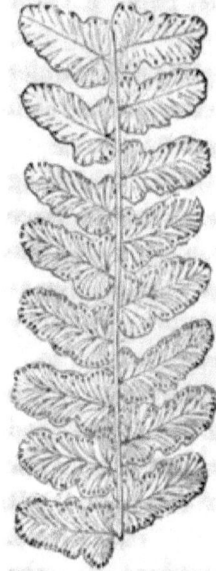

Fig. 47. Nothochlæna trichomanoides. (Part of fertile frond natural size.)

N. TENERA (Slender).—Originally imported from Chili. The fronds are somewhat triangular in form, thrice-divided, about 6 inches long, supported by slender black stalks. The fronds are dusted with white powder, but not to such an extent as in the last-named species. The only way to increase this and the last-mentioned is by spores; they germinate quickly and readily.

N. TRICHOMANOIDES (Trichomanes-like), *Fig. 47.*—Introduced from Jamaica: known also as *Pteris trichomanoides*. It is a handsome, slender plant, 1 foot high. Fronds pinnate, pendulous, powdered white beneath, and with brownish hairs; pinnæ bluntly lobed. Spore-masses terminal, forming a marginal band.

The rest of the stove species are *N. rufa* (rusty); *N. sinuata* (sinuated); *N. tomentosa* (woolly); and some others.

ODONTOSORIA.

So called because the divisions of the frond having the sori are tooth-shaped. It includes only two species, which were at first included under the name of *Davallia:* one of these is a native of the eastern, the other of the western hemisphere. They are both very elegant and graceful plants.

ODONTOSORIA ACULEATA (Thorny).—This is a twining plant, with long wiry stems, which, by means of the hooked thorns with which they are furnished, scramble over other plants in the West Indian Islands, just as the brambles do upon our commons. The fronds are several times divided, and are of a lively green colour. It should be trained round a trellis, or allowed to climb a pillar in the fernery.

O. TENUIFOLIA (Slender-fronded).—This plant differs widely from the last-named kind. The fronds are produced in a cluster from the crown; they are supported upon slender stems, and are divided into very minute divisions. The fronds are about 2 feet high, and droop over on every side very gracefully. It is a native of the East Indies, and was originally raised in Prussia from spores which were sent from Ceylon.

OLEANDRA.

Derivation of the name is unexplained; but as the genus was founded upon *O. neriiformis*, it may refer to its resemblance to the *Oleander*. All the species except that just named have long trailing rhizomes, and are well suited for cultivation in baskets. *O. neriiformis* has rigid upright stems, and forms quite a bush.

OLEANDRA NERIIFORMIS (Nerium or Oleander-like).—This plant has a wide geographical range, having been found in the tropical parts of both the eastern and western hemispheres. Its stems are nearly or quite erect, and branching, growing 2 feet or more in height, and producing numerous lanceolate, undivided fronds, which are about a foot long. This is a perfectly distinct and peculiar species, well worthy of cultivation.

O. NODOSA (Knotted), *Fig.* 48.—Native of West Indian

Islands. Fronds about a foot high, bright green, lanceolate, undivided; margin entire. Stem and stalks black; latter covered beneath with brown scales. Spore-masses scattered.

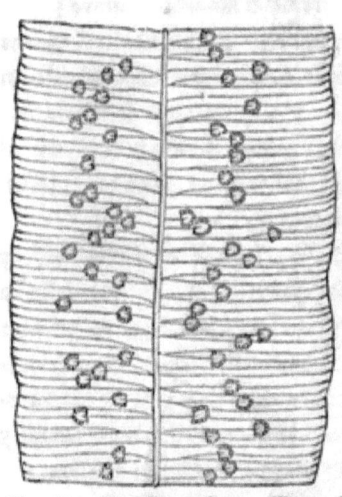

Fig. 48. Oleandra nodosa. (Part of frond medium size.)

Like the other kinds, it can be readily divided.

There are several other species in cultivation, all having creeping rhizomes, and resembling each other in the form of the fronds: *O. articulata*, from Ceylon; *O. hirtella*; *O. Natalensis*, from Port Natal.

OLFERSIA.

OLFERSIA CERVINA, *Fig.* 49. —The only species in cultivation. The first, or generic, name is commemorative of Olfers, a German. The second means stag-horned, in allusion to the appearance of the fertile fronds. Both sterile and fertile fronds are pinnated; the former are beautifully veined, and the latter are covered with spore-masses. It is a fine Fern, and grows about 2 feet long. We have increased it readily by dividing the creeping rhizome, preserving a frond and growing-point to each division.

ONYCHIUM.

For a figure illustrative of the character of this genus, as well as the derivation of the name, &c., see the Greenhouse division. There are only two species in cultivation, one of which must be grown in a stove, the other in the greenhouse.

ONYCHIUM AURATUM (Golden).—This Fern is a native of the East Indian Islands. The fronds are 2 feet in height, and about 9 inches wide; they are divided into narrow linear

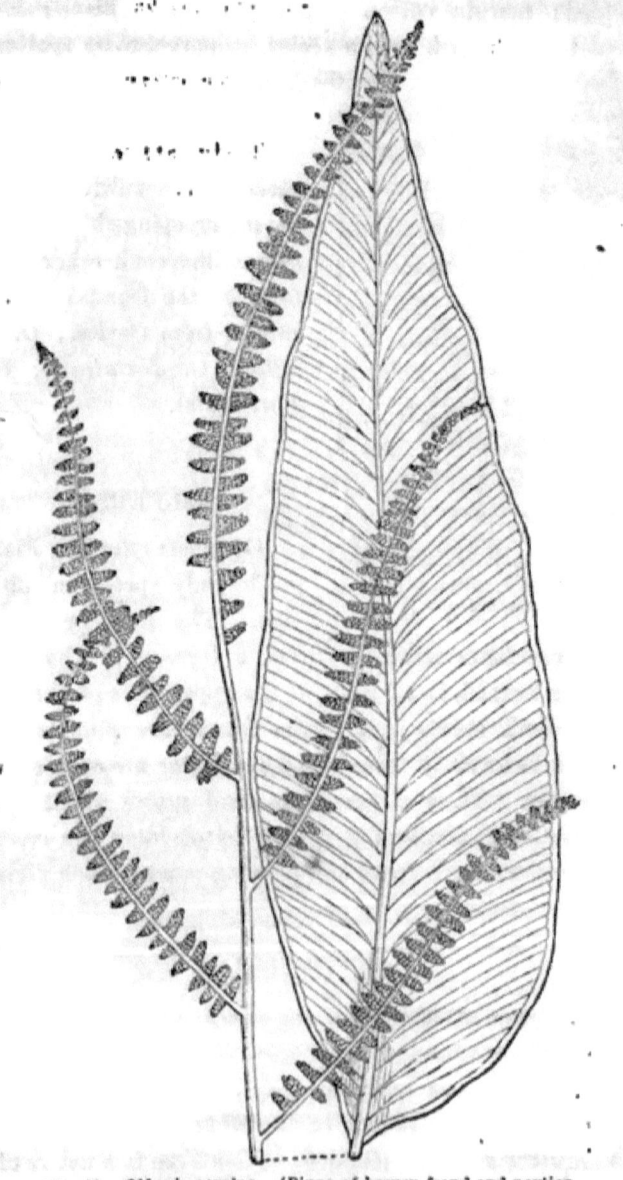

Fig. 49. Olfersia cervina. (Pinna of barren frond and portion of fertile frond medium size.)

segments. The young fronds have a yellowish tinge, but they afterwards become green. It is a very distinct and beautiful plant. It must be increased by spores.

PELLŒA. See *Cassebeera*.

PHLEBODIUM.

A genus of Ferns divided from *Polypodium* by the late Dr. R. Brown. They may be distinguished by the situation of the sori, which are placed distinctly in rows between the midrib and the margin, and by the veins being irregularly branched and very conspicuous.

PHLEBODIUM AUREUM (Golden).—This is the well-known *Polypodium aureum*, and a noble beautiful Fern it is. Fronds pinnate, and drooping, growing 3 feet high. Spore-masses very prominent, and of a golden colour: hence its specific name. Easily increased by dividing-off pieces with fronds attached of the thick creeping rootstock.

P. GLAUCUM (Glaucous), *Fig.* 50.—This is also called *P. sporadocárpum*. It is a Mexican species. Fronds glaucous, pinnatifid, or deeply divided. Spore-masses uniserial, yellowish-brown.

The rest of the species are *P. areolatum, P. decumanum, P. percussum, P. pulvinatum, P. squamulosum*, and *P. venosum*.

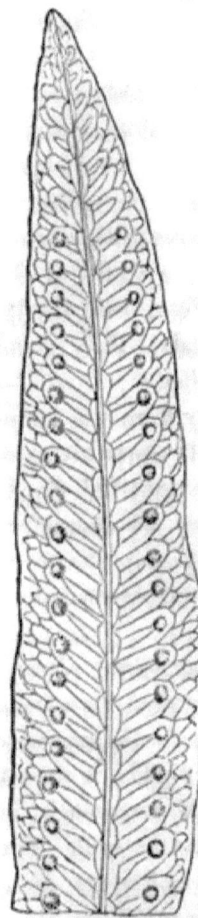

Fig. 50. Phlebodium glaucum. (Part of segment natural size.)

PHYMATODES.

A genus of Ferns formed by the celebrated German botanist, Presl, the type of which is the old *Polypodium phymatodes*. It is very nearly allied to *Phlebodium*, which it resembles in having anastomosing (or netted) veins, and creeping scaly rhizomes. It contains some noble large-growing species, well adapted for growing for exhibition. There are also several very pretty greenhouse species.

PHYMATODES LONGIFOLIA (Long-leaved).—A native of the East Indian Archipelago, with large, deep green, shining fronds. The spore-masses, of a bright golden yellow, are very conspicuous. It has a thick creeping rhizome, like all the species of this genus, and by parting this they may all be readily increased.

P. LONGIPES (Long-footed, referring to the stalks of the fronds). — This, like the last-mentioned Fern, has deeply-divided, thick, dark green, and glossy fronds. They stand somewhat erect. It is a noble and striking plant.

P. SACCATA (Cupped).—This extraordinary Fern was introduced from Java some years ago, but is still somewhat rare. It is a large-growing plant, having deeply-pinnatifid fronds $2\frac{1}{2}$ feet long, besides the stipes by which they are supported. The spore-masses are seated in deep cups, so that on the upper side of the fronds there are rows of raised knobs, corresponding with the spore-masses below.

P. VULGARIS (Common).—This is the *Polypodium phymatodes* of Linnæus. It is a handsome, broad-fronded Fern from the Malay Islands and the Mauritius. The fronds are pinnated, and grow more than a foot long; each division is almost triangular and broad. The rootstock creeps very much, is black and scaly. The spore-masses are round or oval. We once had a large plant of this fine Fern under our care, growing in a large wire basket. The creeping rootstocks grew through the meshes of the basket, and threw out, as they crept round it, their large, broad fronds. It was a noble plant, measuring full 2 feet in diameter, and was much admired. It will, however, grow very well in a pot, or amongst rockwork in the stove. The plant alluded to would have made at least a score of plants had it been divided. This example shows that it is easily increased by that mode. This has also been called *Drynaria vulgaris* and *Pleopeltis phymatodes*.

There are several other stove species in cultivation, the most important of which are *P. cuspidata, P. excavata, P. nuda, P. longissima*, and *P. peltidea*.

PLATYCERIUM.

A singular yet beautiful genus of Ferns, of an epiphytal habit—that is, growing on trees. It is separated from *Acrostichum* on that account, besides its peculiar fructification. The spore-masses are thickly produced in very large irregular patches towards the upper end of the fertile fronds, and have a great similarity to a piece of rough brown cloth. The name *Platycerium* is derived from *platys*, broad, and *keras*, a horn; the fertile fronds being broad and flat, like the elk's horns.

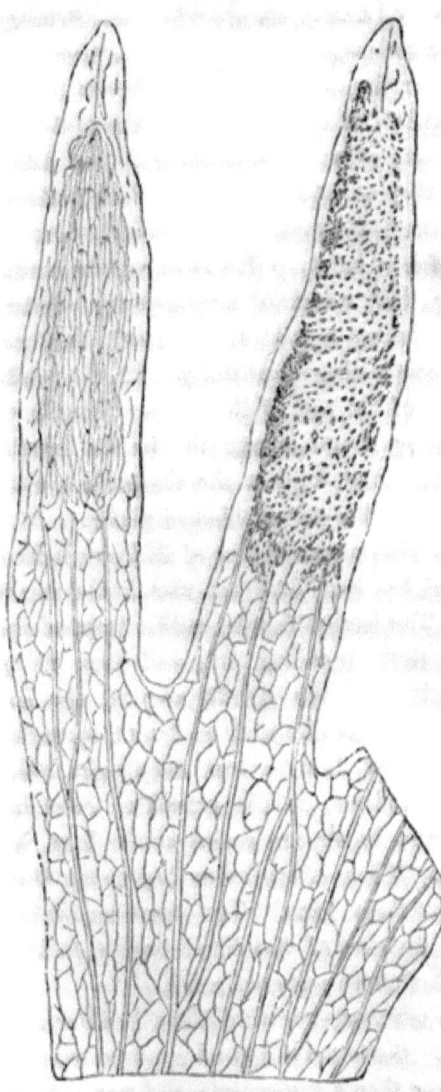

Fig. 51. Platycerium alcicorne. (Part of fertile frond medium size.)

PLATYCERIUM ALCICORNE (Elk's-horn), *Fig.* 51.—This

curious Fern is from the warmer parts of Australia, growing there on stumps of trees and shady rocks. The barren fronds are without stalks, round, or nearly so, spreading horizontally close to the soil, tree, or rock where they grow, or, when the plant is old, spreading over the decaying barren fronds of the previous year. The fertile fronds rise up from the centre of the creeping barren ones, growing sometimes 2 feet high, gradually expanding as they advance in height. Such parts of the fronds as have no spore-masses on them are thickly covered with star-like clusters of short hairs, so fine as to require a magnifying-glass to observe their beautiful arrangement. Spore-masses in patches cover the upper part of the frond; they are of a brownish colour, contrasting beautifully with the white colour on the under side of the rest of the frond. This Fern, when old, produces young plants among the barren fronds. These may be taken off, potted, kept in the shade for a week or two, and then treated like the old-established plants.

P. GRANDE (Noble).—This most singular of all Ferns is likewise from Australia, and has been detected, also, in the woods of the Malay Islands. The barren fronds, unlike those of the preceding species, are first spreading flat, and then rising gradually upwards, and when the plants acquire age and strength they will reach the height of 2 or 3 feet, spreading out towards the upper part into several deeply-cut lobes, forming then some resemblance to the spreading erect tail of some bird. The fertile fronds are entire at the base, but deeply divided upwards. When of some size they droop downwards, assuming a pendulous form. The spore-masses are placed near where the division of the frond begins, and are thickly placed in a kind of three-cornered patch.

The culture of this curiously-beautiful Fern is different to any other Fern known. Some years ago we received one from a friend; it was no larger than a pennypiece, and was as flat as a pancake, growing on a small piece of bark. Having heard that it grew against the boles of trees, we nailed the piece of bark with the plant closely adhering to it to a flat piece of elm wood, about 1½ foot square, and then hung it up against a damp wall in the Orchid-house. It was syringed two or three times every day, and quickly threw out a large, barren, flat, kidney-shaped frond, which gradually crept over and destroyed the one that was on the plant when we received it. The same liberal appliance of moisture was followed-up, and soon after a third frond began to show itself just at the heart of the other. This also advanced, creeping over the last-made one, until it covered it over, and, of course, destroyed it; but this third frond began to spread its wings, as we may say, upwards, and continued growing till the autumn. The plant produced no more fresh fronds that season; but in the spring, as the warmth and moisture gradually increased, the last-made frond spread still higher, so that it seemed to have taken possession of its position, and was determined to keep it. It continued to expand till it was fully a foot high, and continued to advance in size, year by year, till at last a fertile frond was produced. As soon as the spores were perfected this dropped off, and the barren one again advanced in growth, till it was really magnificent, and was parted with for a large price.

Now, any one receiving a small plant of this truly noble Fern should follow exactly the same mode of growing it. It should, however, be affixed to the block or board whilst in a young state, otherwise it would be a difficult matter to fasten it without injuring it. After it is once fixed, its roots, which are produced freely under the spreading barren frond, will cling to the wood, and hold it in its position as firm as a sponge plant on a rock. It is increased by spores sown on small stones mixed with earth, and covered with a bell-glass. The seed-pot should stand in water. Everybody possessing a warm stove ought to grow this most curious and singular of all Ferns.

P. STEMARIA (Garlanded).—This is a West-African Fern, and is so common in the lower levels in the Island of Fernando Po, that it is scarcely possible to find a tree which has not got several plants of it growing upon its trunk. In form and habit it is just intermediate between the two species before-mentioned. It cannot be grown in too hot and moist a place; it enjoys the constant steam from an expansion-box connected with the hot-water apparatus. Like *P. alcicorne*, it produces suckers freely.

Two magnificent species of this genus have been recently introduced from the East Indies by some of our leading nurserymen. These are *P. biforme* (Two-formed), and *P. Wallichii* (Dr. Wallich's). They each of them produce fertile fronds, which are 6 feet or more in length, and the sterile fronds are of a proportionate size. We saw, some little time since, a plant of *P. biforme* at Mr. Low's Nursery, at Clapton, which had been just imported; it was as much as two men could lift. Unfortunately this individual plant had perished upon the journey, but many smaller specimens were growing freely. *P. Wallichii* has also been raised from spores in this country, so that it will soon become more generally cultivated.

PLATYLOMA.

A genus of Ferns with a very significant name, derived from *platys*, broad, and *loma*, a margin; the spore-masses being placed in a broad line on the margin of the fronds. By this character the genus may be known from *Pteris* and other allied genera. The species are mostly from the temperate parts of the world: hence, with the exception of two or three species indicated below, they will all grow in the greenhouse. The species of this genus are sometimes placed under another generic name—*Pellæa*.

PLATYLOMA CALOMELANOS (Beautiful-black).—Though from the Cape, this dwarf beautiful Fern requires the heat of a moderate stove. The fronds grow about a foot long, are bipinnate, with the leaflets of a triangular shape; these are leathery, bluish-green, and heart-shaped at the base, with a thick fleshy margin. Spore-masses long and narrow, continuing round each fertile frond. Increased by dividing the creeping rhizome.

P. FLEXUOSA (Twining), is a Fern from Peru, that loses its fronds annually. It is a twiner, with wiry stems, growing from 4 to 6 feet high, and is very ornamental. Increased by division. It will succeed in a warm greenhouse.

P. TERNIFOLIA (Three-leaflet).—A drooping Mexican Fern, of great beauty. Easily known by its habit. Suitable for basket-culture. The peculiar colour of the foliage makes it very distinct. Increased by division.

PLEOPELTIS.

This name is derived from *pleos*, full, and *pelte*, a shield, and refers to the little umbrella-shaped scales which cover the spore-masses. It is applied to a little group of trailing Ferns allied to *Polypodium*. They all have small undivided fronds, only an inch or two in length, and they all possess long trailing rhizomes, on which the fronds are produced at short intervals. They are well adapted for cultivation in suspended wire baskets, and, grown in this way, they produce a very pretty effect. They can, of course, be rapidly increased by division. They all resemble each other so much in general appearance and habit that special descriptions are unnecessary. The species most generally met with are *P. nitida* (Shining); *P. lycopodioides* (Lycopodium-like); *P. venosa* (Beautiful)—the pretty way in which the veining of this species is shown renders it specially worthy of cultivation; *P. vacciniifolium* (Vaccinium-like), small roundish fronds.

PŒCILOPTERIS. See *Cyrtogonium*.

POLYBOTRYA.

POLYBOTRYA CYLINDRICA (Round), *Fig.* 52.—This is a climbing Fern from the moist woods of Jamaica, where it runs up the trunks of trees to the height of 20 or 30 feet. The climbing Ferns, of which we have already described some species that have the same habit, and shall have one or two more to mention, are not only curious and interesting, but are also useful as a shade to the plants below, whether low-growing Ferns, Orchids, or stove plants. We have had *Lygodium*

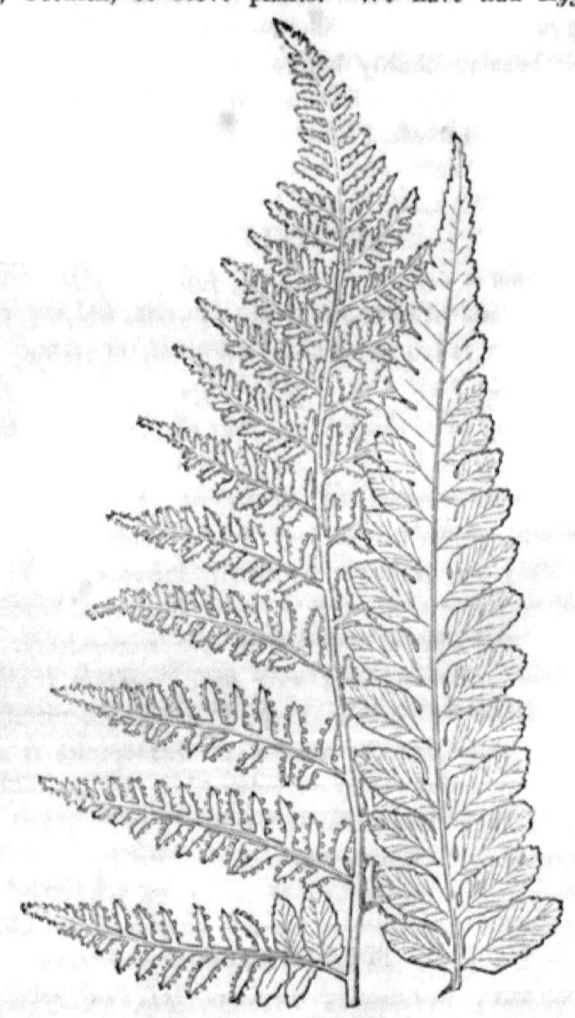

Fig. 52. Polybotrya cylindrica. (Pinnule of barren frond and top of fertile frond natural size.

scandens covering the entire roof of a small Orchid-house, and, seen between the eye and the light of the roof, the spore-masses were perfectly visible and very beautiful. Climbing Ferns are desirable, also, because they take up so little room. They may either be planted in large pots or square boxes, or planted out in a border made for the purpose. As they grow up they should be tied to an upright pillar, and when they reach the roof may be trained any way the fancy of the cultivator may incline. It is a strong-growing Fern, bearing fertile and barren fronds. The latter are doubly thrice-divided, or bitripinnate; contracted and round, growing erect. The sori cover every pinnule of the fertile fronds. Barren fronds grow only 2 or 3 feet high. Easily increased by dividing the creeping rhizome.

There are several species in South America, and one or two more have been introduced, but they are still very rare.

POLYPODIUM.

A large assemblage of Ferns, of which one is a native of this country. It is an ancient genus, having been formed by the celebrated Linnæus. The name alludes to the rootstock—*polys*, many, *pous*, a foot: the rhizome having many divisions. The genus has been much reduced in number of species, being now confined to such as have naked spore-masses with pinnate, forked, or simple veins. As the genus is well known, we shall notice a few of the most interesting or beautiful.

POLYPODIUM EFFUSUM (Spreading).—This is a most elegant Jamaica Fern; the fronds are so finely divided as to give them the appearance of elegant feathers. The fronds are so branched that it is difficult to say how many times they are divided; but generally they are four-times-pinnated, forming almost a perfect triangle in form. Fronds of this fine Fern sometimes measure 6 feet long and 1½ foot broad at the base. It is a noble, beautiful object. It is easily increased by dividing the creeping rootstock.

P. LACHNOPODIUM (Woolly-footed). — Another Jamaica *Polypody*, remarkable for its stem being covered with narrow woolly-like scales. Every part of the plant is of a soft, delicate texture. Fronds doubly thrice-cut, growing 2 feet long, standing upon an upright tree-like stem, or rhizome. A lovely Fern; slow to increase, excepting by spores.

P. PLUMULUM (Feathered).—A West-Indian Fern, and one of the least of the stove species, growing only about a foot high. Fronds of a delicate lovely green, pinnated, with stalks quite black; the leaflets are lance-shaped, and thickly placed on the stalk. Spore-masses in one row, on each side of the midrib, on the upper end of the frond. Increases freely by division.

P. PARADISEÆ (Paradise).—Remarkable for the short stalks of the fronds. A lovely Brazilian Fern, growing 3 feet high. Fronds very slender and drooping, covered with short hairs, lance-shaped and pinnate; the leaflets long and narrow. Spore-masses in one row on each side of the midrib, covering nearly the entire leaf. A handsome Fern, easily increased by division.

P. PECTINATUM (Comb-like, alluding to the arrangement of the leaflets, which are set on the midrib in the manner of the teeth of a comb).—A West-Indian Fern of great beauty. Fronds pinnate; leaflets long and narrow, placed horizontally in parallel lines. It attains the height of 18 inches. The stems are shining black. Spore-masses most elegantly placed in a row on each side of the midrib. This is the most lovely of all the stove *Polypodys*, and ought to be in every collection. Easily increased by division.

P. TRICHODES (Three-footed).—This rare species is from the East Indies; remarkable for having its stalks covered with a fine yellowish-brown down, or small scales. Fronds repeatedly divided, very weak, of a delicate green, and hairy, growing 3 feet high; leaflets narrow, lance-shaped. Spore-masses round, yellow, and medial. Rootstock thick and creeping, by which it may be increased by division.

POLYSTICHUM.

Most of the species of this genus are either hardy or at most only require protection during winter, but there is one or two stove species which deserve mention.

POLYSTICHUM ANOMALUM (Anomalous).—This plant has been well named, for it possesses a peculiarity which is quite unique: there is no other Fern known which absolutely produces its spore-masses on the *upper* side, and on that side only. It is of a bright green colour, with fronds about 18 inches long; but there is nothing striking about it except the curious circumstance mentioned. It is a native of Ceylon, and was introduced to the Royal Botanic Gardens at Kew a few years since.

P. TRIANGULUM (Triangular, referring to the form of the pinnæ).—A native of the West Indies, with elegant pinnate fronds, about a foot in length. It is sometimes called *P. mucronatum*. Mr. R. Sim, of Foot's Cray, has recently imported a very pretty variety of this Fern. It is very suitable for cultivation in a Wardian case.

PTERIS.

Like *Polypodium*, this is a large genus, and was established by Linnæus. The name is derived from *pteron*, a wing, the pinnated fronds having that appearance. Our well-known common *Bracken* is a Pteris. Formerly this was an unwieldy genus, containing nearly two hundred species; but the skill and tact of modern botanists have reduced the number greatly, confining the true Pteridæ to all such species as have veins regularly disposed in lines, not netted across each other. Generally speaking, the plants of this genus are rampant coarse-growers, scattering their spores and coming up thickly wherever there is moisture; yet there are a few that are able to vie in beauty with any other genera of Ferns. These few we shall confine ourselves to in describing.

PTERIS AEGYRÆA (Silvery).—This was the first variegated Fern which was introduced into our gardens. It was imported by Mr. Veitch, of the Exotic Nursery, Chelsea, from central India. It is a remarkably beautiful and striking plant. Its fronds grow to a height of 4 feet or more, but to our taste the plants look more beautiful when only a foot or 18 inches high. As it can easily be increased by spores, there is no difficulty in raising young ones occasionally to replace the larger specimens. The fronds are twice-divided, and each division has a distinct silvery-grey stripe down the centre, which contrasts well with the green margins.

P. ASPERICAULIS (Rough-stemmed).—A small-growing East-Indian, rather difficult to grow well. So far as we have seen, the plant grows best in a hot, damp house, but without ever wetting the fronds; they turn brown if allowed to get wet. The fronds have a beautiful crimson colour, and a tinge of the same remains after they have attained their full size. They are triangular in outline, and twice-divided, about 1½ foot high, including the rough wiry stems upon which they are supported.

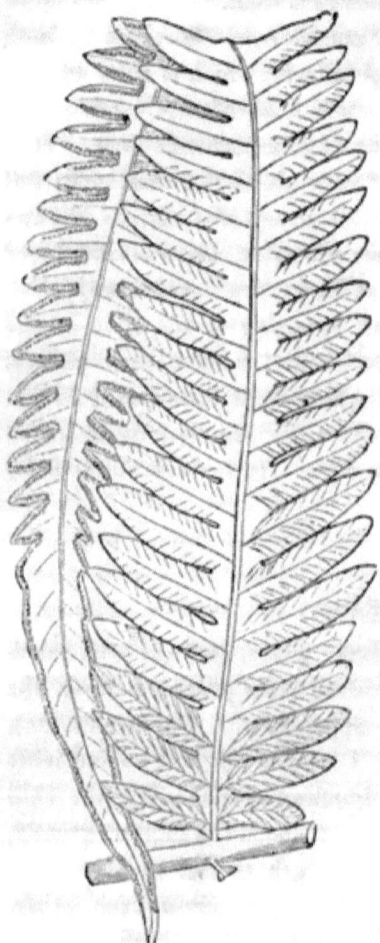

Fig. 53. Pteris felosma. (Pinna medium size.)

The magnificent *P. tricolor*, which was introduced by M. Linden, of Brussels, is in all probability a variety of the species just named. The fronds are of the same triangular form, twice-divided; and when young they are of a deep crimson colour, with a stripe of bright rosy pink up the centre of each division. After the fronds have attained their normal size they gradually change to deep olive green, with silvery stripes where the rose-coloured were originally, the veins still remaining red. No collection of Ferns, however small, should be without this most lovely species. Both it and *P. argyræa* come quite true from spores.

P. FELOSMA (Heavy-smelling), *Fig*. 53.—Native of Jamaica. Evergreen, large and coarse. Fronds 4 feet high, glabrous; pinnæ deeply pinnatifid.

P. HETEROPHYLLA (Various-leaved).—A beautiful Jamaica Fern. Fronds doubly thrice-cut; the lowest leaflet the longest, and gradually shortening upwards, forming an almost triangular shape. Sterile or barren fronds have the leaflets of an oval shape; but in the fertile ones they are bluntly oblong, giving the appearance of two or various kinds of fronds on the same plant: hence its specific name. As it only grows about a foot high, it is a desirable species for small collections.

P. HIRSUTA (Hairy).—Another desirable Fern, native of that island prolific in Ferns—Jamaica. Fronds bipinnate, growing in a triangular form from 3 to 4 feet high, a peculiar light green, and hairy in every part. The stems, as well as the rhizomes, are thick and fleshy. Spore-masses narrow, continued on the margin of the leaflet, a character which is prevalent through the whole genus.

P. LATA (Broad).—A Brazilian Fern, of great beauty, growing 2 feet high. Fronds triangular, and thrice-branched; branches pinnated, and drooping. Leaflets deeply cut, and of a narrow lance-shape. A handsome, broadly-formed Fern, easily increased by dividing the creeping rhizome.

P. LONGIFOLIA (Long-leaved).—A Fern widely spread over

the warmer parts of the world. It has been found in the West India Islands, in Nepaul, and the Philippine Islands. The terminal leaflet is often twice the length of the rest. Fronds 2 feet long, pinnate, dark green, and lance-shaped. Spore-masses continuous, mixed with hairs. A remarkable species, well defined, and easily known. It comes up so readily from spores that it is very common wherever it has been once grown.

P. RUBRA-VENIA (Red-veined).—This Fern, which has recently been introduced by Mr. Bull, the nurseryman of Chelsea, appears to be a free-growing and larger form of *P. aspericaulis*. It looks to possess all the interesting features of that plant without being so difficult to grow; should this prove to be the case, which seems highly probable, it will be a valuable acquisition.

P. SEMIPINNATA (Half-once-divided).—A very interesting and peculiar Fern, perfectly distinct from every other species. It is a native of the warmer parts of China and the islands of the Malayan Archipelago. The fronds are about 2 feet high, and stand somewhat erect; the pinnæ are arranged in pairs, and while the upper side of these is undivided, and looks like the half of a simple lanceolate leaf, the lower side is divided into several lobes, which diminish in size towards the apex. From its peculiarity it is well worth growing.

P. SERRULATA (Saw-edged).—This plant is quite a weed in most ferneries, as it comes up so plentifully from spores, and yet it is a very beautiful plant, and well worthy of attention. The long narrow divisions of its fronds produce a very pleasing effect mixed with flowers and fruit for the decoration of the table; and as the plants are so easily propagated, one has the less regret in cutting the fronds for this purpose.

There are, as before mentioned, many species of this genus, but those above described are most worthy of cultivation; still there are others which are worth a place where there is room for them, as *P. pungens*, *P. quadriaurita*, *P. sulcata*, &c.

SAGENIA.

A genus of large-growing Ferns of great beauty. Most of them are from the East Indies, and, therefore, require the full heat of the stove. The name is derived from *sagene*, a large net, the fronds being covered with widely spread veins. This genus approaches very closely to *Aspidium*. The chief distinction between them consists, in this genus, of the thinly-spread veins and the spore-masses being produced on the top of a small vein.

SAGENIA DECURRENS (Decurrent).—A handsome Fern from Ceylon, bearing barren and fertile fronds separate. The barren fronds half-pinnate—that is, having a small wing at the base. Fertile fronds very curiously turned-up at the edges, contracted, also subpinnate, growing 2½ feet high;

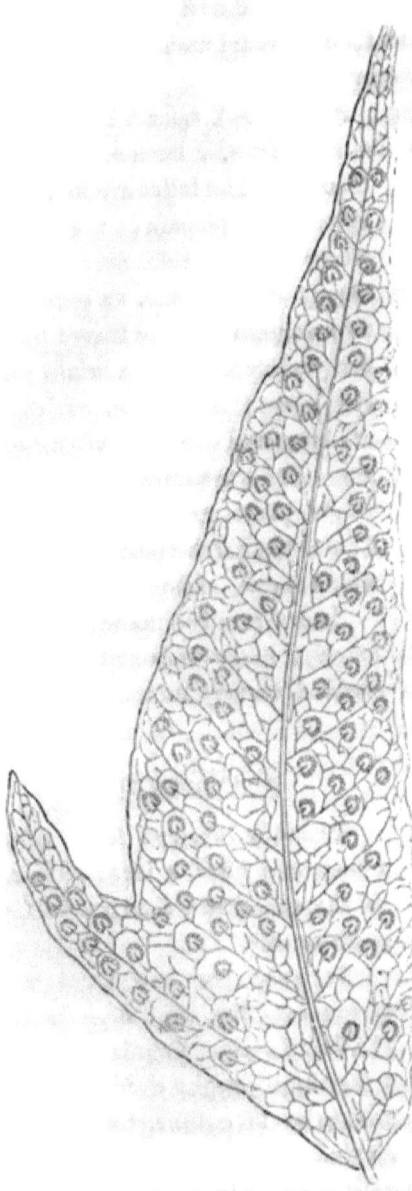

Fig. 54. Sagenia repanda. (Pinna small size.)

the lower part, or wing, runs down almost to the rootstock. Spore-masses very prominent, and covered with a kidney-shaped indusium. Increased by spores.

S. REPANDA (Spreading), *Fig.* 54.—A splendid Fern from the Manillas, with two kinds of fronds, barren and spore-bearing. The latter are half erect, spreading, pinnate; the lowest pinnæ on the side next the soil deeply cut into one, or sometimes two, segments. The barren fronds are pinnated, and of a bright shining green; the pinnæ, or leaves, are large and drooping, often a foot long, with a footstalk to each. The whole plant grows 3 feet high. This is the handsomest Fern of the whole genus. Increased by spores.

There are two more species— namely, S. *coadnata* and S. *hippocrepis*, both very rare.

SITOLOBIUM.

Probably derived from *siton*, wheat, and *lobos*, a lobe; alluding to the shape and situation of the spore-masses.

SITOLOBIUM ADIANTOIDES (Adiantum-like), *Fig.* 55.—Native of West Indies. Fronds from 3 to 6 feet high, bright shining green, triangular in outline, three-times-divided; pinnæ and pinnules triangularly elongate, segments slightly

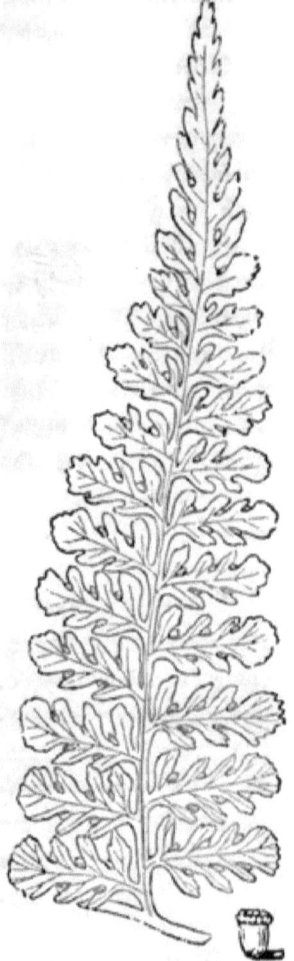

Fig. 55. Sitolobium adiantoides. (Pinnule full size; sorus magnified.)

pinnatifid. A large Fern, but worth growing where there is

room for it. It has a creeping rhizome, and so may easily be divided.

STENOCHLÆNA.

A genus of Ferns divided from *Acrostichum* by Mr. John Smith, of Kew. Name derived from *stenos*, narrow, and *chlaina*, a hood or cloak, because of the narrow covered margin of the spore-bearing fronds. This is a very-well-defined genus, and very remarkable. The spore-bearing fronds are pinnated; and the pinnules are long and narrow, with the under sides densely covered with spore-masses. The habit of the genus is climbing. We have grown the *S. scandens* 5 feet high.

Fig. 56. Stenochlæna scandens. (Pinna of barren frond and part of a pinna of fertile frond medium size.)

STENOCHLÆNA SORBIFOLIA (Sorb-leaved).—A climbing Fern, but not very lofty, from Jamaica. Barren fronds pinnate, with bright green leathery pinnæ. Fertile fronds erect, pinnated, contracted. Increased by dividing the scandent creeping rhizome. It has been also called *Lomariopsis sorbifolia*.

S. SCANDENS (Climbing), *Fig.* 56.—A handsome East-Indian Fern, with the barren fronds pinnated, and each pinna or leaf a foot long, and beautifully veined with a fleshy margin. The fertile fronds are very curious, bipinnated; each pinna long, like a whip, the upper end spreading out and covered with spore-masses. Increased rapidly by division.

There is one or two other kinds to be found in our gardens, as *S. Meyeriana*, which appears to be a little different from *S. scandens*, *S. tenuifolia*, and a variety of it called *natalensis*, which are well adapted for clothing a damp wall in the stove.

STENOSEMIA.

The name of this genus refers to the narrow contracted character of the fertile fronds. There is only one species in cultivation, and it is a very interesting small-growing plant. The fronds are triangular in outline, dark green, deeply lobed, and producing young plants upon their surface. By pegging-down one of these fronds a stock of young plants may soon be obtained. The fertile fronds stand erect, among a cluster of the sterile ones.

TÆNIOPSIS.

Of all the Ferns we have written about, this genus is perhaps the most remarkable. The name is derived from *tainia*, a strap, and *opsis*, like; the fronds being exactly like a long narrow strap.

TÆNIOPSIS GRAMINIFOLIA (Grass-leaved), *Fig.* 57.—A West-Indian Fern of considerable beauty. The fronds are simple, about 10 inches high, long and narrow like a blade of grass, rather erect, but drooping at the end, with wavy margins, and slender at the base. The spore-masses are in continuous lines near the margin, and reaching about halfway down the frond. Veins regular and internal. Increased by division.

T. LINEATA (Line-leaved).—This is also from the West Indies; and is a remarkable, narrow, long-fronded Fern. Fronds simple, 2 feet long, and a quarter of an inch broad, hanging down over the pot-edge; veins thinly strewed, but regular, and placed within the centre of the leaf. The fronds push up thickly from the creeping rootstock: hence it is a very suitable one for a thin rustic basket to hang up in the stove. Increased readily by division. This is sometimes known as *Vittaria lineata*.

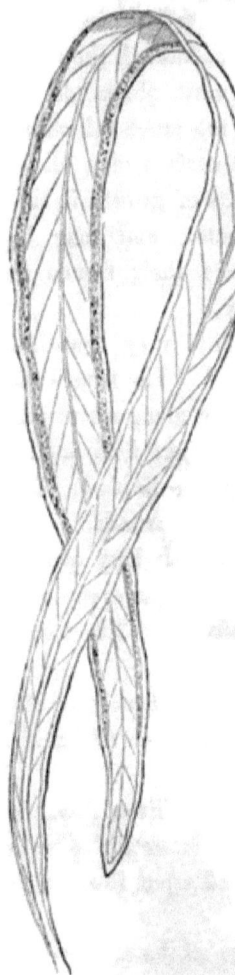

Fig. 57. Tæniopsis graminifolia. (Frond medium size.)

TRICHOMANES.

For the derivation of the name of this genus, and for an illustration of the manner in which it produces its fructification, see the Greenhouse division. Until the last few years it was thought impossible to grow these Filmy Ferns; but now there is a large number which have been introduced, and which may be looked upon as established, but most of them are, and will remain for some time, rare. They are all found naturally growing in the dark and humid recesses of the forest, or in shaded situations where they are kept moist by the spray from a waterfall, or any similar situation where they can obtain the two great necessities of their existence—shade and a moist atmosphere.

I

These points must, of course, be kept in mind in their cultivation. The safest way is to grow them beneath a bell or hand glass, to sprinkle overhead frequently in summer, and to guard against bright sunshine. The shallow boxes or pans in which they are grown should be well drained; for, although they like plenty of moisture, yet they object, as most plants do, to stagnant water. Neither should there be too much soil about the roots; they like to cling to the wet surface of a bit of porous stone. There are two distinct habits of growth in this family: one set produce creeping rhizomes, and may be increased by division; the others produce their fronds in clusters, and can be propagated but slowly.

Trichomanes anceps (Spreading).—This very beautiful species was introduced from the West Indies. The fronds are produced in a cluster from one crown, and not along a creeping rhizome. They are a foot long, spreading out horizontally from the top of the stipes, dark green, much divided. The bell-like spore-masses hang downwards from the fronds.

T. Bancroftii (Bancroft's).—Also a West-Indian species. It is a very small and beautiful plant, delighting to creep over the stump of a tree or a bit of porous sandstone. The fronds are once-divided, and only about $1\frac{1}{2}$ inch long.

T. crispum (Crisped).—The almost pellucid fronds of this plant are about a foot long, once-divided, light green and hairy. It grows in tufts.

T. Kraussii (Krauss's).—A small creeping Fern from the West Indies. The fronds oval in outline, once, or in the lower divisions twice-divided. It is often imported upon the stumps of Palm trees, or tree Ferns.

T. muscoides (Moss-like).—This is one of the most easily-grown kinds; it will bear parting well and grows freely. The fronds are produced thickly, and give one, from their colour and transparency, an idea of a mass of seaweed fresh from the ocean. It came from Jamaica originally, but is now pretty plentiful.

T. SPICATUM (Spike-bearing). — The name is given in reference to the fertile fronds, which are quite different from the others, being reduced almost to a midrib, bearing a line of the cup-like receptacles containing the spores on either side. The sterile fronds are shorter and broader, 3 inches long, divided almost to the midrib. It grows in tufts. There is another species called *T. elegans*, which resembles this one much in form and habit, but is rather larger.

T. TRICHOIDEUM (Hair-like).—A most interesting little gem. The fronds, which are about 3 inches long, are cut up into hair-like divisions. It has a creeping rhizome, and so may be increased by division.

There are now a great number of these Filmy Ferns; perhaps as many as fifty species in cultivation. Mr. Backhouse has introduced many from Chili, the West Indies, and other parts. M. Linden has added some from the Philippine Islands; and Mr. R. Sim, and other nurserymen, have obtained many from New Zealand and elsewhere. There is not one among them all but is well worth cultivating.

This concludes the list of Stove Ferns. We do not by any means consider it a complete one, because we have endeavoured only to notice and describe those that are either remarkable for their beauty, or for being exceedingly curious or singular. Generally, we have mentioned the height they grow; and, consequently, growers that have plenty of room may strive to procure them all, whilst others that have only small space may choose the smaller-sized species.

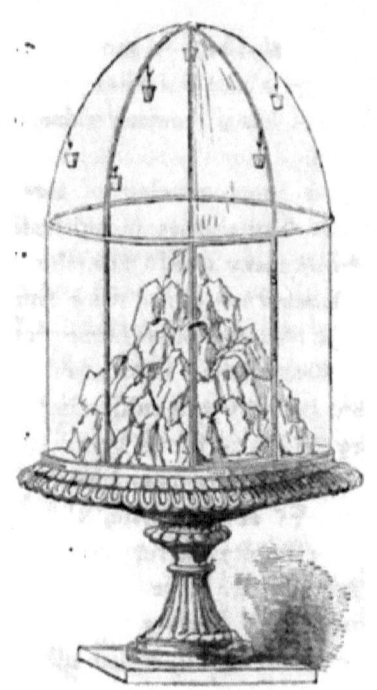

GREENHOUSE FERNS.

It is one of the mysteries of Nature, that one plant will bear the extreme heat of the tropics, and another, of apparently similar form and as delicate a structure, will flourish only in the opposite extreme of cold, whilst a third requires a more temperate clime. Though a mystery to us, it is a wise and merciful dispensation by the Creator and Disposer of all things; for by this adaptation to different climates every part of the earth is furnished with plants yielding food, when cultivated, for the use of man, as well as flowers to gladden his eyes and gratify the love of the beautiful in his heart. Not only are these useful and lovely products of the soil given to man, but also the light of knowledge to collect them together, improve them, choosing some and rejecting others according to his wants or desires.

This knowledge leads men to endeavour to bring together plants that may be useful or ornamental from all parts of the globe; and this is the highest effort of a civilised mind. The mere savage contents himself with the fruits only that yield him food without culture, growing around the place where he was born; and that careless or improvident state of mind constitutes, in a great degree, the difference between the savage and the civilised man. The one lives and feeds like a mere animal, whilst the other labours with his mind and hand, and lays up stores to supply his wants at all times and seasons. In the highest state of civilisation, man not only grows food, but also cultivates some plants merely for their perfume or for their beauty. Such as produce showy, sweet flowers, are the first that he esteems: hence we see cottagers—men without book-learning or science—cultivate as flowers such things as the Stock and the Wallflower; whilst others, possessing a knowledge of the beautiful flowers and fruits of foreign lands, and having wealth to carry out the power of cultivating them, collect together plants from all parts of the world. Then the mystery we have already spoken of appears.

The man of thought and science finds that some plants are more impatient of cold than others, and wonders why it is so; but finding it is so, he understands that he must adopt some means of protecting them, or, rather, he must create, as it were, an artificial temperature and dwelling for them: hence we have our stoves, our greenhouses, and pits, to suit plants of every clime. This provision of suitable habitations for plants has made rapid strides of late years. We have now not only the stove for tropical plants generally, but we have also houses for peculiar tribes of plants—such, for instance, as the Orchid-house, the Palm-house, &c.; then, again, the greenhouse, which, when we were boys, contained every plant requiring its protection crowded together in it. Now, as the science of culture has advanced, it is found necessary to have separate greenhouses for single families of plants, such as Heaths, Pelargoniums, Camellias, Azaleas, and that large assemblage termed New-Holland plants.

Then, again, it is found desirable to grow the tribe of plants we have now under our notice—namely, Ferns, in a separate house, though, from their peculiar habit of growing in the shade, many of them can be cultivated tolerably well amongst other plants, in such positions in the shade where the proper inhabitants would not exist; yet, to grow them to perfection, they ought to have a dwelling to themselves.

Following this train of ideas, we are now brought to the class of plants which, in this highly civilised country, are cultivated not for the love of showy, sweet flowers, but for their beautiful foliage and delicate green colour. We have already written pretty largely on Stove Ferns, and now proceed to Greenhouse Ferns.

CULTIVATION.

In the first place, we would observe that this class of Ferns, during winter, may be grown by the sides of the path under the first step of the stage. We have seen them so growing very well. Advantage may be taken of the summer months, when the regular inhabitants of the house are bivouacing and luxuriating in the open air, to place the Ferns on the stages; thus furnishing the house with beautiful green foliage during the summer months, and giving the Ferns a chance to make finer fronds than they would do if kept during the growing season in the comparative darkness on the side of the path. These fronds would be matured before the autumn, and would keep green in consequence longer through the winter. It would be a good time, also, to give them a shift into larger pots and fresh soil previous to giving them more light.

Following out the idea that there are more persons able to grow Ferns in a greenhouse than in a stove, as such buildings are more common than stoves, we shall, in this division of our subject, treat upon Ferns that will thrive in a house the temperature of which is kept through winter a few degrees above the freezing-point. Many of the more rare or beautiful hardy Ferns will thrive exceedingly well in such a house. Though greenhouses are generally crowded with plants of various kinds through the winter which are set out of doors in summer, yet many Ferns may be kept in it notwithstanding; and on this account, that their fronds die-off in the autumn, and that the plants are dormant through the winter: consequently they may be kept under the stages or platforms, or on shelves against the back wall. In such a state they require but little care, only to be kept moderately moist. The evergreen varieties, however, must have due attention paid to their having a full share of air, light, and moisture.

SOIL FOR GREENHOUSE FERNS.

This section of the Fern tribe requires the same kind of soil as those that are grown in stoves. The compost should consist of that light, open, fibry kind of peat which may be found where the wild Ferns abound—amongst decayed moss, fibry roots, and decaying leaves. The common black peat is unfit for this purpose, being too heavy, and holding water too much; in fact, when thoroughly wet, no Ferns will live in it. Large-growing Ferns would thrive all the better for having added to the fibrous peat about one-third of turfy loam, taken very thinly off a pasture, and chopped into pieces varying from the size of a boy's marble to a hen's egg. Use both the peat and loam without sifting; mix them well together, and add silver sand enough to give the compost a sandy character. For small-growing species use the peat without loam, only adding the sand. For seedlings, or very young plants of any kind, put the compost through a half-inch-meshed sieve.

DRAINAGE.

The best material for drainage is undoubtedly broken pots at least we may say so, without fear of contradiction, for the drainage at the bottom of the pots. Some recommend cinders, others moss, and some oyster-shells. The cinders we object to, because they are difficult to pick out from amongst the roots on repotting; the moss, when decaying, becomes a muddy, stagnant mass, and oyster-shells cannot always be obtained; whereas, unfortunately, broken pots are always (where pots are used in any quantity) handy—they may be removed from the ball easily, they let the superfluous water pass off freely, and the Fern-roots seem to like this kind of drainage the best of any that we have used. To keep the soil in large pots open and pervious to water, we have used moderate-sized pieces of charcoal, and even sandstone, with advantage.

POTTING.

The proper season for this operation is early in spring, just when the young fronds begin to push forth. Examine the deciduous species, and if any show signs of life, give them a good watering to moisten the soil a week previous to repotting. Have the pots in readiness—if new, soak them in water for an hour, and set them to dry for a day; if old, let them be washed thoroughly clean. Then get ready the drainage materials. Break the potsherds into three sizes— a few large enough to cover the holes at the bottom of the pots, a larger number of less size, and a greater quantity about the size of Marrowfat Peas. The compost should be got in and be neither dry not wet.

All these points having been duly attended to, then bring out the plants into the potting-shed. In potting, we always find it advantageous to pot all of one size first. It is immaterial whether you begin with the largest or the smallest. Let this operation be done quickly, we mean all at once. Plants suffer greatly by being kept too long in the potting-shed, exposed, probably, to cold draughts of air, or, if not exposed to that, suffering for the want of light: hence we recommend all to be ready, so that no delay may take place in getting the plants repotted and back again to their home. During the operation see that all decayed fronds are removed, and also any roots that may be dead. Shake off the loose soil and old drainage; and in repotting leave sufficient space, according to the size of each plant, below the rim of the pot, to hold water enough to thoroughly wet the entire ball of earth. *Many a fine Fern has perished by neglecting this point.* When all are finished give a good watering, and return them to their place in the greenhouse, previous to which there will be a good opportunity to wash the stages, platforms, &c., so that all may be fresh, tidy, and clean, giving the plants and the house a cheerful, pleasant appearance.

WATERING.

Attention should now be paid to giving due supplies of water, especially during the growing season. Though the Ferns love water, and must never want it, yet to give them this necessary element in excess is very injurious, especially to the more delicate kinds, such as the Gold and Silver-leaved *Gymnogrammas*, some *Cheilanthes*, and others of like character. Watch such daily, and give water when the surface is dry; give enough at once to wet the whole of the soil in the pots, and let it become dry on the surface again before giving any more. In dry, hot weather use the syringe freely, wetting the walls and floors thoroughly at least twice a-day, morning and evening. Use rain water in syringing over the foliage.

AIR.

We need scarcely direct that air must be given regularly. In spring and summer, indeed, the house should have air both night and day in abundance. Every cultivator will soon find this necessary. A slight shade, such as Shaw's tiffany affords, will be of great service in hot sunshine.

INSECTS.

The thrips is the greatest enemy to Ferns. It may be kept under by frequent moderate smokings of tobacco. In very bad cases cut off the fronds most affected, and burn them, and wash the remainder with tobacco water and sulphur vivum, syringing it off again the next day. The brown scale must be rubbed off, and the plants washed with the above mixture. We have received some plants from abroad so infested with both white and brown scale, that we found it necessary to cut off all the fronds, and watch the young ones, and keep them clean as they advance in growth. Insects will not, however, be found so troublesome in the greenhouse as among the stove Ferns.

Many of the plants which are usually kept in the greenhouse will, it must be kept in mind, succeed sometimes for two or three years in the open air; but then an unusually severe winter comes and they are lost. It is, however, a good plan to plant out all duplicates which may not be required, and this should always be done in spring.

In describing or enumerating the species of Ferns hardy enough to live through the winter in a greenhouse, we need not repeat the generic characters of such as are already given in the first division—namely, Stove Ferns.

ADIANTUM.

ADIANTUM ASSIMILE (Assimilated).—A New-Holland Fern of great beauty, continuing green all the winter. Fronds thrice-divided, or tripinnate, with the leaflets of a rhomboid shape, and the margin slightly cut. The cover of the sporemasses is kidney-shaped. The rhizome creeps very freely, sending up fronds all over and round the sides of the pots: hence it is easily increased by division.

A. CAPILLUS-VENERIS (Venus's Hair), *Fig.* 58.—Though this beautiful Fern is a native of Britain, yet it is too delicate to bear the open air in our gardens. It is identical with *A. Moritzianum* of some authors, who mistook it for a different species in consequence of its growing much larger in warm countries—Madeira, for instance. We have had large patches of it from that island under that name; but we invariably found them, when treated in a similar manner, to assume the character of the true *A. capillus-Veneris;* and then, again, when transported into the stove or Orchid-house, they returned to, or produced the large fronds of, the so-called

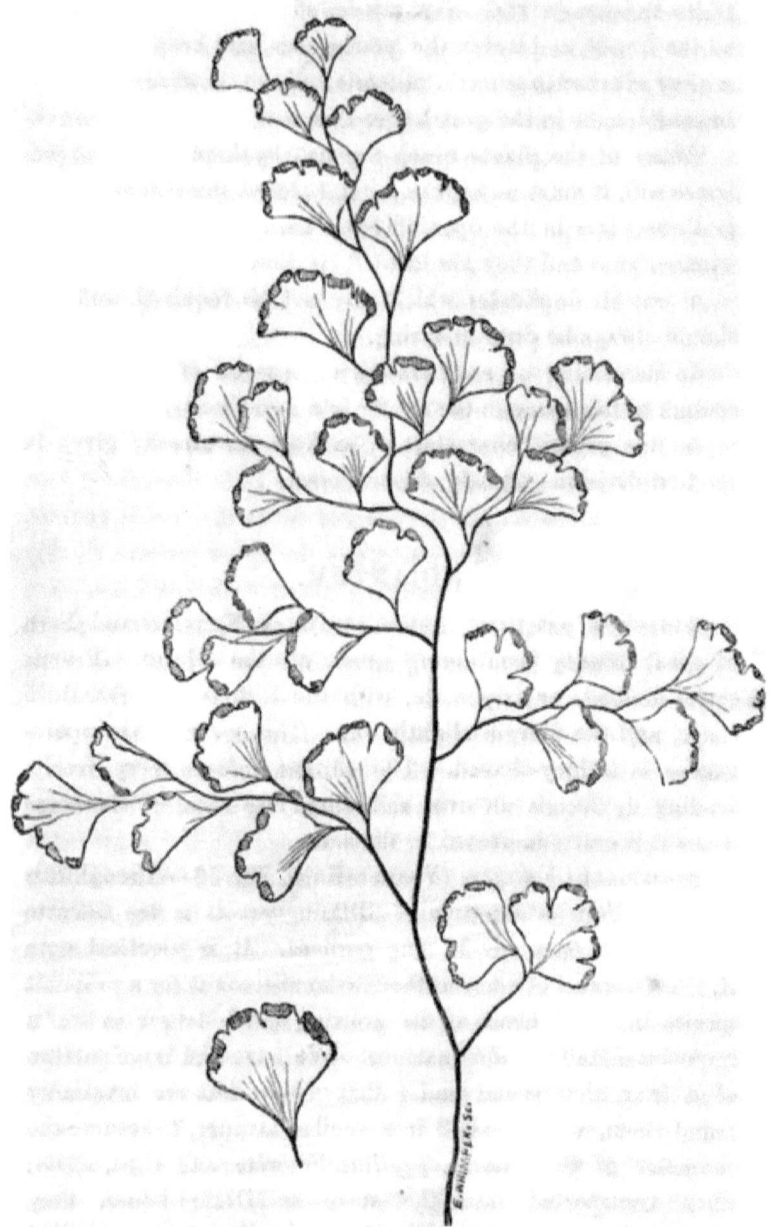

Fig. 58. Adiantum capillus-Veneris. (Frond and pinna.)

A. Moritzianum. This species loves shade and moisture, and, therefore, a close shady part of the greenhouse is necessary to grow it satisfactorily. Fronds bitripinnate—that is, twice-thrice-divided; growing in a greenhouse 6 inches high; pinnæ or leaflets wedge-shaped, bright green, and cut at the edges. Requires a light, sandy, fibrous soil, intermixed freely with potsherds or small pieces of sandstone. Increases freely by division.

A. CHILENSE (Chilian).—Recently introduced by Messrs. Veitch. Fronds with dark polished stalks, a foot high, three-times-divided, with broad pinnules, glaucous green. A very distinct and handsome species.

A. FORMOSUM (Handsome). See *Stove species.*

A. HISPIDULUM (Hairyish).—A pretty little Fern from New Holland, remarkable for the various forms the fronds assume, the lower pinnæ being bipinnate, and the upper pinnate, thickly covered with hairs, and growing about 6 inches high, in a close upright manner. This is often called *A. pubescens* in gardens. There is a very pretty little variety of this Fern called *tenellum.*

A. PEDATUM (Bird's-footed).—This species is a native of a cold country (North America); and, although quite hardy in a favourable situation, yet it shows itself to greater advantage if grown in a greenhouse. It grows splendidly in an intermediate-house, but in rockwork or the open border we have frequently lost it. It is herbaceous—that is, it dies down to the ground in winter. It is a truly elegant Fern, growing a foot high before the branching begins, then spreading its five divisions almost horizontally, something like the claws of a bird. Fronds pedate; pinnæ rather oblong, with a wavy edge, slightly cut. Spore-masses oblong and solitary. Increased readily by division.

A. SCABRUM (Rough).—The Silver Maiden-Hair, introduced by Messrs. Veitch, through their collector, Mr. Pearce, from Chili. It is a dwarf-growing plant; and, what is very remarkable, the fronds are sprinkled with white powder on both sides, like some of the *Gymnogrammas*.

A. SULPHUREUM (Sulphur-coloured).—For this, the Golden Maiden-Hair Fern, we are also indebted to Messrs. Veitch, and we consider these two are the greatest novelties introduced the year 1862. The fronds grow in dense tufts, about a foot high, thrice-divided, and with the under surface sprinkled with golden powder. Both of these plants are well worthy of cultivation.

ALSOPHILA.

ALSOPHILA AUSTRALIS (Southern).—A Fern rare in cultivation, from Van Diemens Land, requiring the warmest part of the greenhouse. It is a tall plant, growing 3 feet high. Fronds bipinnate; pinnæ long and narrow, with smooth edges. Stalks scaly, growing on an upright stem, forming a little tree. Increased by spores sown on sandstones under a bell-glass in a frame.

A. CAPENSIS (Cape of Good Hope).—This is also a tall Fern. Fronds 3 feet high, bipinnate, form oval lance-shaped; pinnæ or leaflets also lance-shaped, with wings at the base, edges deeply cut. Stalks scaly. Spore-masses small. Stem forming a little tree, with the fronds seated on the summit. This is sometimes very curiously covered with short deformed leaflets. Increased by spores only.

ANTIGRAMMA.

A genus of Ferns with broad fronds and regular veins at the back. The name means *anti*, against, and *gramma*, a line, the spore-masses being arranged opposite to each other on each side of the midrib.

ANTIGRAMMA RHIZOPHYLLA (Frond-rooting), *Fig.* 59.—A North-American Fern, of a dwarf, compact habit. It will live in a cold frame, but is safer in a good greenhouse. Fronds simple, growing 9 inches high; heart-shaped at the base, but lengthened-out above and rooting at the point.

ASPLENIUM.

There are no less than twenty-two species of this genus that require greenhouse treatment. Some certainly grow more freely in a stove, and others will exist in the open air—*A. marinum*, for instance; but the more tender ones may be placed in the warmest part of the house, and the others in the coolest.

ASPLENIUM APPENDICULATUM (Appendaged).—A Fern from Van Diemens Land, of great beauty. Fronds tripinnate, a foot high, or more, and rooting at the extreme point; pinnæ or leaflets oval-shaped, sharply cut into segments at the edge. Spore-masses oblong, covering the under surface of the fronds. Stalks scaly and winged. Rootstock creeping, but slowly increased by division, and the rootbulbs formed at the ends of the fronds. This is now generally looked upon as one of the many forms of *A. bulbiferum*. As several species propagate themselves by these self-formed appendages, we may just as well describe for all how to manage these proliferous fronds. When the tufty bulb or knob has become of a moderate size, fill a small pot with the proper compost, and place it so near the proliferous frond as to allow the end just to reach the centre of the pot. Then either peg it down with a hooked stick, or lay a small stone upon the frond, just behind the knob, pressing it down close

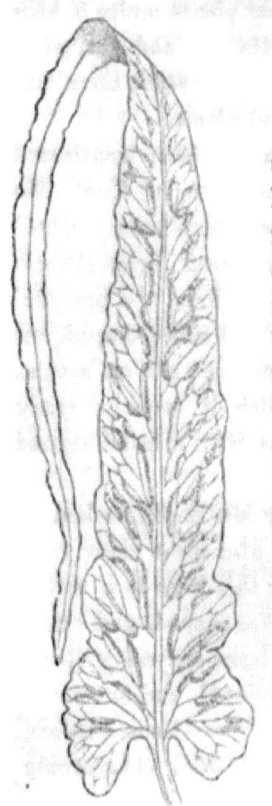

Fig. 59. Antigramma rhizophylla. (Frond natural size.)

to the soil; water it gently, and let it alone till roots are formed, and young fronds have made some progress. Then cut it off, and place the young plant or plants under a bell-glass till fairly established; give a little air, and gradually inure them to bear the open air; afterwards repot them and treat them exactly like the old-established plants.

A. AXILLARE (Axillary).—This Fern has been transferred from *Aspidium* and *Allantodia* by Mr. Smith, of Kew. No doubt it is a true *Asplenium*, by its linear spore-masses placed on the upper side of the veins. Fronds oval, lance-shaped, bending forwards, thrice-cut, growing 2 feet long, of a beautiful lively green; pinnæ wide apart, narrow and sickle-shaped, cut at the edges. Spore-masses narrow, sometimes two on a vein. Rootstock thick and creeping, by which it may be easily increased by dividing the rhizome across, with a frond beyond the cut. It is a native of Madeira.

A. BROWNII (Brown's), named so by Mr. Smith, in honour of Mr. R. Brown, the eminent botanist, who spent many years in New South Wales, of which country this Fern is a native. Fronds 2 to 3 feet long, dark green, lance-shaped, and rather drooping, and partly thrice-cut; pinnæ lance-shaped, with the pinnules largest next the stem, sharp-pointed, and cut at the edges into oval segments. Stem scaly. Spore-masses oblong, with a rising cover or indusium. Rootstock thick and creeping. Increased by division.

A. BULBIFERUM (Bulb-bearing).—From that great storehouse of Ferns, New Zealand. Fronds 2 feet high, erect two-thirds of their length, then gracefully bending downwards, partly thrice-cut, producing living plants plentifully on the leaflets, to manage which see *A. compressum* below. This Fern is remarkable by having the under surface of the leaflets covered with small heart-shaped scales of a dark colour.

A. COMPRESSUM (Compressed).—A Fern from the rocks of St. Helena. Fronds 2 feet high, pinnate, very stout and leathery, main stem winged; pinnæ broad and compressed, nearly every one producing plants, bluntly cut at the margin. Rootstock erect. Increased by the young plants produced on the fronds. These should be taken off and laid on the soil, and covered with a bell-glass, and when fairly rooted and fresh fronds produced, they should be potted-off into small pots, and repotted as they require it. All the viviparous Ferns should be treated in a similar way, in order to make sure of good plants quickly.

A. DIVERSIFOLIUM (Various-leaved).—A Fern discovered by the late A. Cunningham in Norfolk Island. This plant will succeed in a warm greenhouse; but see what is said of it in division devoted to Stove Ferns.

A. EBENEUM (Black-stalked).—The habitat of this Fern is rather wide. It has been found at the Cape of Good Hope, in Mexico, and North America. It is a neat, rather dwarf species. Fronds 9 inches high, long, lance-shaped, and pinnated; pinnæ overlapping, heart-shaped, rounded at the top, and notched at the margin. Stalks black, shining, and rather hairy. Increases readily by spores. Keep a sharp look-out for insects on this Fern: it is somewhat subject to the attacks of thrips.

A. FLACCIDUM (Feeble). — A New-Zealand Fern, of a drooping habit: hence it may be grown in rustic baskets. Fronds long, lance-shaped, 2 feet or more long, often tripinnate, and dull green; pinnæ very long and narrow, producing plants on the apex and ends of the segments. Increased by division, as well as by the young plants on the leaflets. There is a variety of this species with more erect habit, which produces very few or no young ones on the fronds.

A. FLABELLIFOLIUM (Fan-leaved).—From New Holland. This is also a drooping, or, rather, weeping Fern, and is proper to be placed in baskets to hang from the roof; or it should at least be placed upon a tall pot turned upside-down, to allow room for the fronds to droop, and be seen their full length. Fronds long and narrow, growing a foot long, pinnated about

K

two-thirds of the length of the frond, the rest being naked. It produces roots and a plant at the end of each full-grown frond: by these it must be propagated.

A. FURCATUM (Forked).—A native of the Cape of Good Hope, India, and Malayan Archipelago, of great beauty. Fronds bipinnate or twice-divided, growing 1½ foot high; pinnæ sharp, oblong. Leaflets wedge-shaped, with a deep incision at the top. Stalks covered with brown scales. Root-stock round, slender, and creeping. Increased by division.

A. HEMIONITIS. See *A. palmatum.*

A. LUCIDUM (Shining), *Fig.* 60.—Native of New Zealand. Fronds 2 feet long, leathery and shining, pinnated and lance-shaped: pinnæ with long-stemmed leaflets, wedge-shaped and serrate, or cut.

A. MARINUM (Sea-side).—Though a native of Britain, on the rocks near the sea, this Fern never thrives well in gardens in the open air. In the greenhouse, on the contrary, it grows remarkably fine, much larger than it is ever found wild. We have had plants with fronds 18 inches long. At Sion House, the seat of the Duke of Northumberland, it may be seen forming quite a bush, 2 feet high and as much through. It is found, also, in the Channel Islands, the south of Europe, Madeira, Teneriffe, in India, and the North of Africa. Fronds long, lanceolate, pinnate, and dark green; pinnæ oblong, rounded at the apex, sharply cut at the edges. Stalk winged. Increased by division. There are several varieties of *A. marinum*, and, like the parent

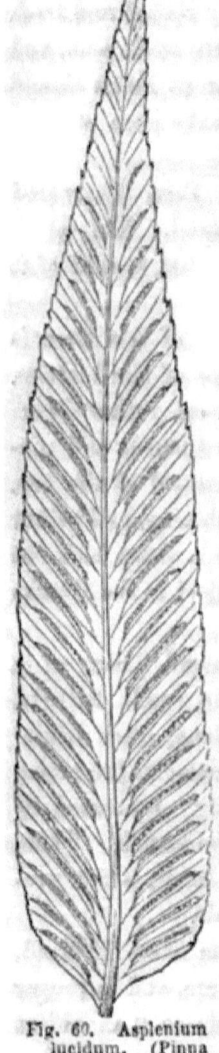

Fig. 60. Asplenium lucidum. (Pinna natural size.)

species, they all grow the better for a little extra heat: even the stove does not seem too hot for them, especially while young. The most distinct of these varieties are *A. marinum ramosum*, fronds usually forked so as to appear like two fronds joined; *A. marinum trapeziforme*, with more triangular fronds; and *A. marinum sub-bipinnatum*, with the pinnæ deeply divided.

A. OBTUSATUM (Blunt-fronded).—A very handsome Fern, native of New Zealand. Fronds rigid, erect-growing, leathery, bright green, and pinnated. It is a dwarf species, seldom growing more than 9 inches high; pinnæ bluntly oblong, rounded and serrated at the margin. Stalk always winged, covered with scales. A very remarkable and well-defined species. Messrs. Osborne, of Fulham, cultivate this handsome Fern on the floor of their greenhouse very successfully. Increased by division.

A. PALMATUM (Hand-shaped).—A handsome Fern, native of the Canary Islands. Fronds simple, but deeply divided into five lobes, hence its specific name; growing only 10 inches high. Increased by dividing the creeping rootstock. This Fern is more generally known as *A. hemionitis*. There is a variety with the points of the lobes divided and almost tufted.

A. POLYODON (Many-toothed).—Another handsome Fern from New Zealand. Fronds pinnated, lance-shaped, growing 2 feet long; pinnæ nearly square, with long stems. Each pinna is divided into segments, and each segment has two divisions or teeth; hence its name—Many-toothed. Stems scaly. Increased by division.

A. RECLINATUM (Reclining).—A very pretty small-growing Fern from the Island of St. Helena. The pinnate fronds droop gracefully on every side of the central crown, and young plants are produced at their points. It may therefore be readily increased.

A. UMBROSUM (Shady).—This plant will succeed in a warm greenhouse. See what is said of it in the Stove division.

Like *A. marinum*, there are several other British Ferns which may with more ease be cultivated in a greenhouse than out of doors. It is only in favourable positions that such plants as *A. trichomanes*, *A. fontanum*, *A. septentrionale*, *A. lanceolatum*, *A. germanicum* (or *A. alternifolium*), *A. viride*, or even the more common *A. Ruta-muraria*, can be induced to grow freely in the hardy fernery; but they make very pretty little ornaments grown in pots in the greenhouse.

There are some other greenhouse Aspleniums, among which are *A. acutum*, a South-European species, *A. rutæfolium*, from the Cape of Good Hope and Natal, *A. pinnatifidum*, a small-growing species, and others.

BALANTIUM.

BALANTIUM CULCITUM (Cushion), *Fig.* 61. — A curious, scarce, handsome Fern, the only one of the genus in cultivation. It is a native of Madeira. The fronds are many-times-divided, growing 3 feet high; the pinnæ are nearly triangular, with sharp points, and deeply toothed at the edges. The spore-masses are curious, in the shape of an oblong purse: hence the generic name, *balantium*, a purse. The rootstock is decumbent, or laid down in the earth, is very thick, and rather creeping. By this it may be increased wherever there is a bud formed below the leading shoot.

Fig. 61. Balantium culcitum. (Pinna natural size; indusium magnified.)

BLECHNUM.

The genus *Blechnum* is well defined, and easily distinguished by its spore-masses, which run in continuous lines on each side of the midrib of the fertile fronds. The genus *Lomaria* has the spore-masses in the same way; but the fertile fronds in that genus are contracted—that is, turned up at the edges; whereas in *Blechnum* the fronds are all even and flat.

BLECHNUM AUSTRALE (Southern).—Known also as *B. cognatum*. It will do in a greenhouse, but thrives better in a stove. See the other divisions of this work.

B. CARTILAGINEUM (Fleshy-edged).—A New-Holland Fern of considerable size. Fronds 3 feet long or more, lance-shaped and pinnated; leaflets or pinnæ longest at the base, gradually shortening upward; the lowest 8 inches long, cut sharply at the edges, and of a dark green. Increased slowly by dividing the thick creeping rhizome.

B. HASTATUM (Spear-headed).—A Fern from Chili. Fronds a foot long, and pinnated; pinnæ narrow, lance-shaped, light green; the lower ones spear-shaped, the upper sickle-shaped. Increased by dividing the creeping rootstock.

B. TRIANGULARE (Triangular).—A Mexican Fern of great beauty. Fronds a foot long, triangular in form, pinnated; the pinnæ are generally alternate, not stalked—the end one is entire, running out very narrow. Increased by division.

CASSEBEERA.

A name adopted by Mr. Smith, to commemorate J. H. Cassebeer, a German botanist. The plants arranged under this name have been collected from *Pteris* and *Cheilanthes*, to which they are closely allied. There are a few handsome species which will thrive well in a greenhouse.

CASSEBEERA CUNEATA (Wedge-shaped). — From Mexico.

This elegant Fern has already been mentioned in the Stove division; but we have inserted the name here because it will succeed with care in a warm greenhouse.

C. GERANIIFOLIA (Geranium-leaved).—This has been well named, as the fronds are very like the leaves of the wild Geranium, known as Herb Robert, which grows so plentifully on our hedgebanks. The stems are dark brown and wiry. It succeeds well in a Wardian case. If grown in the stove it is very subject to the attacks of thrips, from which it almost escapes if grown in a warm corner of the greenhouse.

C. HASTATA (Spear, or Halbert-shaped).—This is the well-known *Pteris* (or *Pellæa*) *hastata*, a native of the Cape. We once raised from spores a variety with very broad fronds, and we now find this variety frequently appears amongst seedlings of the true species. It is of a much larger habit in every way, and we value it more than the true species. We have now some plants of it that are really noble specimens. We find them both thrive well in Wardian cases. Fronds from a foot to 2 feet in length, bipinnate; the lowest pinnæ heart-shaped, the upper halbert-shaped. Spore-masses situated on the margin, narrow and continuous. Stalks very dark brown. Rootstock short and creeping. Increases plentifully by spores; also by dividing the creeping rootstock.

C. INTRA-MARGINALIS (Inside the border, referring to the spore-masses).—This is a most beautiful Fern from Mexico. It has been described among the Stove Ferns; but those who only possess a greenhouse may yet grow it with a little extra care.

CHEILANTHES.

Name derived from *cheilos*, a lip, and *anthos*, a flower; the cover of the spore-masses being that shape. A very handsome tribe of Ferns, deservedly favourites with all Fern-growers; but they require close attention, and should have no water over their fronds at any time of the year. The soil they do best in is very sandy peat, with small pieces of potsherds and charcoal intermixed; the pots to be well drained, and rather under-watered when not growing in winter.

CHEILANTHES MICROMERA (Small-parted).—A dwarf Mexican Fern, very neat, and of a pleasing green colour. Fronds 9 inches high, bipinnate; pinnæ short and narrow, deep milky green; the sterile are notched at the edges. Spore-masses long and narrow. Stalks black and scaly. Increased by dividing the slowly-creeping rhizome.

C. MICROPTERIS (Small-winged).—From the hills of Mexico, and a neat beautiful species. Fronds pinnated, 6 inches long, very slender and hairy; pinnæ small, almost round, and thickly placed on the stalks, which are dark brown and smooth. Increased by division.

C. ODORA (Sweet-scented).—This is a European Fern, but is not hardy. Fronds bipinnate, growing 6 inches high; pinnæ distant on the fronds. When dried the fronds give out a pleasant odour: hence the specific name. Stalks thickly covered with long narrow scales. Increased chiefly by spores, the rootstock creeps so slowly. Called also *C. fragrans*.

C. TENUIFOLIA (Slender-leaved).—For a description see *Stove Ferns*.

CYATHEA.

Of this genus there are several kinds which succeed very well in a greenhouse. Even *C. dealbata* and *C. medullaris* (mentioned among the Stove Ferns) will grow in a moderately warm conservatory, but not so fast, of course, as in the warmer house. The stems should be moistened with a syringe in hot and dry weather.

CYATHEA CUNNINGHAMII (A. Cunningham's).—This Fern is said to attain a height of 20 or 25 feet in its native country— New Zealand. It has a stem usually covered with brown roots, and the upper part clothed with whitish scales. The fronds are about 5 or 6 feet long, according to the strength of the plant; they are thrice-divided.

C. SMITHII (J. Smith's).—This is another New-Zealand tree Fern, many stems of which have been recently imported by our leading nurserymen. It has a stout stem, covered at the upper part with brown scales. The fronds are twice or even three times divided, of a bright glossy green colour.

CYRTOMIUM.

From *kyrtos*, convex; the veins being prominent and in that form. There is only one species, and a remarkably handsome Fern. It is perhaps the finest of all the greenhouse species.

CYRTOMIUM FALCATUM (Sickle-shaped), *Fig.* 62.—A Fern from Japan. Fronds 2 feet high, spreading, and of a bright shining green, twice-cut; the pinnæ are broadly falcate, very stout, and slightly waved at the edges, veins very conspicuous, convex, with the spore-masses on central veins. Increased readily by spores only. We have seen them coming up freely under the stages, if the floor becomes mossy or is formed of earth.

One or two other species have been recently introduced from Japan. One of these is called *C. Fortunei*, after its discoverer. It has narrower pinnæ, and is certainly very distinct.

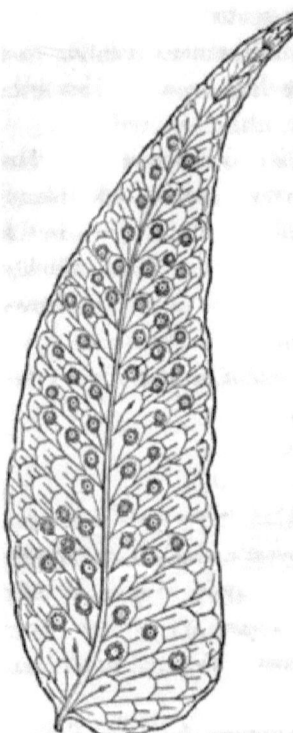

Fig. 62. Crytomium falcatum. (Pinna medium size.)

CYSTOPTERIS.

A genus separated from *Aspidium* by Bernhardi. Name derived from *kystos*, a bladder, and *pteris*, a Fern. Distinguished by spore-masses being roundish in the middle of the back of a vein or veinlet, covered by a thin membranous indusium, inserted by its broad base at the under side of the spore-mass and covering it; opening by a free, usually long extremity, pointing towards the apex of the segment, ultimately reflexed.

Fig. 63. Cystopteris tenuis. (Pinna natural size and pinnule magnified.)

CYSTOPTERIS TENUIS (Slender), *Fig.* 63.—Native of North America. Fronds 12 to 15 inches long, oblong-lanceolate, nearly three-times-divided, light green; pinnules ovate-oblong, deeply cut into segments, which are bluntly toothed.

DAVALLIA.

Commemorative of Edmund Davall, a Swiss botanist. Spore-masses contained in a cup-like cavity. Most of the species, being natives of the tropics, require a stove for their cultivation: consequently most of them will be found described in the first part of this work.

DAVALLIA CANARIENSIS (From the Canary Islands).—This, the well-known Hare's-foot Fern, is too well known to need description. It grows very well in the greenhouse; but, like many other Ferns, enjoys more heat and moisture when it can be got. A variety called *pulchella* was introduced some time ago, and at first it was a very dwarf form, but it would not keep this character under cultivation, though it still remains somewhat distinct.

D. PYXIDATA (Shining), *Fig.* 64.—Native of New Holland. Shrubby and deciduous. Requires a warm greenhouse. Fronds 18 inches high, smooth, dark green, three-times-divided. The rhizomes are as thick as one's finger, and as they stand erect they give a shrubby character to the plant.

Fig. 64. Davallia pyxidata. (Part of barren and fertile fronds full size and portion of fertile magnified.)

DICKSONIA.

This genus commemorates James Dickson, a British cryptogamist. It contains some of the best greenhouse tree Ferns. They require a good deal of room to exhibit their proportions to advantage, but where they can be accommodated they make truly noble objects.

DICKSONIA ANTARCTICA (Antarctic), *Fig.* 65.—A tree Fern, requiring a warm greenhouse. Native of Van Diemen's Land. Fronds about 5 feet high, dark green, lanceolate, several-times-divided; pinnæ linear-lanceolate. Pinnules same, deeply cut; segments ovate, toothed at the margin. Stipes and rachis covered with hair-like scales. The erect stem is thick and usually clothed with brown rootlets.

There are two or three other kinds of *Dicksonia* introduced, but at present they are extremely rare, only a specimen or two xisting in some of the largest collections of Ferns. They are

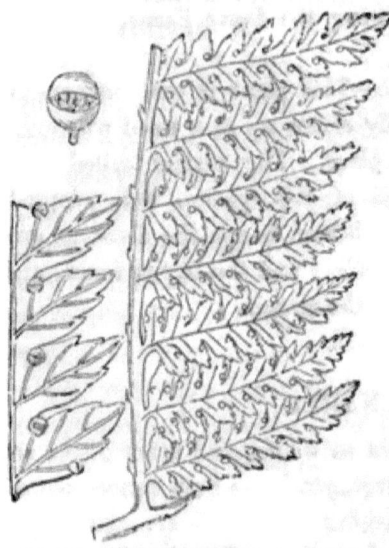

Fig. 65. Dicksonia antarctica. (Fertile part of frond; a smaller portion, and a sorus or spore-mass magnified.)

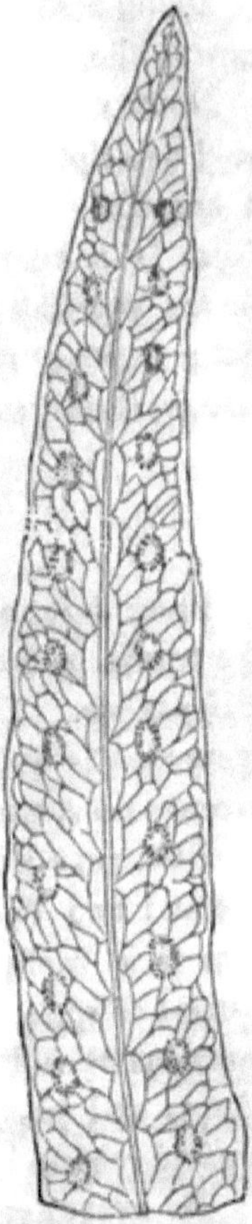

D. lanata (Woolly), *D. fibrosa* (Fibrous); the plant called sometimes *D. squarrosa* is generally *Cyathea medullaris*.

DICTYMIA.

From *dictyon*, a net: the veins are very much netted.

DICTYMIA ATTENUATA (Attenuated), *Fig.* 66.—A New-Holland Fern of great beauty. Fronds simple—that is, not divided, growing a foot high, thick and leathery, narrowed or attenuated at the base.

Fig. 66. Dictymia attenuata. (Top of frond natural size.)

The veins of this fine Fern are very beautifully and regularly arranged. The spore-masses are in rows on the upper part of the frond. Rootstock creeping. Increased by division.

DOODIA.

D. lunulata, described among the Stove Ferns, will also grow in the greenhouse.

DOODIA CAUDATA (Tailed).—This plant is too common to need description. It generally comes up as a weed wherever it can find an undisturbed place. The variety called *confluens* is a very pretty form of the species, well adapted for the Wardian case. In the barren fronds the divisions are closer together than in the species; and the fertile fronds are narrow, linear, and wavy along the margin.

DRYNARIA.

From *drys*, a tree: it lives in woods, and often grows on the trunks of trees. This large genus has been formed out of *Polypodium*. The distinguishing characters are the naked spore-masses and the crooked veining. There are only two greenhouse species. Sometimes called *Phymatodes*.

DRYNARIA BILLARDIERI (Billardier's), *Fig.* 67.—From New Zealand and Van Diemen's Land. This Fern creeps so fast that it is useful to cover naked damp walls, rockwork, or stumps of trees, or to plant in rustic baskets; in any of which positions it will thrive well if frequently syringed. Fronds simple and pinnated. Spore-masses large and round. Increased readily by division.

D. PUSTULATA (Pimpled).—From New Zealand. A very dwarf Fern. Fronds from a few inches to a foot long, simple occasionally; pinnated veins, obscure and immersed. Spore-masses round, and in one row or series. Increased by division.

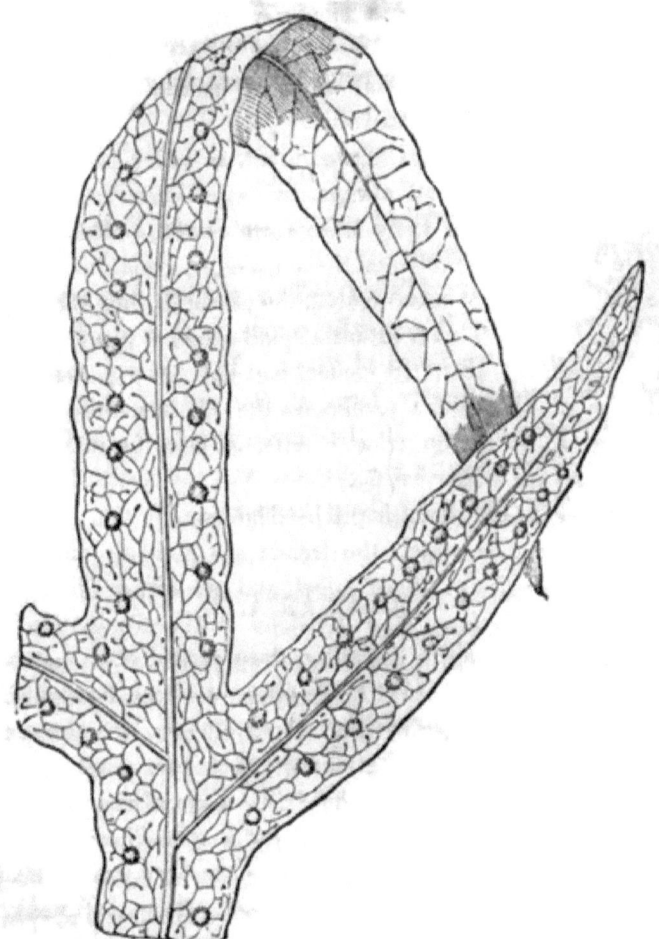

Fig. 67. Drynaria Billardieri. (Part of frond natural size.)

GLEICHENIA.

Of this beautiful and remarkable genus there are several species which grow as well or even better than in the stove. There seems to be a good deal of confusion among the names of this family, the same *Gleichenia* being known under various titles in different gardens, or slightly different varieties being known by distinct names. They have all got wiry stalks, and can be increased only by spores, or, with some difficulty, by division. See what is said of them in the Stove division. They are all natives of Australia.

GLEICHENIA DICARPA (Two-fruited, so called because there are frequently, but not always, two spore-cases in each little pouch in which the spore-masses are seated).—The branches divide always into two equal divisions—*i.e.*, dichotomously, and the little fronds are once-divided, the pinnæ looking like strings of green beads. This is rather a small-growing plant, attaining only a height of about 18 inches, and making a dense bush in old plants. In mature specimens the old stems require now and then to be cut out; but it must be done carefully, as the young ones are rather brittle.

G. FLABELLATA (Fan-shaped).—The name in this case refers to the manner in which the fronds are divided. The stems rise to the height of about 4 feet, and are rather thicker than in most *Gleichenias*. The divisions of the fronds are from 6 to 9 inches in length, drooping, deeply-divided. One of the most distinct and beautiful kinds often seen in our exhibitions. Mr. R. Sim, of Foot's Cray, the well-known nurseryman, who pays such especial attention to Ferns, pointed out to us, a short time ago, that there is a very distinct and good variety of this species which he calls *Lætevirens*. It may easily be distinguished from the true species by the rhizomes being always buried beneath the surface, while in *G. flabellata* they are always on the top. It is a free-growing and very useful variety.

G. HECISTOPHYLLA (Smallest-leaved).—This is somewhat similar to *G. dicarpa*, but is a taller grower. Like it the spore-masses are contained in little cup-like cavities on the under surface of the frond. In this point it differs from the next species.

G. MICROPHYLLA (Small-leaved).—The same kind of habit and appearance characterises this species as that last named; but it grows to a greater height, and will attain as much as

3 feet. The spore-masses are upon the surface of the frond, and not in a cavity. It is sometimes known as *G. circinalis.*

G. RUPESTRIS (Rock).—The fronds of this species are thick, and might almost be called leathery; they are light green above, and whitish on the under side. It is much rarer than most of the other kinds, and will probably long continue so.

G. SEMIVESTITA (Half-clothed).—This is probably a variety of *G. microphylla,* which it somewhat resembles. Its stalks are rather more downy. It grows to a height of about a yard.

G. SPELUNCÆ (Cave, probably from its growing in caves or dells).—This is another rare and very beautiful Fern. The fronds are very glaucous, almost white beneath, giving it a lovely appearance. It is a very distinct plant, and one of the best of the family.

HYMENOPHYLLUM.

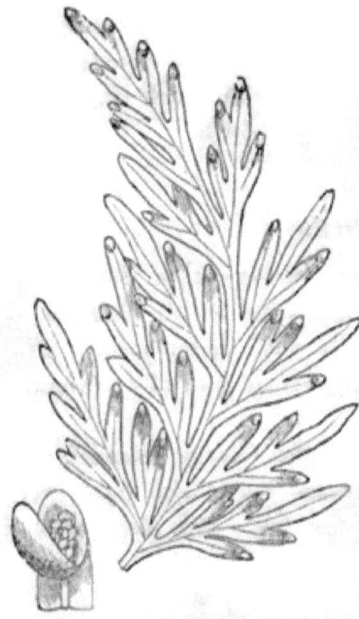

Fig. 68. Hymenophyllum dilatatum. (Pinna natural size; indusium magnified and turned.)

HYMENOPHYLLUM DEMISSUM (Hanging-down).—A very beautiful Filmy Fern from New Zealand. The fronds are a foot or more in length, twice-divided, smooth, and half transparent. For culture see what is said of *Trichomanes* in the Stove division.

H. DILATATUM (Spread-out), *Fig.* 68.—Native of New Zealand. Requires protection in the winter, and succeeds best treated as a greenhouse Fern. The fronds are sometimes as much as 18 inches in length.

Several nurserymen have recently imported new species of this beautiful genus from

Chili and New Zealand, and other cool parts of the world, so that we shall soon have quite a group of Filmy Ferns; and we hope then to see our horticultural societies offering special prizes for them, which will much encourage their cultivation.

HYPOLEPIS.

A genus of Ferns separated from *Polypodium* and *Cheilanthes* by Bernhardi. Name derived from *hypo*, under, and *lepis*, a scale; the spore-masses being partly covered by a scale. The genus may be distinguished by that character, and by the situation of the spore-masses, which are placed in the hollow or sinus of the frond. There is only one species in the genus in cultivation that will thrive in the greenhouse.

HYPOLEPIS RUGULOSA (Rather rough).—From Van Diemen's Land. Fronds 2 feet high, thrice-cut; pinnæ lance-shaped. Spore-masses round, and covered by a reflexed crenule of the frond. Rootstock very rough with scales, much lengthened, and creeping. Increased readily by division.

LASTREA.

Mr. Moore, one of the ablest writers upon Ferns, says that this name was "given in honour of M. Delastre, of Châtelheraut, a zealous botanist and microscopist." This group is one of the best known, but is not generally a favourite for in-door culture.

LASTREA CANARIENSIS (From the Canary Islands).—A strong-growing and rather distinct Fern, with light green fronds, twice-divided, about 2 feet high, with stems covered with light-coloured scales.

L. DECOMPOSITA (Much-divided).—A native of Australia and New Zealand. Fronds triangular in outline and nearly as wide as they are long, repeatedly divided, dark green, spreading horizontally not more than a foot above the pot. One of the most distinct and desirable of the family.

L. ELONGATA (Lengthened).—This is a native of the same part of the world—Madeira and the Canary Islands; and is often confounded with the foregoing, which it much resembles.

L. KAULFUSSII (Kaulfuss's).— Fronds erect, supported by long stalks, about 6 inches wide and nearly a yard high (including the stipes), once-divided, but with the pinnæ deeply cut, light green.

L. TENERICAULIS (Slender-stemmed).—This is the name under which *Polypodium* (or *Phegopteris*) *trichodes* is known in some gardens. It will be found under the latter name among the Stove Ferns, though it will also grow in a greenhouse.

LITOBROCHIA.

This a remarkable genus of these elegant plants. They are allied to *Pteris*, from having the spore-masses in a line close to the margin of the frond. For the derivation see Stove Ferns.

LITOBROCHIA VESPERTILIONIS (Bat-winged).—This plant has already been mentioned among the Stove plants, but the name is inserted here to show that it may be grown in the greenhouse.

LOMARIA.

This is a genus containing many species. They are chiefly suitable for the greenhouse; and are generally of a moderate size, and easy to cultivate. The name is derived from *loma*, a border, from the position of the spore-masses. Here, again, is an affinity with *Pteris:* the difference consists in the fertile frond being contracted, and turned-up at the edges. This character distinguishes it also from *Blechnum*.

LOMARIA ALPINA (Alpine).—From New Holland, and nearly hardy. Fronds of two kinds; the fertile, or spore-bearing, grow 6 inches high; the barren only 4 inches: hence the fertile ones are very conspicuous. They are of a lively green, and both pinnated. It is a desirable species, and easily increased by dividing the rhizome. We have grown this neat little Fern well in a Wardian case, and also in a cold frame.

L. ATTENUATA (Attenuated, or Thin).—A rather tender greenhouse species, from the Mauritius. It should have but little water in winter, or it will perish. Fronds of both kinds pinnated; fertile ones a foot high, barren ones 6 inches taller, both slender-growing or attenuated. The rhizome sometimes grows erect, with branches at the foot that creep. By this the species may be easily known. It is increased by cutting off one of the creeping rhizomes.

L. AURICULATA (Eared).—This is a remarkable Fern from the Cape of Good Hope. We saw a few years ago three or four fine specimens in the Birmingham Botanic Gardens, placed behind a north wall, as a summer habitation. The fronds on them were, in some instances, nearly 2 feet long. We know that most of our hardiest greenhouse Ferns would be much benefited if set out of doors in a shady place during the summer. Fronds of both kinds pinnate; the barren ones are lance-shaped, and of a pleasing green, the others broader at the base, with the pinnæ long, narrow, and terminating with a sharp point. Very slow of increase. The rootstock does not creep, but sometimes sends out a branch at the base, which, when rooted, may be taken off, potted, and placed under a hand-glass for a week or two, till it makes fresh roots and new fronds.

L. CAPENSIS (Cape of Good Hope).—Undoubtedly this is the giant of the genus, growing 3 feet or more high. Sterile fronds coarse and strong, dark green, pinnated; pinnæ 6 inches long, wavy-edged, and heart-shaped at the base, with notched edges. Fertile fronds pinnate; pinnæ long and narrow, and entire at the edges, though contracted. Stalks scaly.

Increased by dividing the thick creeping rootstock; but the divisions must be well rooted, with a frond or two on each.

L. FRAZERI (Frazer's).—So named by A. Cunningham, in honour of his friend, A. Frazer, a fellow traveller. Native of New Zealand, and a very handsome Fern. Fertile fronds twice-cut; pinnæ narrow and oblong, growing a foot high; the others are shorter. Increased by dividing the creeping rhizome.

L. GILLIESII (Gillies's).—From Chili. This handsome Fern is hardy enough to thrive in the greenhouse. Fronds of both kinds pinnated. Barren fronds a foot high, of an oval lance-shape; pinnæ obliquely heart-shaped at the base—that is, one side is shorter than the other. The margin is cut. Fertile fronds a foot high; pinnæ narrow, contracted, and sharp-pointed. The rhizome produces many heads: hence the plant may be increased by division.

L. MAGELLANICA (Magellan).—So named because it is a native of Terra del Fuego, a country on the borders of the Straits of Magellan. Fronds of both kinds pinnate. Sterile fronds 2 feet long, lance-shaped; pinnæ narrow and sharp-pointed, with the margin entire. Fertile fronds also a foot long, narrow, contracted, and sharp at the point. Fronds standing on the top of an erect thick rhizome, which, Dr. Gardiner says, makes a dwarf tree Fern. He saw many specimens 4 feet high, at a great height on the Organ Mountains in Brazil. It can only be increased by spores. Nearly hardy.

L. NUDA (Naked).—A Fern found in Van Diemen's Land, or, as we now call it, Tasmania. Fronds of both kinds pinnate. Sterile ones broadly lance-shaped, growing 1½ foot high, and of a beautiful dark, shining green. Fertile fronds, with pinnæ of a sickle form, narrow, and sharp-pointed. Rhizome many-headed, and rather creeping. Increased by division. One of the best of the genus.

L. Patersoni (Paterson's).—Another species from Van Diemen's Land. Fronds simple, sometimes, when well grown, slightly pinnatifid. Barren fronds stiff or rigid, growing 6 or 9 inches high, long, lance-shaped, with the edge notched. Fertile fronds a foot high, long, narrow, simple. Increased by dividing the plant when it has many heads.

Among the new Ferns which have been recently introduced from New Zealand by Mr. Standish, of Ascot, and Mr. Lee, of Hammersmith, and which are recommended as hardy, there are several very beautiful *Lomarias*. There is no doubt but that they will prove hardy in favourable situations, but while young it would be advisable to grow them in the greenhouse. Among these we have *L. fluviatilis*, with long narrow fronds with roundish divisions; *L. elongata*, with stout pinnate fronds 2 feet in length; *L. Frazeri*, a very beautiful and distinct kind, but rare yet; *L. discolor*, producing tufts of dark green fronds with a tinge of reddish-brown; *L. crenulata*, with fronds about 6 inches long; *L. Banksii*, somewhat like *L. fluviatilis* in form and habit; *L. lanceolata*, very small.

MICROLEPIA.

Microlepia novæ-zelandiæ (New Zealand).—This beautiful little Fern has been called by several names—as *Leucostegia*, *Davallia*, and *Acrophorus hispidus*; but it is now generally known by the one we have used, which was given it by Mr. J. Smith. Its fronds are not more than 3 or 4 inches high, finely-divided, and of a dark green colour. It should be grown in a shallow pot, and protected from draughts. It is well suited for a Wardian case, as it never grows too large.

MOHRIA.

This name was given to commemorate M. Mohr, a German botanist. It contains only two species, but they are both very beautiful greenhouse Ferns, and deserve to be more generally known than they are.

MOHRIA ACHILLEÆFOLIA (Yarrow-leaved).—The name of this plant gives a very good idea of the form of the fronds. They are about 6 inches long, short-stemmed, and rising from a tufted crown. The fertile fronds are longer and stand more erect than the sterile fronds, which surround them.

M. THURIFRAGA (Frankincense).—This very attractive and beautiful Fern is a native of South Africa. The fronds somewhat resemble those of the other species, but they grow to a greater size, and their divisions are broader. Both of them should be grown on a shelf near the glass.

NEOTTOPTERIS.

NEOTTOPTERIS VULGARIS (or *N. australasica*), the common and beautiful Bird's-nest Fern, which is described among the Stove plants, will succeed pretty well in a greenhouse, and should form one of the collection, however small it may be.

NIPHOBOLUS.

Whoever grows any species of this genus may be much gratified by a microscopic view of the under side of the fronds. There will, when so viewed, be seen a white, starry set of short, fine hairs, giving the leaflet a mossy appearance.

NIPHOBOLUS LINGUA (Tongue-like).—A Chinese Fern, of a neat habit, but rarely seen in fructification. The only time we ever saw it was on the rockwork in the Fern-house in the Botanic Gardens at Sheffield. We imagine the reason has been because it has generally been kept too warm in the stove. Fronds simple and of two kinds. Barren fronds long, oval-shape, with a sharp point, growing 9 inches high. Fertile fronds turned-up at the edge a little, and rather less than the other. Spore-masses thickly strewed on the under surface, giving the frond the appearance of a piece of brown cloth. Veins placed between the two surfaces of the leaflet: these, to be seen in their wondrous beauty, should have the tissue of substance of the leaflet destroyed and removed by soaking in water. If this be delicately done, one of the most beautiful examples of elegant veining will be seen. Increases fast by dividing its quickly-creeping rhizome.

N. RUPESTRIS (Rock).—One of the tiniest of all Ferns. We have kept it in a three-inch pot for years. Native of Australia. Fronds of two kinds. Fertile, narrow and blunt at the top, and not more than 3 inches high. Barren ones thick, oval, and not more than 2 inches high. This pretty little Fern might be grown in those tiny pots in which we see Sedums, and small Aloes, and Mesembryanthemums cultivated and sold in Italian warehouses in London, generally termed baby plants. It might also be planted on a hollow stone, and hung up in a Wardian case. Increases freely by dividing the creeping rhizome.

NOTHOCHLÆNA.

The greenhouse species belonging to this genus are amongst the loveliest of the tribe; they are also like *Cheilanthes*, somewhat tender and impatient of wet over the fronds. We have found them thrive best placed on a shelf, about a foot from the glass, kept moist in summer and rather drier in winter. The soil should be rough sandy peat, and half-decayed leaves, freely mixed with silver sand.

NOTHOCHLÆNA DISTANS (Distant). — So called from the pinnæ being wide apart. A delicate New-Holland Fern of considerable beauty. Fronds bipinnate or twice-cut, growing 6 inches long; pinnæ without stalks and hairy. Pinnules opposite and distant. All the stalks are thickly covered with scales. Spore-masses placed on the margins of the fronds. Increased by dividing the creeping rhizomes.

N. LANUGINOSA (Woolly).—From Madeira. Fronds covered with fine, woolly hair, the under side quite brown, bipinnate, growing 6 inches high; the pinnæ are almost round, except the end one, which is lobed or hollowed, as it were, into two or three parts. Spore-masses circular, and placed at the end of the pinnæ. Increased slowly by dividing the slow-creeping rootstock.

N. VESTITA (Clothed).—A nearly-hardy North-American Fern. Fronds bipinnate, 5 inches high; pinnæ roundish, and thickly set on the midrib. The whole plant is densely clothed with rather long hairs, very conspicuous even to the naked eye. We have had this Fern exist through a mild winter, plunged in coal ashes behind a low west wall; but in a very severe winter it perished. It is safe in a good greenhouse if treated carefully. Every one of the above species is a very elegant plant, and will try the skill of the best cultivator.

ONYCHIUM.

Derived from *onichion*, a little claw: divisions of the fronds resembling a claw.

We formerly grew this Fern under the name of *Cænopteris japonica*. It is now made a separate genus. There is only one greenhouse species in cultivation, and it is a very elegant one. We find it quite hardy enough for greenhouse temperature.

ONYCHIUM LUCIDUM (Shining), *Fig.* 69.—Native of various parts of the East. Fronds slender, and of two kinds, fertile and barren, both forming almost a triangle. The fertile fronds grow 3 or 4 inches longer than the barren ones; the latter are a foot long, bright green, and finely-divided. Spore-masses small, but when magnified may be seen in clusters between the midrib and the margin; when nearly ready to burst they are spread out, almost covering the under side of the pinnæ. Easily increased by dividing the creeping rhizome.

Fig. 69. Onychium lucidum. (Parts of barren and fertile fronds natural size, and a smaller portion of a fertile one magnified.)

PHYMATODES.

P. Billardieri and *P. pustulata* will be found described under the name *Drynaria*, by which they are more commonly known.

PLATYCERIUM.

P. alcicorne, the common Elk's-horn Fern, succeeds very well, but does not often produce fructification in a cool house. For a description and mode of culture see Stove Ferns.

PLATYLOMA.

From *platys*, broad, and *loma*, margin. It is well named, as the spore-masses form a broad margin to the under side of the frond. Allied to *Pteris*; not very distinct from *Pellæa*.

PLATYLOMA ATROPURPUREA (Dark purple).—Though this elegant Fern is a native of North America, it is not hardy enough to bear our winters, but thrives well in a good greenhouse. Fronds 10 inches high, bipinnate; pinnæ bluntly oval, and heart-shaped at the base, the end one lengthened-out. Colour a purplish-green: hence the specific name. Spore-masses continued on the margin, forming a broader band than the *Pterides*. Increased but slowly by dividing the slow-creeping rhizomes. A very beautiful Fern, and ought to be in every collection.

P. CORDATA (Heart-shaped).—A beautiful Mexican Fern. Fronds bipinnate, delicate, and erect, growing 1½ foot high; pinnæ halbert or heart-shaped, with a sharp point, beautiful light green, and hairy. Stalks light brown. Increased by dividing the thick, scaly, creeping root-stock. This species loses most of its fronds in winter, and should then be kept only just moist enough to keep the roots alive.

Fig. 70. Platyloma falcata. (Part of frond medium size.)

P. FALCATA (Sickle-shaped), *Fig. 70.*—A rather tall Fern, from New Holland. Fronds pinnate and lance-shaped, 2 feet high, growing nearly upright; pinnæ oblong, suddenly coming to a point, heart-shaped at the base, but sickle-shaped upwards, dull green and leathery. Spore-masses long and narrow, placed transversely on the pinnæ, thus forming a broad belt close to the margin. Stalks scaly. Increased by dividing the creeping rootstock.

P. ROTUNDIFOLIA (Round-leaved).—From New Zealand.

Fronds pinnated, growing a foot or more long, and reclining. We never saw them, however strongly grown, stand upright. Pinnæ nearly round, stout, and dark green, and slightly hollowed-out at the edges. Stalks covered with brown scales. Increased readily by dividing the creeping rootstock. This is also a most desirable Fern, and thrives well in a Wardian case. It is also very suitable for cultivation in a basket.

POLYPODIUM.

Under this name there were formerly arranged a great number of species of very various forms and habit of growth—in fact it was an incongruous assemblage; but they have now been divided into many distinct genera, so that under the old name there are but comparatively few species left.

POLYPODIUM PLEBEJUM (Homely or Simple).—A native of Mexico, and a very interesting little Fern. It is somewhat rare yet, but well deserves a place in every greenhouse collection of Ferns. The fronds are not more than 4 inches in length, dark green, and sprinkled with brown scales, which make very interesting objects under the microscope.

P. SUBPETIOLATUM (Short-stalked).—A Mexican Fern of considerable beauty. Fronds pinnate, growing, with ordinary care, 2 feet high, narrow, lance-shaped, covered with very fine short hairs; pinnæ quite smooth, with very short footstalks. Easily increased by dividing the scaly creeping rhizome. Even this species is sometimes put into the genus *Goniophlebium*, and, strictly speaking, perhaps *P. plebejum* is the only true greenhouse Polypody.

POLYSTICHUM.

This name is derived from the Greek *polys*, numerous, and *stichos*, order; the spore-masses being in many regular lines. This genus is nearly related to *Lastrea*, but may easily be distinguished from it by the indusium or covering of the spore-masses being round and attached by its centre.

Fig. 71. Polystichum capense. (Part of frond full size.)

POLYSTICHUM CAPENSE (Cape), *Fig.* 71.—Native of the Cape of Good Hope. Sometimes called *Aspidium coriaceum*. It requires a warm greenhouse. Fronds about 3 feet high, dark green, smooth, tripinnate. It makes a noble specimen where there is room enough to grow it to its full size. It is well adapted for exhibition, as it is so striking and distinct.

P. CONCAVUM (Concave).—A very beautiful greenhouse or perhaps hardy Fern, with large, spreading, ovate, quadripinnate fronds, having crowded obliquely-ovate lobed pinnules, with recurved margins, so that the surface is concave.

P. CORIACEUM (Leathery).—Somewhat similar to *P. capense*, but not so striking a plant. The fronds are smaller, and of a dull green. It is a native of Mauritius.

P. FLEXUM (Bent).—This species is very nearly hardy. It is thick, shining, thrice-divided. Fronds about 18 inches or 2 feet high. It is a native of St. Juan de Fernandez.

P. ORDINATUM (Regular).—A handsome bold-habited greenhouse Fern, with erect stem, and a plume-like tuft of bold bipinnate dark green fronds, with oblique trapeziform biserrated pinnules. South America.

P. PUNGENS (Spiny).—This is a South-African Fern, but nearly hardy. The fronds of this plant are erect, spiny, dark green, about 2 feet high. It is a very pretty species.

P. VESTITUM (Clothed).—A New-Zealand Fern. The fronds are about 2 feet high, dark green and shining, and the stems and crown covered with scales. The *Polystichum* called *proliferum* is said to be a variety of this plant. It bears a cluster of two or three little plants at the apex of the frond.

PTERIS.

The most familiar name of all the genera of Ferns with, perhaps, the exception of *Polypodium*. There are a few handsome species that belong to our division of Greenhouse Ferns.

PTERIS ARGUTA (Sharp-notched).—Native of Madeira, the Canary Islands, and St. Helena. Fronds 3 feet long, spreading, and triangular in form, many-times-divided, and of a pale green colour; pinnæ bluntly oblong, and sharply cut at the edges. Stalks a foot or more long, and of a rich brown colour. Spore-masses narrow, and close to the margin. Increased easily by dividing the creeping rhizomes, or by spores. This fine species requires a large space to show off its large, beautiful fronds.

P. CRETICA (Cretan).—Though found in the Isle of Crete, this Fern is widely spread in various parts of the globe. It has been found in the East and West Indies, in China, and in Southern Europe. It will however grow in a greenhouse, but should be kept at the warmest end in winter. Fronds pinnate, a foot or more high, and of a beautiful lively green; pinnæ of the fertile fronds narrow, and very long; of the barren ones long lance-shaped, with the lowest pair often divided in the centre. Stalks light-coloured. Increased by spores.

P. CRETICA ALBO-LINEATA (White-lined).—This extremely beautiful variegated Fern was introduced from Java a few years ago. The plants were forwarded to the Royal Botanic Gardens at Kew, where the plant was rapidly increased from spores, and in less than a year had been widely distributed through the country. It is now pretty plentiful; and as it will bear being cultivated in the greenhouse, though it by no means objects to stove heat, it is a great and valuable acquisition. While young it looks very beautiful in a Wardian case.

P. KINGIANA (Capt. King's).—Found in Norfolk Island only. Fronds partly bipinnate, 2 feet high, and rather spreading; pinnæ long lance-shaped, hanging down with sharp cut edges.

P. SCABERULA (Roughish).—A perfect little gem, introduced a few years ago from New Zealand. The fronds, which are not more than 8 or 9 inches long, are divided into very fine segments; they are triangular in outline, spreading horizontally, and of a light green colour. It can only be satisfactorily divided in the spring. It should be grown near the glass in the greenhouse, but by no means exposed to cutting draughts of air.

P. SERRULATA var. ANGUSTA (Finely-serrated).—A pretty miniature arching Fern, in which the acuminate divisions of the bipinnate fronds are much smaller and narrower than in the common state of the plant. Very desirable for small Fern cases. Garden variety.

P. TREMULA (Shaking).—A common New-Zealand Fern. Fronds many-times-divided, spreading, growing 2 or 3 feet long; pinnæ broadly line-shaped, and hollowed-out at the edges. We find this very handsome free-growing Fern springs up from spores freely on the soil, in the pots, wherever it grows.

P. UMBROSA (Shading).—This handsome Fern is very common in New South Wales. Fronds 2 feet high, bipinnate on the lower part of the frond, and only pinnate on the upper fertile pinnæ are remarkably long, often as much as 10 inches. Sterile fronds shorter, and deeply cut throughout. Increased by spores or division.

TODEA.

This genus was named in honour of a botanist of Mecklenburg, who paid a good deal of attention to cryptogamic plants—his name was H. Julius Tode. It contains several species, and they differ most remarkably from each other.

TODEA AFRICANA (African).—A native of the Cape of Good Hope. It has a short, thick, erect stem, so that it approaches nearly to a tree Fern. The fronds are 3 or 4 feet in height; and are twice-divided. As the fronds stand somewhat erect, with tops gracefully arching over, the plant makes a truly noble specimen, well suited for exhibition. *T. rivularis* very closely resembles, if it is not identical with, the African species. It is a native of Australia.

T. HYMENOPHYLLOIDES (Filmy-Fern-like).—It is also quite as often called *T. pellucida*, and both of these names give a very good idea of the appearance of the plant. It is a native of New Zealand, and grows in great masses in the swamps there, just as the Royal Fern (*Osmunda*) does in Europe. It was one of the last novelties introduced by Messrs. Loddiges, whose name will long retain a place in the horticultural history of our country. The finely-divided, light green, semi-transparent fronds of this plant make it a universal favourite. We have cultivated this plant under a hand-glass; but we have also tried it without, and find it succeeds quite as well, though the fronds looked so very delicate that we were at first afraid to try it.

Under the name of *T. superba*, Mr. Veitch has introduced another exquisite Fern, even more beautiful than the last, and nearly related to it, though it will probably be considered a distinct species.

TRICHOMANES.

Derived from the Greek *trichos*, hair, and *mania*, excess: referring to the hair-like appendages to which the spore-masses are attached, and which spring from the bottom of little cups along the margin of the frond. The species figured below is one of the few in which this hair is not developed beyond the point at which the spore-masses are growing. These, however, project beyond the cup, as will be seen in the figure. There are many kinds in cultivation now, but most of them are stove plants.

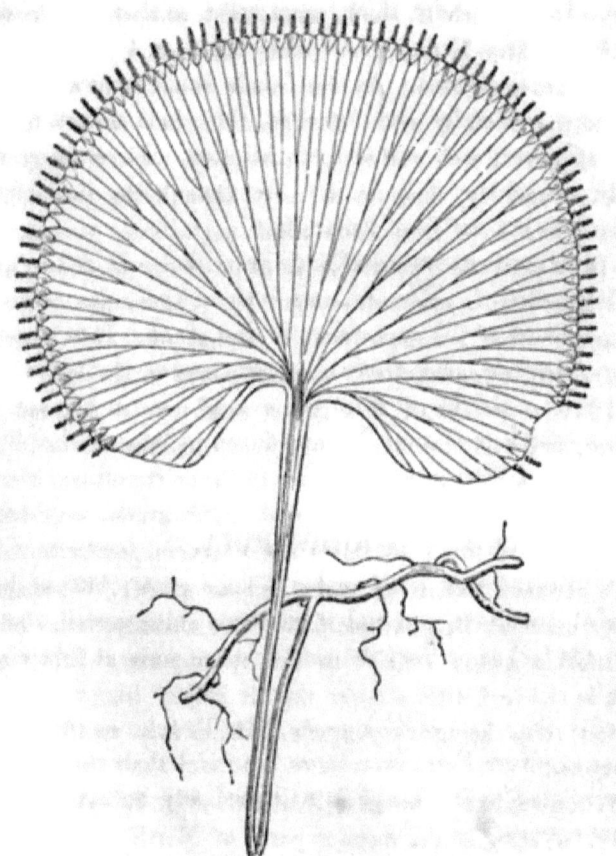

Fig. 72. Trichomanes reniforme. (Frond full size.)

TRICHOMANES RENIFORME (Kidney-shaped), *Fig.* 72.—Native of New Zealand. Fronds about 6 inches high, shining dark green, smooth and semi-transparent, simple, kidney-shaped. Rhizome slender, creeping, and wire-like. It may be increased by division. For the mode of treatment see what is said of the Stove kinds.

T. RADICANS (Rooting).—So named by Swartz; Willdenow, however, called it *T. speciosum,* and R. Brown *T. brevisetum.* It is not only a native of Ireland, as the popular name (Killarney Fern) would lead us to believe, but is found also in many other parts of the world—in fact it grows almost everywhere where a warm and moist atmosphere is to be obtained. Fronds triangular, many-times-divided, light green and almost transparent, growing about 9 inches or a foot long; ribs of the frond winged. Stalks having narrow brown scales. This elegant Fern is always in request with Fern-growers. It was formerly considered very difficult to manage, but recently we have seen some most magnificent specimens of it. It is perfectly impossible to grow it out of doors, and it even likes the stove better than the greenhouse. There is a variety with narrower fronds named after Mr. Andrews (*Andrewsii*), an enthusiastic lover of Ferns in Dublin.

All the species of this genus need to be covered with glasses, and during summer to be kept constantly moist.

WOODWARDIA.

A commemorative name in honour of Mr. Woodward, a rather eminent British botanist. The characteristics of this remarkable genus consist in the spore-masses being much sunk in the leaf with a cover that is hollow like a vault, and by the veins being very much divided into small irregular polygons.

WOODWARDIA RADICANS (Rooting), *Fig.* 73.—Very nearly hardy. Native of the warmer parts of North America. It is a large-growing Fern. We have had it 3 feet high, and as much through, the fronds spreading very much. Unless the space in the greenhouse is large, this Fern should not be introduced. Fronds irregularly pinnate, of a lively green; pinnæ irregular in breadth and length, with the edges cut into pointed segments. The fronds form at the top a large knob, which soon sends forth roots (hence the name *radicans*), and forms new plants. It is a common, rather coarse, but curious Fern. There is a variety of this Fern which is more curious than beautiful; it is called *interrupta*, from some of the pinnæ being depauperised or altogether wanting. It is interesting, but by no means so beautiful as the true species.

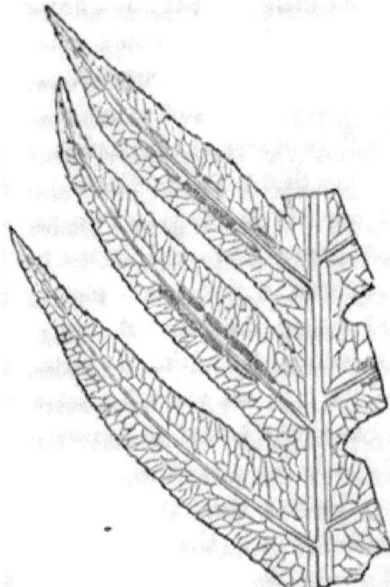

Fig. 73. Woodwardia radicans. (Part of pinna natural size.)

Two species have been recently introduced from China and Japan under the names of *W. orientalis* and *W. japonica*. They will in all probability prove hardy, or very nearly so; but as we have not ourselves tried them out of doors (in fact with us they have been growing in a stove, and evidently enjoying it), we refrain from placing them among those which are proved to be truly hardy. They are very proliferous, and consequently will soon be plentiful. They appear to be much smaller plants than *W. radicans*, and therefore more suitable for cultivation where room is scarce.

This completes our list of Greenhouse Ferns. We have only to add a few hints on their culture. Like most other arge classes of plants, they thrive best in a house by themselves; but, as we remarked before, many of them may be grown by the sides of the path, just under the first shelf of the stage. The more tender kinds, such as *Cheilanthes* and *Nothochlæna*, must be placed on a shelf near the glass, because the drip from greenhouse plants on the stage would quickly destroy them. If convenient, a nearly upright mass of rockwork at one end of the greenhouse would suit many of the species. The soil for them, unless otherwise specified in the catalogue, should be stronger than that for stove Ferns. We found the following a good mixture for them:—Two parts mellow turfy loam, one part fibrous peat, and half a part partially decayed tree leaves, with a few small pieces of charcoal regularly intermixed among the compost, together with plenty of sand. We generally prefer mixing the compost a day or two previously to the one set apart for potting. We think if it is mixed some months before, it becomes so solid that the fine roots of the Ferns cannot so readily, if at all, run through it; and, besides that, it sooner runs together, and will not so readily permit the water to pass through and thoroughly wet the interior of the ball of earth in the pot. Excepting for very delicate kinds, we find they do best in rather large pots, providing they are thoroughly drained. The best season for potting is in early spring, just before the new fronds begin to shoot.

The mode of potting is simple, yet requires care. Bring the plant to the potting-bench, reverse it, and place one hand under it close to the ball; then thrust the finger or a blunt stick through the hole at the bottom of the pot, pressing hard to force the ball out of the pot. The roots of the strong-growers cling to the sides of the pot very tenaciously, and require considerable force to separate them. In very obstinate cases it may be desirable, rather than injure a valuable plant, to break the pot, but the stroke to do it must be gentle, or the roots will be bruised. Having got the ball out of the pot, then pick out carefully all the old crocks used for drainage; the roots in a healthy plant will be here very numerous. Then with a sharp-pointed stick pick out some of the old soil all round the ball, and give it a smart stroke or two on the hand. This will loosen some roots, and make them ready to enter into the new soil. Have ready the pot well drained with a few pieces of the rougher parts of the compost (or a thin layer of moss) on the drainage. The pot should be so much larger than the ball as to allow the operator to thrust the soil down between it and the sides of the pot. Fill in as much compost upon the covered drainage as will raise the ball rather above the level of the rim of the pot, so that when it is pressed and shaken down the ball will be below the rim, about the thickness of a finger or more, if the pot is very large. Then fill in the compost round the ball, and finish by a smart stroke or two on the bench. Level the soil, and then the operation is finished; and so proceed till the whole are gone through. Give a very gentle watering through a fine-rosed pot, and replace them in the greenhouse. By potting them at the season above indicated, they will not require shading, and will be slowly making new roots to sustain the new growth.

This potting time is a good season for increasing all such as will bear dividing, but all plants so divided-off should be placed either in a close frame or in a shady part of the house.

SUMMER MANAGEMENT.

Where Ferns are grown under the stage, and the greenhouse-stage is occupied through the summer with flowering-plants, the Ferns will be greatly benefited if placed out of doors from the end of May to the middle of September, only remembering to keep in such as we have indicated as being rather delicate with regard to wetting their leaves. The situation for their summer residence should be one where they will be shaded from the midday sun, and if the pots are plunged in moss over their rims the Ferns will thrive all the better for the cool, moist qualities of the moss; only keep a good look-out for slugs and destroy them. Remove them in-doors early in September, and then give them plenty of water, gradually reducing the quantity till in the depth of winter the soil is only just moist enough to keep them from drooping. By following these simple rules, Ferns in the greenhouse will thrive and be very ornamental.

HARDY FERNS.

It is with great pleasure that we commence writing about these lovely plants—the Hardy Ferns; and that pleasure arises chiefly from the fact that any one possessing a few perches of ground may grow most of the species that we shall treat upon; and therefore we are somewhat sanguine that our remarks, the result of many years' experience, will be, or may be, useful to a great number of our readers. It also pleases us to write about them, because they are great favourites with ourselves, as much so or more than any other tribe of plants, always excepting the Orchids. "The labour we delight in physics pain," was said by one of our greatest poets; by which he meant that any trouble we bestow upon what we delight in, is compensated for by the pleasure we anticipate and receive in doing it. Though these charming plants are at this day grown by many persons, yet we think the cultivation of them is on the increase; and, we trust, when our instructions are completed, and, we hope, understood, that many more persons will be induced to turn their attention to and enjoy the pleasures of growing them.

They may be grown on the highest hills and in the lowest vales. Many of them will bear the smoke of large towns, flourishing where few other plants will live. They will grow in the shade of trees or shrubs, and on the naked exposed rock. Some will only thrive in boggy wet swamps, whilst others will grow on old walls; in fact there are few places where a judicious selection of the proper species for right situations will not thrive. These selections and situations for them it will be our business in the forthcoming pages to point out.

To grow the greatest number of species two methods may be resorted to. The first, which is the best, is to form a spot to grow them in the open air, by imitating the various positions in which they are found growing wild. This includes rockwork formed with stones, scoria, and stumps of trees, with a plot of ground in front, in which to plant such as are found in wet or shady places. This rockery, if judiciously formed, will of itself be a pleasing object, and in many situations, where the materials are plentiful, will not be very expensive.

The other method is to grow them in pots, plunging the commonest and hardiest species in ashes or old tan, and placing the more tender or rock-inhabiting species in a cold pit or frame. This plan has its advantages and disadvantages. The first is that a greater number may be grown in a small space, and the tenderer kinds protected both from the cold and damp of winter, and the scorching rays of the sun in summer. The drawbacks on this method are that they cannot possibly make such fine fronds in pots, unless grown in a greenhouse, as they will in the open air, on a fernery formed purposely for them. Now the choice between these two ways of growing them rests upon the space the cultivator has at command. If he has a place in his grounds where a fernery can be formed, we would say, By all means set about it at once, if you wish to see them thrive well; but if your space is limited, and a rockwork impossible to be formed without interfering with the arrangement of the garden, then, if you are still desirous of having a collection of Ferns, grow them in pots; but, for your comfort, let us tell you that a great number of species will grow in the common soil and borders of your villa garden.

We once saw, in the garden of Mrs. Priestley, the Grove, Chalfont, Buckinghamshire, the finest specimen we ever met with of that beautiful Fern the *Ceterach officinarum*, growing in the open border. It was 9 or 10 inches high, and 6 or 7 inches across, forming a dense little bush of exceedingly fine fronds. The soil is stony, but had been mixed with heath mould, and the plant had thriven well in it undisturbed and unprotected for many years. Now, this species is generally found wild, growing in crevices of rocks and on old decaying stone walls. We have seen and gathered it in the latter on the roadside leading to and from the railway-station at Tetbury, in Gloucestershire; but the wild specimens were pygmies compared with the one in the border of Mrs. Priestley's garden. We from this fact are inclined to think that a dry border would grow many species that we usually consider require rockwork to grow them on; but, as every rock species has not been tried in such a border, it would not be advisable to risk the entire stock in such an experiment. More common species, such as *Polypodium vulgare*, *Scolopendrium vulgare*, and the common Male and Female Ferns, and many others, where the stock is plentiful, might be planted out at once in common borders.

A third method of growing a collection of Ferns may be adopted where rockwork cannot be formed and the trouble of growing them in pots is objected to, and that is to throw up a bank of earth 3 or 4 feet high, either in a circle or longitudinally, forming it into, as it were, narrow terraces some 9 inches or a foot wide; the face or upright part to be built with small stones or flints. If the circular form is adopted, then an opening should be left through the bank to enter within the circle, and the inner sides of the bank should be planted with Ferns loving shade; and a circular flat bed within the walk, formed at the foot of the bank, would be an excellent place for Ferns growing in wet places, the *Osmunda regalis* for instance. The outside terraces of the bank would be an excellent position for Ferns found wild on high grounds or rocky situations.

If a long straight bank should, from choice or space, be considered preferable to a circle, then let it be formed to run east and west, the side facing the south to receive Ferns that are naturally found on rocks exposed to the sun; but, as these are few in number compared with such as grow in shady moist places, the bank should be formed much broader on the north side than the south, a thing easily done by carrying it out further on that side. The material of the bank may consist of almost anything; even clay would not be objectionable, only let there be a sufficient bed of good proper soil for the Ferns to grow in. The soil for each species we will mention when we describe them; but a general compost, which will suit the greater part, consists of sandy peat, leaf mould, and loam, in equal parts. Great care, however, must be taken, that neither in the material of which the bank is formed nor the soil there are any roots of perennial weeds, such as Thistles, Nettles, the Creeping Convolvulus, Coltsfoot, or Couch-grass. When any of these are left in, they are very difficult to eradicate. Avoid them as you would the plague.

CULTURE IN POTS.

The species that are found in dry situations, such, for instance, as the *Asplenium trichomanes*, should be well drained, and potted in sandy peat and loam, thoroughly mixed with broken potsherds or small stones—limestone is the best. Whilst those which grow in damp places, such as *Osmunda regalis*, should be potted in strong loam. Others that are found in shady woods or banks, should have a free admixture of leaf mould, not too much decayed, added to the compost. The moisture-loving species should be plunged behind a wall or low hedge, on the north side; the others require a free exposure to the sun; but the pots should always be plunged, to protect the roots from the burning rays of the sun. They should be repotted every year, in the spring, and be supplied with water as they require it. The size of the pots must be in proportion to the size of the plants. The *Osmunda regalis*, for instance, will require, when a good size, pots from 10 to 12 inches in diameter; whilst the small species, such as *Allosorus crispus*, will seldom need a pot more than 6 inches wide, even for the largest specimens.

In the situation we have mentioned these hardy Ferns may remain all the year; but where there is that convenience we would recommend them to be removed into a cold pit or frame. In woods they are sheltered by the fallen leaves or low shrubs; and the removing them into a winter shelter is a similar protection to them from the severe winter's frosts and heavy snows or rains.

CULTURE IN A FERNERY.

A situation for a fernery should be chosen in a retired spot, and should be formed by throwing up a mound of earth, and facing it on both sides with rocks and roots of trees; or two banks of earth, faced similarly, and facing each other, with a walk between, would answer admirably. One bank should face the north, and the other the south. On the side facing the north, near the base, the moisture-loving species should be planted, and higher up on the bank such as love shade. On the opposite bank plant towards the base all that grow on hedgebanks; and towards the top such species as inhabit mountainous rocks, old walls, &c. By these judicious arrangements nearly the whole hardy species may be grown successfully in a comparatively-speaking small space of ground. Suitable soils for each species must be put in for them. The dead fronds should be allowed to remain through winter to protect the roots from the frost. In the spring cut them all away, and make the fernery neat, adding a little fresh soil around the plants.

PROPAGATION.

By Spores (or Seed). — It is only for very rare species that this mode of increasing the number need be resorted to, such, for instance, as the *Woodsias* and the American and other foreign kinds. Save the spores as soon as ripe; this may be known by the bursting of the spore-cases. The spores are extremely minute, but every particle must be preserved carefully. Though so small as to be invisible without the aid of a magnifier, yet their powers of germinating are remarkable. The elder Mr. Shepherd, of the Botanic Gardens at Liverpool, succeeded in raising some Ferns the spores of which were brushed off fronds that had been in his herbarium for ten years. We would not, however, advise the cultivator to keep his Fern-spores any such length of time. If they have been saved early in the summer, sow part immediately, and the rest in spring, about April. To insure success, prepare a sufficient number of shallow garden-pans, with bell-glasses to fit. Drain them well, and fill them with sandy heath mould, sifting a small part very fine for the surface. Press it down firmly, and lay on the surface a number of very small sandy stones; then sprinkle the spores on the whole and cover with the glasses. Pack some moss round the rim of the pans, at the bottom of the bell-glasses, to keep in the moisture. This moss also prevents the washing-away of the soil. Water must be given only upon this moss. It will enter the soil inside by capillary attraction, and keep it sufficiently moist. To prevent it drying, the glasses must be shaded from the sun. The best position for these seed-pans will be in a cold frame, where the sun does not shine till towards evening. We choose evening for the reason that a little heat will be thrown into the frame, and serve to keep up a rather warmer atmosphere than the open air.

There is a difficulty about this mode, or, indeed, any other mode of raising Ferns from spores, and that is the pulling-up any weeds that will spring up from the spores. We have prevented this by baking, not burning, the soil on a flue, or in an oven, till all the seeds in it were effectually destroyed. This fiery process also kills the eggs and larva of insects. The soil, when sufficiently baked, may be moistened gradually by laying upon a moist cloth and covered with another cloth: gardener like, we always used a bast mat for that purpose. It will take several days to moisten it sufficiently. We prefer this gradual moistening to the more ready one of wetting it by means of the water-pot.

Supposing all these points have been strictly attended to, and everything gone on well, the Ferns will soon make their appearance. The soil and stones will appear as if covered with green scales, from the base of which the first tiny frond will spring. It is very curious and exceedingly interesting to watch the progress of the germination and development of these young Ferns. Be very careful, however, to keep the soil moderately moist, and keep the glasses constantly on, to keep up an internal moist atmosphere. It has often been to us a matter of surprise how Fern-spores germinate and grow in their native localities. It can only be accounted for by the immense number of spores each plant produces. Thousands and tens of thousands must perish for want of a proper pabulum and of circumstances favourable to their growth; but the profusion of spores renders the entire loss of any species impossible.

To return to our seedlings. Under our careful management, as soon as the third frond appears, it will be time to think about potting them off—a most delicate operation. Take off the glass and examine the small stones first; there is no difficulty with them. Take up each stone that has a Fern on it, and plunge the stone just within the soil in the tiny pot you have prepared for it, leaving the frond just above the soil. For such delicate rock-loving species as *Woodsia hyperborea*, a native of the Scotch mountains, we have added to the heath mould some pieces of sandstone about the size of swan shot. This keeps the soil open both to the influences of the air and the water. After potting all off, replace them in the frame, and keep them close for a month; then gradually inure them to bear the open air, and when large enough plant them out in the fernery.

This may appear a tedious process, but the results, when successful, will repay all the trouble. The owner may if he chooses dispose of his surplus stock to some nurseryman; or he may exchange with other growers that have not the means of raising seedlings.

Another rougher mode of propagating hardy Ferns from spores is to place some small pieces of sandstone, or even bricks, on the soil, in a shady moist place; then sprinkle the spores upon them and cover the whole with a hand-glass. Many good kinds of Ferns have been raised in great numbers by this method.

Mr. Glover, of Smedley House, near Manchester, an enthusiastic admirer of plants in general, but more particularly of Ferns, adopts the following mode of raising seedlings:— In the house where the seed-pots are placed there is such a moist air kept up that even the outsides of the pots are thickly covered with young Ferns. He does not sow the spores in pans, but in pots about 5 inches wide, and mixes the compost with old bricks, broken very small, instead of sandstone, as we recommend. The seed-pots are placed in saucers, and they are kept full of water, the moisture from which, ascending through the drainage and compost, and confined by bell-glasses set within the pots, causes a regular moisture—just the thing to encourage the spores to grow. The success of this mode is very great. Some species, however, even baffled him, especially the *Asplenium marinum;* but, determined not to be beaten, he shed some of its spores on the earth border, under the front platform, and on the front wall inside; and, curious enough, there they germinated freely.

Another mode of raising Ferns from spores is that practised by Mr. Frazer, gardener to John Shaw Leigh, Esq., of Luton Hoo Park, near Luton, Bedfordshire. In a communication on the subject he says:—

"I have been reading with much interest this morning your mode of propagating hardy Ferns. I am now raising many seedlings of the exotic species. The *Bird's-nest* (*Neottopteris australasica*), I have long tried without success till lately. I find it can with me only be induced to germinate when sown on *pieces of mossy bark;* or, I daresay, as you recommend, on pieces of brickbats or sandstone. It is impatient of too much moisture when young; indeed I have had thousands germinated in the usual way, but I lost them after they got the first leaf perfected."

Where natural rockstones are difficult or expensive to obtain, then these conglomerated bricks come in very well as a substitute. Clay for brickmaking abounds much more than stone: hence there is no difficulty in getting them. Indeed they might be so burned and run together purposely to form rockwork for a fernery or for alpine plants; and in that case might be formed into larger blocks than the usual size when made for building purposes.

By Division.—Many species of Ferns send forth creeping rhizomes or rootstocks; such are easily increased by taking off one or more of their offshoots. They may either be planted in a bed by themselves, and shaded till they are established, or, which is the better plan, be potted in suitable-sized pots, placed in a cold frame, and kept close and shaded for a week or two, and, when fully rooted, planted out in the fernery where they are required to grow. Other kinds, that do not have creeping roots, will, when of a considerable size, produce small side shoots, which, as soon as they produce roots, may be taken off with a sharp knife, potted, and treated like those mentioned above. Some other species grow in a compact form, of which the Parsley-leaved Fern and Wall

Rue Fern are examples. These must be taken up and divided into as many pieces as will give a fair share of roots to each pot; put each division into a small pot, and shade them till fresh fronds and roots are produced. All these operations are pleasant and recreative, giving useful and innocent amusement to many persons in every rank of life.

It should be kept in mind that although the number of *species* of Ferns which are truly hardy is rather limited, yet the *varieties* are almost without number, and in many cases these are as distinct in appearance as though they belonged to different species. As an instance of this, look at *Asplenium Filix-fœmina Frizelliæ* and *A. Filix-fœmina plumosa*; two plants could not be less alike. In the following pages we have mentioned the most striking varieties of each species; but in most cases there are a number of others which resemble more or less one of those named. Where it is wished to make the collection as large as possible, of course the grower will obtain these; but where space is not too plentiful, those kinds mentioned will be found to give a great variety of form and habit.

ADIANTUM.

ADIANTUM PEDATUM (Divided like a Bird's Foot).—*Adiantum* contains many beautiful species, but this is the only species that is decidedly hardy. Sir Oswald Mosely, at Rolleston Hall, near Derby, has a very fine collection of hardy Ferns, planted in a rather open part of a plantation, on a raised bank, and there this *Adiantum* has lived for several years, protected by a slight covering of decaying leaves. The last time we were there, we saw it producing fronds 18 inches high, and spreading nearly a foot across. Let any one possessing a plant try a similar situation, and he will find it thrive equally well. The *Adiantum capillus-Veneris*, though a native of Britain, is not so hardy.

ALLOSORUS.

A genus of Ferns containing a solitary species. The name means *allos*, various, and *sorus*, a heap: the sori or spore-masses presenting varied appearances as they develope themselves.

ALLOSORUS CRISPUS (Curled), *Fig.* 74.—This pretty Fern is found plentifully on the blue slate rocky hills of Wales and Cumberland. It has two kinds of fronds, one barren, and the other spore-bearing or fertile. Barren fronds twice-divided or bipinnate; pinnæ often divided again, and twice-cut at the edges, giving the plant a parsley-like appearance. From this circumstance collectors often call it the Parsley Fern. Fertile fronds are also bipinnate, and even tripinnate at the lower part of the frond; pinnæ contracted on one side. The plant is very dwarf, seldom reaching 6 inches high. It forms a pretty, neat, evergreen patch, and should always be planted amongst small stones, considerably elevated. Increased readily by dividing the creeping rhizome.

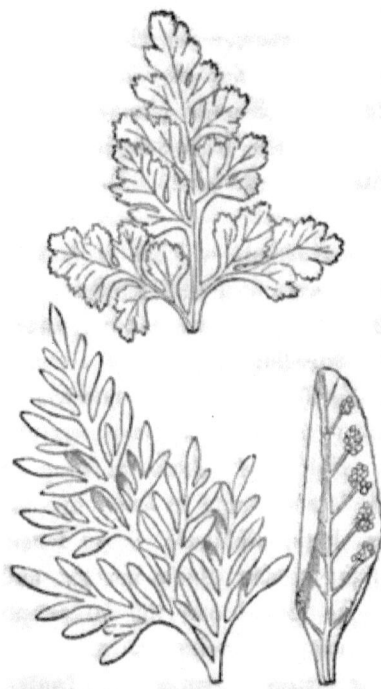

Fig 74. Allosorus crispus. (Tops of barren frond and fertile frond; segment of fertile magnified.)

ASPLENIUM.

ASPLENIUM ADIANTUM NIGRUM (Black Adiantum).—A neat

dwarf Fern, a native of Britain, on old walls and hedgerows. Fronds triangular-formed and variously-divided; when the fronds are in fructification the spore-masses (nearly black) cover the under sides of the pinnæ. Very hardy, but requires a dry situation, rather shaded. Increased readily by offsets that form themselves round the tufted crowns. There are several forms of this species varying in the forms of the pinnæ, and one which is irregularly blotched with white, and is thence called *variegatum*.

A. ALTERNIFOLIUM (Alternate-leaved).—An elegant little Fern found on the Scottish mountains, and also in Germany, France, Sweden, and Switzerland. Fronds pinnated alternately, growing only 3 or 4 inches high, in a compact patch; pinnæ lance-shaped. Increased by division. Difficult to manage out of doors.

A. ANGUSTIFOLIUM (Narrow-fronded). — This is a very distinct North-American Spleenwort. Quite hardy. The fronds are about 18 inches high, light green, standing somewhat erect, once-divided, with lanceolate pinnæ.

A. FILIX-FŒMINA (Female-Fern).—So named because of its graceful appearance. There is no Fern that surpasses this in its elegant feathery habit. Native of Britain, growing on hedgebanks in shady lanes. It is also found in every quarter of the globe. Fronds 2 feet high, bipinnate, broad lance-shaped, and of a beautiful light green; pinnæ narrow, and thickly placed on the stem, the lowest one the largest in size. Stems scaly. Spore-masses kidney-shaped. Increased slowly by division. There are numerous permanent varieties of this beautiful Fern. One is particularly handsome, and has been named *multifidum* (Many-times-cut)—that is, the pinnæ at the end of the fronds are finely divided or tasselled. This was discovered in Ireland by Mr. D. Moore, of the Glasnevin Gardens. Another variety is sometimes named *crispum*, and also *Smithii*. It was also found in Ireland by Mr. Andrew Smith, gardener at the Holme, in Regent's

Park, a very successful cultivator of hardy Ferns, even in that locality. A third variety has been named *ramosum;* the pinnæ branching out, flat-shaped, not particularly handsome, but very curious. Found in Ireland by the late Dr. Mackay, the curator of the Trinity College Gardens, Dublin. This is one of the most variable of all Ferns, and there are a number of well-marked and distinct forms of it. *Frizelliæ* (Miss Frizell's) is a very narrow-fronded variety, in which the fronds are simply pinnate, and the pinnæ small and fan-shaped. In *plumosa* (Feather-like), we find just the other extreme: here the frond is very broad and repeatedly-divided. This is a very beautiful kind for pot-culture, as is also the last-named. Then again we have another variety, also brought out by Mr. Veitch, and called *multiceps* (Often-divided). In this we find the much-branched frond combined with another interesting character—that is, with all the points of the frond tasselled. On strong plants the tassel at the apex of the frond has been seen as much as 5 inches across. In the curious form called *depauperatum* (Depauperised), we find the divisions of the fronds reduced almost to their midribs, a mere skeleton as it were; but then at the points spreading into fan-shaped tassels. This is a very striking and remarkable plant. Most of these varieties come true from spores, or nearly so.

A. FONTANUM (Fountain).—A British Fern of a neat, dwarf, compact habit. Fronds long and narrow, lance-shaped, and twice-cut, growing 6 inches long. We have had plants of this pretty Fern nearly a foot across. Should be grown in moist shady places. Increased readily by division when the plant is large enough. This is really a desirable Fern, and no collection ought to be without it.

A. LANCEOLATUM (Lance-shaped).—Another elegant British Fern, something like the *A. fontanum*, but the pinnæ are placed much more distant from each other, and the fronds grow taller, often attaining a foot in length, and the pinnæ are more deeply notched or toothed. Decidedly a rock Fern. Increased by division.

A. MARINUM (Sea-Fern).—So named because it is found in the clefts of rocks on the seashores of Britain. We described this as a greenhouse Fern; but where the cultivator resides near the sea it may be cultivated in the open air.

A. MICHAUXI (Michaux's).—A North-American Fern, but perfectly hardy. It loses its fronds in winter, being what is termed deciduous. It is a tall-growing Fern, reaching 2 to 2½ feet high. The whole frond forming a broad, lance-like shape, and many-times-divided; pinnæ flat and widely apart, and deeply-cut at the edges. Increases readily by dividing the creeping rhizome. We may as well just mention here that all hardy Ferns that will increase by division should have that operation performed just before they begin to grow. If divided after the fronds have made some progress the young fronds are almost sure to perish. There is a variety with purple stems.

A. RUTA-MURARIA (Wall-Rue).—In some parts of England this pretty Fern clothes old walls with its dark green tufts of fronds. Fronds bipinnate, only a few inches high; pinnæ roundish, something like the leaves of Rue: hence its specific name. To grow this pretty Fern well, mix some old lime amongst the soil, and plant it on the top of a pyramid of small stones or broken bricks, or place it in the crevices of rockwork. Increased readily by division.

A. SEPTENTRIONALE (Northern).—This very neat Fern formerly grew plentifully in the crevices of the rocks on the mountain named Arthur's Seat, near Edinburgh; but ruthless collectors have nearly stripped that locality. The last time we were in Scotland, we climbed to the top of that mountain, but could not find a single plant. Fronds bipartite, or twice-parted, three-toothed at the extremity. Spore-masses long, covering the entire under surface of the fronds. This truly elegant little Fern should be planted in pure loam, and placed on the highest point of the rockwork. A plant or two should always be kept in pots, under a cold frame, as it is apt to die for want of its pure native mountain air.

A. TRICHOMANES (Maiden-hair).—One of the prettiest of our British Spleenworts, often found growing on the walls of old buildings. The fronds, about 2 or 3 inches long, are pinnate, with the little roundish pinnæ. The stems are dark brown and wire-like. Of this, too, there are several varieties —*multifidum*, with the fronds several-times-divided, and the points crisped; *depauperatum*, in which the pinnæ are very much reduced; *incisum*, with the pinnæ cut so as to resemble a miniature form of *Asplenium formosum*.

BOTRYCHIUM.

This name is derived from *botrys*, a bunch, in reference to the shape of the fructification, which is not unlike that of an erect bunch of Grapes.

BOTRYCHIUM LUNARIA (Moonwort).—This is the only British species of the genus; and, although not uncommon in our island, it is extremely difficult to cultivate artificially; indeed we have never yet seen a person who had been entirely successful. It is more likely to succeed in loam than in peat, but even in loam it never grew well with us a second season.

CETERACH.

CETERACH OFFICINARUM (Official, used formerly in medicine), *Fig.* 75.—The name is *Cheterak* in Persian. A Fern not uncommon in Britain. We have found it growing on the north side of old walls near Tetbury, in Gloucestershire, in great abundance. This shows how it ought to be cultivated— namely, on shady rocks. Fronds simple, but so deeply cut as almost to be pinnate, lance-shaped, about 6 inches long, densely covered with long loose scales. Spore-masses placed between the veins on the upper part of the frond. The veins are beautifully placed on the fronds like network. A very beautiful Fern, easily cultivated, and increased by dividing the tufted plants.

CYRTOMIUM.

CYRTOMIUM FALCATUM, the plant described among the Greenhouse Ferns, is hardy in favourable situations, unless it is in winters which are unusually severe. As it is easily raised from spores, it should be tried; for if it succeeds, its dark glossy fronds make quite a feature. Do not plant it in too moist a situation.

Fig. 75. Ceterach officinarum. (Frond medium size; portion magnified.)

CYSTOPTERIS.

CYSTOPTERIS BULBIFERA (Bulb-bearing).—A fragile-looking Fern from North America, with twice-divided fronds, which stand nearly erect, about a foot high; and bearing towards the top numerous little bulbs, about the size of a Pea, which drop off and reproduce the plant.

C. FRAGILIS (Fragile).—A British Fern, with fronds from 1 foot to 1½ foot high, and thrice-divided. It will succeed on a shady part of the hardy fernery. The variety called

Dickieana has shorter fronds, with the pinnæ crowded together.

C. MONTANA (Mountain).—This is also a native of our own country; and, like many other alpine plants, is rather difficult to manage. It has triangular, bipinnate fronds; the rhizomes creeping. It should be kept moist while growing freely. It may be more safely grown in a frame, and therefore duplicates only should be trusted on the open fernery.

C. SEMPERVIRENS (Evergreen).—Unlike the last-named plant, this Fern keeps its fronds nearly perfect all winter. Mr. Moore thinks it is only a variety of *C. fragilis*.

C. TENUIS is described among the Greenhouse Ferns, and, like the last, it is only safe there; though if there be a plant to spare, it may be tried out of doors.

DIPLAZIUM.

DIPLAZIUM THELYPTEROIDES (Thelypteris-like).—This Fern is from North America, and is the only one of the genus which is hardy. The fronds are lanceolate, 2 feet high, twice-divided, hairy below, with thick creeping rhizome and scaly stalks. It is very distinct, and well worth a place in the fernery.

HYMENOPHYLLUM.

A genus of very delicate Ferns, containing only two species which are indigenous to Britain. The name is derived from *hymen*, a membrane, and *pteron*, a leaf.

HYMENOPHYLLUM TUNBRIDGENSE (Tunbridge Fern).—So named because it was formerly found there in great quantity, and that locality was supposed to be the only one where it grew; but it has been found in the hill districts of Yorkshire, and is so plentiful in Ireland, that we have received a large batch of *Trichomanes radicans* from thence, packed in large patches of *Hymenophyllum*. Fronds pinnate, from 1 to 4 inches long, dark green; pinnæ narrow, forked, pointing edge upright, spiny. Cups or involucres single, on the points of the pinnules, compressed; when opened they divide in two parts, showing the spore-cases in a cluster. Stalk winged. Rootstock creeping and thread-like. Increased readily by division.

H. WILSONI (Wilson's Hymenophyllum).—This is also a British species, often found growing in the same locality, and mixed with the former species, to which it bears a close resemblance. Fronds lance-shaped, pinnate, dark green, from 1 to 4 inches long; pinnæ recurved, and divided into hand-shaped segments, which are cut into thorny points at the edges. Cups containing the fructification entire at the edges. Stalk winged. Rootstock round, like a thread, and creeping Increased by division. The differences between these two closely-allied species are, in the latter the pinnæ are recurved or rolled back, whereas in the former the pinnæ point their edges vertically or upwards; then, again, the latter has the cups or involucres quite smooth at the edge, the former being spiny or fringed. To find out the differences the cultivator must use a good magnifier.

As we have succeeded very well in cultivating these two Filmy Ferns, we have great pleasure in detailing the means we used, and the method we followed. The first plants we had under our care were those we alluded to above as coming from Ireland, wrapped round the emphatically so-called Irish Fern. We were informed by the collector, an Irish gardener of the name of Doran, that they grow there on a sloping wet bank near waterfalls, generally on the north side: consequently there were two things they did not like—dryness and sunshine —on the contrary, a moist climate, with plenty of wet at the root, and plenty of shade, were necessary adjuncts to their well-being. Acting upon this information, we filled several large flat pans with sandy peat and small stones intermixed; upon this we laid the patches of *Hymenophyllum*, packing some soil round the edges, and pressing the whole firmly down to the soil. We then fitted a hand-light to each pan, gave a good watering, and placed them in a shady part of a stove. There we sprinkled them with water every day, and soon had the satisfaction of seeing new fronds springing up over every part of the plants. We had them over from Ireland in the spring, and before the autumn we had almost every pan covered with beautiful healthy fronds. During the summer we removed them into a deep pit, placed them close to a wall on the south side, so that the sun never shone upon them till the evening. Whilst in the pit we removed the hand-lights, as the shade was quite sufficient to keep them from drying-up too quickly. In this pit we have no doubt they would have done well through the winter, but we wanted them to be seen, and so we removed them back again into the stove, placing them at the north side, where no sun could reach them. We have but little hope that these delicate Ferns can be grown in the open air, unless a similar situation can be had as that of their native locality. Such cultivators as do not possess a frame or pit should place them behind a low hedge or a wall, and keep a hand-light constantly over them, excepting in rainy weather, only bearing in mind that they are not aquatics, and will not exist long in a swamp: therefore the place, however favourable in other respects, should have the surface covered with small stones, as well as being well undermined.

LASTREA.

LASTREA CRISTATA (Crested). — A British Fern, growing 2 feet high. Native also of various parts of Europe, and also of North America. Very hardy and deciduous. Fronds pinnate, lance-shaped; pinnæ distant, deeply-cut and heart-shaped at the base. Spore-masses placed in rows on each side of the midrib, midway from the margin. Stalk scaly. Scales broad. Rootstock slowly creeping. Increased by division.

A free-growing species in almost any situation, and well worthy of general cultivation.

L. DILATATA (Enlarged-crested). — This handsome Fern decorates the hedgebanks of many a pleasant country lane in Britain. We have found it plentifully in shady lanes about Macclesfield, in Cheshire, a part of England rich in Ferns. In one particular lane we counted ten species of these pleasing plants in twenty yards. Fronds, in favourable spots, fully 3 feet long, dark green, oval lance-shaped, bipinnate, and graceful, bending in arch-like manner. Pinnules with thorny lobes. Spore-masses medial—that is, in rows at equal distances from the midrib and the margin. The indusium fringed. Stalk very scaly and dark-coloured in the centre. Increased by dividing the slow-creeping rootstock. There are a crested variety and one or two other forms of this Fern.

L. DECURRENS (Decurrent).—Until recently it was seldom that we had to record a Fern from that distant country China. Mr. John Smith, of Kew, very correctly placed the plant in this genus, under this appropriate specific name. It is somewhat tender, but will live in the open air if covered with leaves during severe frost. Fronds a foot high, rather drooping, lance-shaped and pinnate, light, beautiful green; pinnæ without stalks, sinuated and decurrent, winging the stalk, which is covered with chaffy scales. Spore-masses at the end of each vein. Increased by dividing the tufted rhizomes. This Fern forces beautifully. We have it with beautiful light green fronds, 6 inches high, growing circularly round the rootstock, forming a kind of hollow like a bird's nest.

L. FILIX-MAS (Male-Fern).—This Fern is the most common of any, excepting the common Brake, throughout Britain and all the four quarters of the globe. It will grow in almost any soil and situation, but thrives best in shady moist woods. We have seen it in Ireland in such a situation, 5 feet high, forming quite a bush. Fronds bipinnate; pinnæ narrow and lance-shaped, deeply cut at the edges. Spore-masses medial.

L. FILIX-MAS CRISTATA (Crested).—This is a most beautiful variety, with the ends of the frond and each of the pinnæ most beautifully tasselled. It was originally found wild in Cornwall, and has been kept by division ever since in cultivation. It also comes true from spores. We consider it one of the most beautiful and elegant of all hardy Ferns in cultivation. It makes a splendid pot-plant. A sub-variety, called *cristata angustata* (Narrow-crested), was raised by Mr. R. Sim, the celebrated Fern-grower at Foot's Cray, a few years since, and it is as well worth growing as its predecessor. Its fronds are very narrow, not more than 2 inches in width, and beautifully crested. *L. Filix-mas paleacea* has a yellowish tinge on the fronds, and scales with which the stalks are covered, are of a bright yellowish-brown. The form called *pumila* is, as the name indicates, a very pretty dwarf plant; the fronds not more than 6 inches high. The plant called *Schofieldii* proves, says Mr. Sim, to be "an elegant little variety of *L. Filix-mas*, and not as was previously supposed, of *L. spinulosa*." Its fronds are only 2, or at most 3 inches long, with the points usually once or twice-forked.

L. GOLDIANA (Goldie's).—This handsome scarce Fern is a North-American one. Fronds 2 feet high, broadly lance-shaped, half of the frond twice-cut, the other half of the frond pinnate; pinnæ broad lance-shaped, deeply-cut, and serrate at the margin. Stalks scaly. This is a very handsome, noble Fern, but slow to increase. A young plant is sometimes produced on one side of the rootstock, and as soon as it has roots belonging to it, it may be carefully divided-off, potted, and kept in a cold frame for a few weeks until it is established.

L. MARGINALIS (Margined), *Fig.* 76.—This is also a North-American hardy Fern, and is very handsome, growing 2 feet high. Fronds bipinnate throughout, lance-shaped, and a peculiar colour—greyish-green, with a shade of blue, when seen in strong sunshine; pinnæ sharp-pointed and oblong. Pinnules oval, blunt-ended, the largest next to the stem, and notched on the edge. Stalk chaffy. Spore-masses placed near the margin. Rootstock tufted and very large. This rare Fern is very slow to increase except by spores.

L. NOVEBORACENSIS (New York).—As its name imports, this Fern is from North America, growing about a foot high. Fronds very slender, covered with short hairs, lance-shaped, and pinnated; pinnæ lance-shaped, without stems, deeply-divided, narrow. Spore-masses medial. Rootstock creeping. Easily increased by division: hence this pretty dwarf Fern is by no means rare.

L. OREOPTERIS (Mountain Fern).—A pretty British species, with an agreeable perfume. Fronds 2 feet high, pinnate, and the pinnæ beautifully divided into oblong flat segments. Spore-masses near the margin. Stem very short and chaffy. Rootstock tufted: hence it is slow of increase. This is one of our handsomest Ferns, and is found pretty plentifully in high situations, on the shady sides of hills. Known also as *L. montana*.

Fig. 76. Lastrea marginalis.
(Pinna natural size.)

L. RECURVA (Bent-back).—Mr. Watson names this *Lastrea Fanisecii*: it is generally known by Mr. Newman's name, *recurva*. It is a native of this country, and is a neat, compact, evergreen, hardy Fern. We have several plants of it that have been fully exposed in pots unplunged during a very hard winter, and the fronds are now quite fresh and green. Fronds triangular, tripinnate, a foot high, and of a lively green. Examined with a good magnifier, the under side will be seen covered with glands. Pinnules oblong, curved upwards, with spiny divisions. Spore-masses medial. Stalks and ribs of the fronds covered with narrow scales. Rootstock tufted: hence it is slow of increase; but old large plants have many heads or tufts, and by dividing these a plant may be made into several.

L. SIEBOLDI (Dr. Siebold's).—This is now quite as commonly known under the name which Mr. J. Smith gave the plant, *L. podophylla*. It was introduced from Japan. The fronds are about a foot long, leathery, of a dull green colour, once-divided, the divisions being broad and having entire margins. It is so unlike any other Fern that no hardy collection should be without it.

L. SPINULOSUM (Crested-prickly). — A common British species, ornamenting many a woodland lane with its yellow-green fronds, growing in favourable situations 3 feet high. Fronds bipinnate, narrow, lance-shaped, growing erect; pinnæ oblong, deeply-cut, and spiny. Spore-masses medial, with entire covers. Stalks covered with light-coloured broad scales. Rootstock tufted, slow to increase; but that is of little consequence, for it is plentiful enough in almost every part of Britain.

L. THELYPTERIS (Lady-Fern).—Another Fern common in Britain, and in the four quarters of the world. The only Fern in this genus that has barren and fertile fronds. Fertile fronds erect, contracted, growing a foot or more high, pinnate. Barren fronds pinnate, shorter than the other. Spore-masses medial. Rootstock creeping: hence the species is easily increased by division. It grows generally in wet boggy places.

L. ULIGINOSUM (Moor-Fern).— A strong-growing Fern, native of Britain, said to be only a variety of *L. cristata*.

Mr. Newman, however, thinks it quite distinct. Fronds 2 feet high, bipinnate at the base, pinnate on the upper part; pinnæ triangular, deeply cut. Stalks scaly. Rootstock creeping. Increased by division.

LOMARIA.

Most of the species of this genus of Ferns were formerly arranged under that of *Blechnum*, a genus that had become quite unwieldy. The Lomarias are easily distinguished by their contracted fertile fronds, of which our *L. spicant* is a familiar example. None of the *Blechnums* as now arranged are hardy.

LOMARIA ALPINA (Alpine).—This is a pretty dwarf Fern from the hills of Van Diemen's Land. It is generally kept in a frame; but it will live through the winter if covered in severe frost with dry Fern-fronds or a hand-glass. We have had it live through severe weather close to a wall without any protection. Spore-bearing fronds contracted, and distantly-pinnate, growing 6 inches high. Barren fronds lance-shaped, erect, 4 inches high, pinnated, and bright green; pinnæ oblong and round at the top, with the edges quite entire. Increased readily by dividing the creeping rhizome.

L. CRENULATA (Notched).—This Fern has recently been introduced from Chili by Mr. J. Veitch; and by him it is stated to be quite hardy. The fronds are narrow, lanceolate, with acute divisions. The plant makes a dense tuft about 6 inches high, with the fertile fronds on their reddish stalks standing rather taller.

L. SPICANT (Spiked).—This is a common Fern throughout Great Britain. We have found it very finely grown at the foot of rocks in Derbyshire: hence in culture it should be planted in a moist place. Fertile or spore-bearing fronds a foot high, distantly-pinnate, contracted; pinnæ curved. Barren fronds lance-shaped, a foot long, spreading, deeply cut into lance-shaped segments. Increases freely by the side underground shoots from the tufted rhizome or rootstock. Mr. A. Stansfield, the nurseryman of Todmorden, has been very successful in the discovery of varieties of this interesting Fern, and about two years ago read a paper before the Botanical Society of Todmorden upon the subject. Since that time we have seen most of the sorts he had found, and they form a very curious and pretty little group, not differing so widely as do those of the *Hart's-tongue* or the *Lady Fern* but still well worth growing. First, then, we have *concinnum* (Neat), with narrow fronds about 9 inches long; *imbricatum* (Overlapping), the fronds short and ovate, with the pinnæ "overlapping each other so as to make the frond appear double," as Mr. Stansfield says; *crassicaule* (Thick-stemmed), another small ovate-fronded form; *anomalum* (Anomalous), the fronds in this case are fertile above and sterile below; *ramosum* (Branched), fronds branched and crested at the points. There are many more varieties which differ more slightly from the normal form or from each other; but those mentioned are the most distinct, and some of the others we believe will hardly retain their characters under cultivation.

LORINSORIA.

LORINSORIA AREOLATA (Divided into spaces).—This North-American Fern is known also by the name of *Woodwardia areolata*. It has two kinds of fronds; the fertile ones being much contracted. The barren fronds are broad and divided nearly to the midrib, the divisions lance-shaped and toothed along the margin. They rise to about a foot or 18 inches from the soil, and stand somewhat erect. It has a thickish creeping rhizome.

ONOCLEA.

This is a genus of Ferns from North America. There is only one recorded species. The name *Onoclea* is derived from *onos*, a kind of vessel, and *kleis*, to shut or close: the spore-masses being shut up or covered by the lobes of the pinnæ on the fertile fronds.

ONOCLEA SENSIBILIS (Sensitive), *Fig.* 77.—A most beautiful hardy Fern from North America. There are in the garden of the Warden of Winchester College large tufts a yard across of this beautiful Fern. Our good friend Mr. Weaver has the charge of that garden, and grows foreign hardy Ferns very successfully, cultivating them in light soil composed of peat and leaf mould. *O. sensibilis* has two kinds of fronds, fertile and barren. The fertile spring up amongst the other, growing from 1 to 2 feet high, contracted very much, and bipinnated in opposite pairs; the pinnules on the pinnæ curling over the spore-masses. Barren fronds triangular, very broad, of a most beautiful delicate green, pinnated, with lobed margins. This is a most elegant Fern, but was supposed not to bear handling: hence its specific name. It grows well in a wood where the trees do not stand

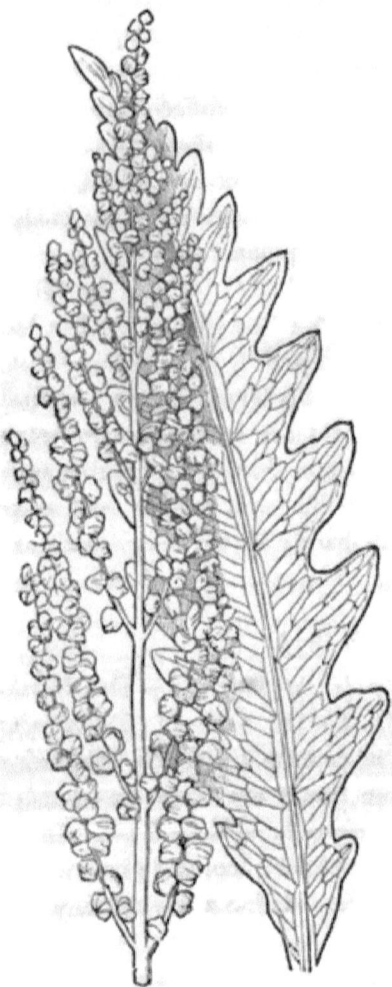

Fig. 77. Onoclea sensibilis. (Part of barren frond and nearly all of fertile frond medium size.)

too thick; the rhizomes running freely amongst the decaying leaves. There are examples in such situations at Mrs. Bosanquet's, Broxbournbury, and at Sir Oswald Moseley's, Rolleston Hall, Derbyshire. Increases rapidly by dividing the creeping rhizomes.

ONYCHIUM.

ONYCHIUM LUCIDUM (Shining). — Described among the Greenhouse Ferns; but we have seen it stand the winter with a little protection, and it would be worth the trial wherever there is a duplicate plant; and as it is easily increased by division, this is soon obtained.

OPHIOGLOSSUM.

OPHIOGLOSSUM VULGATUM (The Adder's-tongue). — This little British Fern seldom finds a place in the fernery, and when it does rarely gives satisfaction. It never seemed happy but when growing amongst grass. The still smaller one found a short time since in Guernsey, and called *O. lusitanicum*, has fronds only about 1½ inch long. If grown at all it should be kept in a pot, in a cold frame.

OSMUNDA.

The derivation of this name, given the plant by Linnæus, is doubtful. Mr. Moore tells us that "there is a legend that it commemorates Osmund, a waterman of Loch Tyne. It is also said to come from the Saxon *osmund*, domestic peace." It contains some of the noblest of the hardy Ferns; and they all delight in moist boggy places.

OSMUNDA CLAYTONIANA (Clayton's).—This is also known as *O. interrupta*; and it has been so called because the fertile parts are found here and there interrupting the frond as it were. It is a native of North America. The fronds are a yard in height, once-divided, but with the pinnæ again divided almost to the base. They are of a lively green colour.

O. CINNAMOMEA (Cinnamon-coloured).—This plant is found in both North and South America, and we have specimens which were collected in the West Indies. In this plant the fructification is produced upon a frond by itself: in other words the sterile and fertile fronds are distinct. The name refers to the colour of the fertile fronds, which stand up in the centre, and are taller than the green barren ones. It is a very beautiful plant.

O. REGALIS (The Royal Fern).—The well-known Flowering or Royal Fern, the best and most beautiful of our native species. Good strong old plants will sometimes make fronds 4 feet high. The demand for old plants has been so great that it is only in out-of-the-way nooks and corners that one now has the chance of seeing this plant growing wild. We once saw it growing most luxuriantly on the margin of a bit of swampy ground hidden in the centre of an old forest among the South Downs: the effect it produced was grand beyond description.

O. SPECTABILIS (Showy).—Somewhat similar to the last, of which indeed it may, perhaps, be an American form. It does not grow to more than half the size of *O. regalis*, but has a purplish tinge while young.

O. GRACILIS (Slender), is somewhat like the species last named. It is very delicate in its appearance, and grows about 2 feet high.

POLYPODIUM.

A large genus distributed throughout every quarter of the world. A considerable number are natives of Britain, and some of North America, all of which are hardy and worthy of cultivation.

POLYPODIUM ALPESTRE (Mountain).—A Fern found but rarely in Scotland. It grows plentifully on the mountains of Switzerland. Though that country is often visited by tourists and plant-collectors, they bring home only flowering plants, such as the beautiful blue-flowered Gentian; hence the Ferns of that country are comparatively scarce, and would well repay some future collector if he would bring home a good batch, especially of the beautiful *P. alpestre*. Fronds lance-shaped, growing a foot high, bipinnate; pinnæ or side wings sharp, lance-formed, shortest near the stalk; the leaflets deeply-cut and oblong in shape. Spore-masses in the middle of the leaflet in one row, and round in shape. Rootstock short and creeping. Increased by division. There is a good plant of this interesting scarce Fern at Kew. It is deciduous—that is, dies down or loses its fronds in winter.

P. CALCAREUM (Limestone Polypody).—Though this delicate Fern is common in some parts of Britain, it is also widely distributed over Europe, and is even plentiful in North America. The fronds grow 9 inches high, are triangular in form, stand erect, the frond lying almost horizontal, with three branches. Each branch is twice-cut, or doubly pinnate; pinnæ crenated or hollowed. Spore-masses round, placed just within the edges of the leaflets. Veins simple, or rarely forked. Rootstock rough, scaly, creeping very much: hence it is easily increased by division. It is deciduous: therefore the best time to increase it is in spring, just before the new fronds appear. We have found it in great abundance growing near rocks in the neighbourhood of Pately Bridge, in Yorkshire, a locality rich in Ferns.

P. DRYOPTERIS (Three-branched Polypody, or Oak Fern).—This British Fern is found also plentifully in all four quarters of the globe. There is no hardy Fern more lovely than this: the green is peculiarly beautiful. We can distinguish it at once by its lovely colour. It is also very easy to cultivate; all that is required is a dry, rather shady situation, with a light soil to run in. Fronds ternate—that is, with three branches, broad and deflexed, bipinnate; leaflets distant and partially crenate. Spore-masses somewhat oblong—a rare circumstance in this genus, as now constituted. Increases very freely by division. It is, fortunately, for such a beautiful Fern, plentiful and cheap.

P. HEXAGONOPTERUM (Winged Polypody).—We are indebted to North America for this hardy, deciduous, handsome Fern. Fronds $1\frac{1}{2}$ foot high, triangular, bipinnate, with the pinnæ opposite, and without stalk, or sessile. Pinnules bluntly oblong and scalloped. The whole plant is covered thinly with hairs. Spore-masses round and placed near the margin. Rootstock creeping. Increased by division.

P. PHEGOPTERIS (Beech Fern).—A British Fern, very hardy, being found in the northern parts of Europe, as far as Sweden and Lapland. Fronds bipinnate, 9 inches high; the lower pinnæ project forward and reflex. Pinnules entire and very narrow. Seed-vessels incline to oblong, and are placed near the margin. Rootstock scaly and creeping freely; by it the species may be easily increased.

P. VULGARE (Common).—This is the Fern we see so common on hedgebanks, fallen trees, and low walls near to woods. The fructification is very conspicuous and beautiful. There are several varieties—one called *P. v. cambricum*, or *Welsh Polypody*, is the most distinct. In the garden at Winchester, before referred to, we noticed a variety with the pinnæ very deeply and sharply cut into segments. We have ventured to name this *P. vulgare dentatum*. It is true the *Welsh Polypody* has its pinnæ deeply cut, but they are very irregularly so, and are frequently curled both upwards and backwards—circumstances that never occur, that we are aware of, in the *P. v. dentatum*. Mr. Weaver could give no account where it came from, but stated that it was very constant in its varied character. In a garden near Barnet (Wrotham Park), Mr. Thomson, who was then gardener there, showed us a lot of common Ferns growing in a raised bed, and, to our great surprise, we observed a few fronds of the *P. vulgare* that were dentated, like the one at Winchester. We drew Mr.

Thomson's attention to it, and he promised to separate that part, to try if the dentation would be permanent. Another variety is in cultivation, named *P. v. bifidum* (Twice-cut)— that is, with the apex of each pinna divided into two parts, all the other parts remaining the same as the common one. All these are readily increased by dividing the creeping rhizomes. *P. v. omnilacerum* (All-cut), is another very distinct and beautiful form of this species. All the divisions are lengthened-out and toothed along the margin. There is also a crested form of the *Polypody*, called *cristatum*.

POLYSTICHUM.

A large assemblage of Ferns, separated from *Aspidium* by M. Schott, a German botanist. The distinguishing characters of this genus consist in round spore-masses, with round cover, and leathery, thick, spiny fronds, and a certain rigidity of habit. Many well-known Ferns are included in this genus. The hardy ones are—

POLYSTICHUM ACROSTICHOIDES (Acrostichum-like). — A North-American Fern of great beauty. It has the advantage, also, of being evergreen—that is, the fronds do not die-off in autumn. Fronds lance-shaped, 2 feet high, and pinnated: the leaflets are narrow, with short stalks, with long spiny hairs. Spore-masses on the upper part of the frond, where it contracts. Stalks scaly. Rootstock tufted: hence it is slow to increase by division.

P. ACULEATUM (Thorny Fern).—A British Fern, and also found in every quarter of the globe. Fronds 2 feet high, broad, lance-shaped, bipinnate; pinnules dark green, rigid and thorny, the one nearest the base generally the largest. Spore-masses thickly placed on the upper part of the frond. Stalks thickly covered with brown scales. Rootstock tufted. Increased by dividing large many-tufted plants. Common on hedgebanks about Burnham Beeches, in Buckinghamshire, and other parts of England. A very handsome Fern, keeping its fronds green through the winter. Grows well on old stumps of trees in rockwork. There are several varieties of this fine Fern, of which *P. a. lobatum* is the most distinct.

P. ANGULARE (Angular).—This is also a British Fern, and has been found also in some parts of Germany. Fronds soft and drooping, growing 2 feet long. This species is easily known by its stalks being very woolly or chaffy. Spore-masses numerous. Evergreen, and increased by dividing large, many-tufted plants. It is a fine Fern, and grows well in not-over-shady woods, in leaf mould and loam. Of this plant again there are several well-marked varieties, as, for instance, *P. a. cristatum* (Crested), and *P. a. polydactylum* (Many-fingered). In the first-named all the pinnæ terminate in tassels, while in the latter the terminations are forked into two or three divisions. *Wollastoni* (Mr. Wollaston's), is a very pretty and distinct form. *Proliferum*, as the name implies, produces many young plants upon its fronds. There are still several other forms of this Fern, as *dissimile, decompositum, grandidens, &c.*

P. LONCHITIS (Holly Fern).—A stiff-growing, fine species, native of England and some parts of Scotland, but by no means common. Fronds pinnate, a foot high, very hardy, and evergreen, narrow, lance-shaped, and of a deep green colour; pinnæ short and thickly set on the frond, very thorny, like the leaves of the Holly. Stalks covered with chaffy scales. Slow to increase; but sometimes a second tuft is produced on the rootstock, which may be taken off when rooted. Found chiefly amongst rocky regions: hence it should be grown on a little hillock of stones, in peat and loam. It is one of the finest of our native Ferns, and should be in every collection.

P. SETOSUM (Bristly).—From Japan. A very handsome hardy evergreen Fern, with ovate-acuminate bipinnate fronds, 2 to 3 feet high. The pinnules trapezio-oblong, acute, auricled and fringed with stiff hairs.

PTERIS.

Our readers will have noticed many names of Ferns ending with *pteris*, such, for instance, as *Callipteris*, *Ceratopteris*, *Cystopteris*, and others. The original name *Pteris* is derived from *pteron*, a wing, because the fronds have the appearance of the wings of a bird. The compound names describe different sorts of wings, as horn-winged, ostrich-winged, &c. The genus *Pteris*, as originally formed, contained a great number of species. It is now restricted to such only as have forked veins, with the spore-masses on their points close to the edge of the leaflet. The only hardy species left in the genus is—

PTERIS AQUILINA (Eagle-like Fern).—This is the very common Bracken or Brake that so beautifully clothes many of our wild wastes, affording shelter to all kinds of game. The question has been asked, Can this Bracken be transplanted? We say, Yes, very easily, and certainly. Take up, in early spring, the rhizomes or creeping rootstocks in quantity; dig the ground well, draw drills, and lay the long roots in thick, covering them 2 inches deep, and they will certainly grow the following summer, and soon form a thick plantation; but the ground must be dry, or if not, well drained to make it so, because this Fern will not thrive in wet places. There is a variegated form of this plant, which is beautifully dotted with clear white; it is at present very rare. There is also another with a tendency to become tufted at the points.

SCOLOPENDRIUM.

A genus of handsome Ferns represented by only one species, but a very large number of varieties. They may be distinguished easily by their spore-masses slanting upwards and being placed between the veins at some distance from the midribs, where they are sometimes in one line and sometimes in two. The spore-mass-cover (indusium), also is special, sometimes linear, and in other cases hollow or vaulted. They may be known also by their long sword-like fronds. The generic name is derived from *scolopendra*, a centipede: the long lines of spore-masses are supposed to resemble the feet of that insect.

SCOLOPENDRIUM VULGARE (Common Hart's-tongue Fern), *Fig.* 78.—A British Fern of great beauty, common almost everywhere, clothing sloping hedgebanks. It is also frequently seen growing out of the bricks in old wells, where it flourishes very freely. On the hedgebanks the fronds are short, seldom exceeding 8 inches in length. Fronds simple, shining, of a lively green, long, strap-shaped, tapering to a point, and heart-shaped at the base. Margin smooth and entire. Stalks scaly. Rootstock creeping slightly. Increased readily by division.

S. VULGARE POLYSCHIDES (Many-cut).—A variety known generally by the name *angustifolium* (Narrow-leaved), found near Bristol. Fronds simple, though sometimes they will come pinnatifid. They are then very curious, long and narrow, cut into segments overlapping each other. Spore-masses very narrow, and placed in the hollows, and sometimes on the segments, only occupying three-fourths of the under side of the frond. Not commonly in cultivation. We have only seen it in one place in Glou-

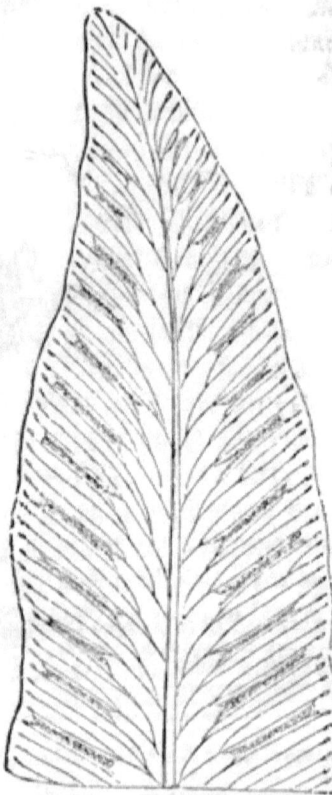

Fig. 78. Scolopendrium vulgare.
(Top of frond natural size.)

cestershire. A very distinct variety, and may be increased, though very slowly, by division, when the plant becomes large.

S. VULGARE MULTIFIDUM (Many-times-divided).—Fronds split up at the apex into many irregular divisions. Sometimes the frond has many branches from the base, and each branch is multifid at the top, and often quite tasselled, and becomes so heavy as to droop downwards. This singular variety is often varied again, by the midrib dividing at the apex, and again by being divided in another style without tassels. These two latter varieties are, however, not constant on the same plant. We noticed in Ireland many plants with forked branches, and this variety is sometimes called *furcatum;* but none of the three are distinct enough to be separated from *multifidum.* Increased by division.

S. VULGARE UNDULATUM (Waved).—Frond simple, strap-shaped, tapering to a point, where it is sometimes, but rarely, divided. The margin is beautifully waved, almost plaited, like a shirt-frill. We never met with this variety bearing spores. It is the most distinct and most beautiful of all the varieties. Grown in a peat border, it forms quite a bush, and is then very ornamental throughout the year.

Without a doubt this is the most variable Fern in existence; there seems to be no end to the various forms it assumes. The fronds are forked and divided, crested and lobed, fringed and plaited, reduced or enlarged, in every conceivable way. It is quite a protean Fern. Many of the varieties, were they imported from a foreign country, would be named as distinct species without a question. Mr. Sim, of Foot's Cray, has got the finest collection of them that we ever saw; and any of our readers who have the chance should visit his nursery, were it only to see the host of forms of the *Hart's-tongue* which he possesses. (We need not add that they will find many other things in the Fern way to interest them.) The *Scolopendriums* are a host in themselves. *S. v. marginatum*

(Margined), has fronds only an inch wide and about a foot long; the margin appears double, as though one frond was laid on the top of the other. *S. v. fissum* (Cut), fronds deeply and regularly cleft along the sides. *S. v. macrosorum* (Large-fruited), fronds a foot or more long, with irregular margin, often showing the spore-masses on the upper side. *S. v. cristatum* (Crested), points of the fronds divided into wide-spreading tassels. *S. v. cornutum* (Horned), the midrib in this case is developed into a sort of horn, projecting from the upper surface of the frond a little way from the apex. *S. v. subcornutum*, the fronds branch irregularly, and often produce a horn-like projection of the midrib on the under side. *S. v. reniforme* (Kidney-shaped), this is sufficiently described by the name; the fronds are reduced wonderfully in size. *S. v. proliferum* (Proliferous), fronds only a few inches long, sometimes reduced even to the midrib without any blade at all. *S. v. fœcundum*, this is another small-fronded form, which often produces young plants upon the fronds. *S. v. rugosum* (Rough), the upper surface of the fronds, which are 6 or 8 inches long, rough, with numerous blunt projections. *S. v. palmatum* (Divided like a hand), fronds very variable in shape, often divided near the base into two or three, and then again divided towards the apex. These are a few only of the most marked varieties, and these at least should be in every collection. Those who have the space, and wish for it, may largely increase their number; we therefore add the names of a few more:—*Undulato-lobatum* (wavy and lobed), *ramo-marginatum* (forms a dense tuft), *fimbriatum* (fimbriated along the narrow fronds), *glomeratum* (forming a close mass of fronds 2 or 3 inches long), *variabile* (a name which might be applied to many of the varieties), *supralineatum* (with two lines along the upper surface midway between the midrib and margin), &c.

When a plant has become large it may be increased readily by division. Take the plant up, and shake off all the soil, then pass a knife through between each crown, and with the hand disentangle the roots from each of the other divisions; pot them in suitable-sized pots, in any open fibrous soil mixed with leaf mould and sand, place them in a cold frame, and shade them from the light for a few days, and from the sun for a month; they will then have made fresh roots, and will bear to be fully exposed. All the *Scolopendriums* should be propagated in a similar way. If these curious varieties are grown in a greenhouse, they display their diversities to the greatest advantage, and make splendid fronds. As they are all evergreen, and very handsome, very hardy, and not easily lost, every grower of hardy Ferns should try to procure all the varieties.

SITOLOBIUM.

Divided from *Dicksonia* chiefly on account of the species being deciduous, more delicate structure, and having a creeping rootstock. There is only one species that is hardy. The name is derived from *sitos*, corn, and *lobos*, a lobe: the fructification, or spore-masses, being placed on the segments or lobes of the fronds.

SITOLOBIUM PUNCTILOBUM (Spotted-lobed). — A North-American Fern of great beauty. It is the *Dicksonia pilosiuscula* of Willdenow, and by that name was formerly known amongst cultivators. Fronds 2 feet high, lance-shaped, and thrice-divided, and of a light green colour; pinnæ deeply-cut, dentated or toothed at the margin. Rootstock creeps much: consequently it is easily increased by division. In the Botanic Garden at Birmingham there is a border 3 feet wide and several yards long, thickly covered with this handsome Fern. The border is composed of sandy peat, and is on the north side of a Hornbeam hedge. In this situation this Fern thrives most remarkably, forming a dense mass of fronds. Though so easy to increase and so easy to grow, we do not meet with it in many places, yet we know no Fern that would give greater pleasure to the Fern-fancier.

STRUTHIOPTERIS.

From the Greek *struthios*, an ostrich, and *pteris*, a Fern: the fronds in form like that bird's plumes. A genus containing two noble hardy species. The fertile fronds are contracted, and not produced until after the barren ones, among which they are quite hidden. One species is American, the other European, but both perfectly hardy.

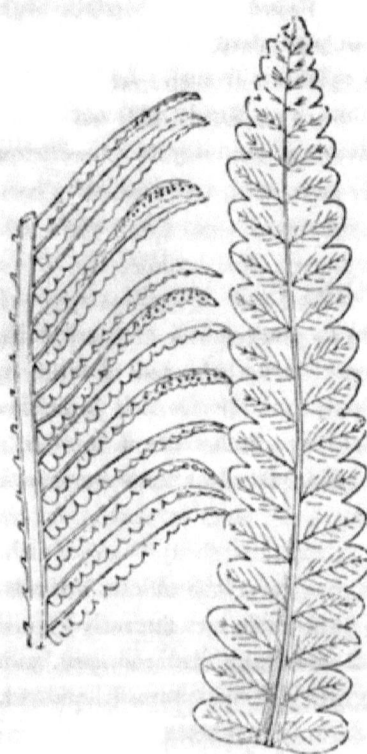

Fig. 79. Struthiopteris pensylvanica. (Sterile pinnule and part of fertile frond natural size.)

STRUTHIOPTERIS GERMANICA (German). — This plant makes a glorious tuft of fronds, 3 or 4 feet high. It does not materially differ from the other species, but the two are quite unlike any other Fern, and at least one of them should find a place in every hardy fernery—both where there is plenty of room.

S. PENSYLVANICA (Pensylvania), *Fig.* 79.—Native of North America. Deciduous. Sterile fronds about 3 feet high, pinnate; pinnæ acuminate, deeply-divided, with segments rounded. Fertile fronds about 1 foot high, contracted, pinnate. This makes a noble specimen, and may be propagated like the other by division.

WOODSIA.

Commemorative of Joseph Woods, a British botanist. Spore-masses circular, surrounded by an inferior involucre, the edge of which is divided into many hair-like incurved segments.

WOODSIA HYPERBOREA (Northern), *Fig.* 80.—Native of Great Britain; hardy, yet does better under a frame in winter. Fronds 2 to 6 inches high, narrow-lanceolate, pinnate, dullish green, with a few scales on the under side. Sori medial, finally confluent, or covering the surface. Indusium deeply laciniated, terminating in hair-like articulated segments. Stem articulated near the middle, the upper part falling off when mature. It should be planted in a dry part of the fernery if it be intended to try it in the open air. *W. ilvensis* sometimes succeeds in similar situations, but a spare plant should always be kept in the frame in case it should not do well.

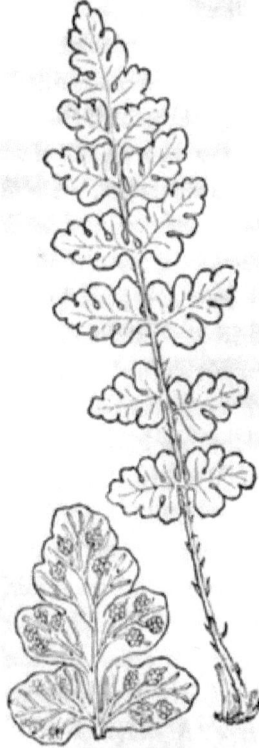

Fig. 80. Woodsia hyperborea. (Frond full size; pinna magnified.)

W. POLYSTICHOIDES VAR. VEITCHII (Mr. Veitch's Polystichum-like Woodsia).—Introduced by the gentleman after whom it is named, and who found it near Yeddo, in Japan. It has narrow pinnate fronds, 6 or 8 inches or more in height, with both the upper and lower surfaces covered with short close hairs. It will probably prove hardy, but is safer for the present in a frame.

CONSTRUCTION OF A FERN CASE.

GLAZED cases for the cultivation of Ferns in the windows of our dwelling-rooms are now so popular that our work would be incomplete without a few words upon their construction and management. First as to the way in which to make one.

We require a planed, well-seasoned deal board, 21 inches by 12 inches, and $1\frac{1}{2}$ inch thick; also other two planed deal boards, 12 inches by 10 inches, of the same thickness. These latter are firmly morticed perpendicularly into the ends of the former, 1 inch from the edge. Grooves a quarter of an inch by three-eighths of an inch are, in each case, cut in the inner side of the uprights, and carried in a right line along the base pieces half an inch from their edges.

This framework may be covered all over with oil paint, three coats in thickness; or, if preferred, it can be (as in our case) coloured with oak stain, and thoroughly varnished thrice with shell-lac dissolved in spirits of wine. When dry, the grooves are filled with white or red-lead putty, and glazed with one-eighth-of-an-inch sheet glass. The putty having set, the joints can be varnished, and a frame of deal moulding screwed on the top; the screws passing downwards into the uprights. Ornamental finials of turned deal are fixed by wire pegs to the upper rail at its four corners. A sheet of glass lies loosely on the top of the moulded rail. Thus, with the addition of a few perforations in the vertical pieces above soil-level, *the ventilation necessary can be arranged to a nicety.*

The fernery is now complete, and when filled and fitted with back scene, forms an interesting ornament. A few pieces of tile should be spread at the bottom, and on them the undulating sanded charcoaled bog earth.

Ferns may then be introduced (the smallest varieties being the most suitable), with pieces of pumice stone, Roman cement, rockwork, &c., to taste. Should the light be too intense, a screen may be placed at the back.

We find the most suitable watering-pot for Wardian cases is an engineer's oil-can. (They can be procured at any ironmonger's for 6*d.* each.) When filled, the pressure of the forefinger at the bottom causes an ejection of the water, which immediately stops running on withdrawing the finger. One at the price mentioned holds about a quarter of a pint. A few good specimens of Mosses add greatly to the appearance of a fernery of this description, particularly if some of the scarlet cups so common in spring upon our hedgebanks be introduced. Ferns and Mosses seem naturally inseparable companions, and should not be parted.

The case is wide enough to allow three rows of Ferns placed alternately, and will hold about eighteen plants. The centre row should be planted with the following six species in this order:—*Adiantum pedatum, A. brasiliense, Onychium lucidum, Adiantum formosum, Davallia canariensis,* and *Doodia aspera.*

The next row may be planted with the following:—*Adiantum tenerum, Doodia media, Platyloma rotundifolia, Adiantum capillus-Veneris, Lycopodium stoloniferum,* and *Grammitis ceterach.*

The row on the other side may contain the following:—*Adiantum hirsutum, Pteris cretica, P. serrulata, Lycopodium variabile, Allosorus crispus,* and *Cystopteris fragilis.*

There is a very neat form or arrangement for Fern glasses wherein rockwork and liliputian ruins are introduced and planted with Ferns and other cryptogamic plants. They are prepared by Mr. W. F. French, of Bristol, and specimens, at very moderate prices, are on sale at the flower-shops about Covent Garden. To look at them in their unfurnished state they are not very attractive; but when placed under a glass shade and appropriately planted, they are very effective. We have one before us most strikingly so. The base or groundwork, composed like the ruin, of fragments of various calxes and stones, is covered with growing Lichens; and grouped about the ruin are *Adiantum formosum, Adiantum capillus-Veneris, Asplenium ruta-muraria, Pteris serrulata, Lycopodium densum,* &c.

The following are Mr. French's directions for keeping them in a healthy condition:—

"The best situation for the case is in a window open to the north; but the plants will grow and flourish in other aspects, if due care be taken to shade them from *direct sunlight*, which causes Ferns to grow too rapidly, and to become deformed. Twice a-week in summer, and once a-week in winter, the glass cover should be removed for a few minutes, and occasionally the inner side of the glass and the rim of the case may be wiped dry.

"A small quantity of rain water must be added, from time to time, to replace that subtracted by evaporation and by wiping the glass cover. About a wineglassful at a time, and five or six times a-year, will generally be found sufficient. The best way to apply the water is with a small piece of sponge, or a small syringe; care being taken to avoid wetting the fronds, which causes them to rot away.

"Dead fronds and branches must be cut out neatly. The same side of the case should be always kept turned towards the light."

We ought not to omit mentioning that wherever Mr. French has exhibited his Fern-adorned rockwork it has been generally admired. It forms one of the most elegant of room-adornments.

One of the best forms of Fern cases is that called "The Bijou," an elegant and ornamental structure for drawing-rooms and sitting-rooms, made by Mr. Stocks, 14, Archer Street, Kensington Park, W.

INDEX.

[N.B.—*Synonymes are printed in italic.*]

INTRODUCTION	v
Fern-house, position and construction of	vi
construction of rockwork for	vii
ground plan of	viii
heating	x
Ferns, soil for	xii, xiii
watering	xiii
potting	xiv
propagation by spores	xvi
by division	xix
insects injurious to	xix
Fern Pillars	xx
Rockwork, construction of, in Fern-house	vii
arrangement of	viii

ACROPHORUS, 73
  hispidus, 148
Acrostichum, 1
Adiantum, 2, 123, 174
  asarifolium, 5
  assimile, 123
  betulinum, 6
  brasiliense, 2
  capillus-Veneris, 123, 174
  cardiochlœna, 2
  caudatum, 3
  chilense, 125
  concinnum, 3
  cristatum, 3
  cuneatum, 3
  curvatum, 3
  Feei, 6
  flexuosum, 6
  formosum, 4, 125
  Foveanum, 3
  Adiantum hispidulum, 125
  hispidulum tenellum, 125
  intermedium, 3
  lunulatum, 4
  macrophyllum, 4
  Moritzianum, 123
  obliquum, 6
  patens, 6
  pedatum, 125, 174
  pentadactylon, 4
  polyphyllum, 2
  pubescens, 125
  pulverulentum, 6
  reniforme, 5
  scabrum, 125
  setulosum, 5
  sulphureum, 126
  tenerum, 5
  trapeziforme, 6
  Wilesianum, 6

Adiantum Wilsoni, 6
Allantodia umbrosa, 16
Allosorus, 175
   crispus, 175
Alsophila, 6, 126
   articulata, 7
   australis, 126
   capensis, 126
   ferox, 7
   pruinata, 7
   villosa, 7
Anemia, 8
   adiantifolia, 8
   collina, 8
   Dregeana, 8
   flexuosa, 8
   tomentosa, 8
   villosa, 8
Anemidictyon, 8
   hirtum, 9
   fraxinifolium, 9
   phyllitidis, 9
Anetium citrifolium, 9
Anthrophyum lanceolatum, 9
Anthropteris, 9
   albo-punctata, 9
Antigramma, 126
   rhizophylla, 126
Aspidium, 9
   apiifolium, 11
   cicutarium, 11
   coadunatum, 11
   ebeneum, 11
   macrophyllum, 11
   trifoliatum, 10
Asplenium, 11, 127, 175
   adiantum nigrum, 175
      variegatum, 176
   acutum, 132
   Aitoni, 16
   alatum, 16
   alternans, 12
   alternifolium, 132, 176
   angustifolium, 176
   appendiculatum, 127
   auritum, 11
   axillare, 128
   bachypteron, 12
   Belangeri, 16
   bifidum, 12
   brasiliense, 12
   Brownii, 128

Asplenium bulbiferum, 128
   ceylonense, 16
   cicutarium, 12
   compressum, 128
   Dalhousieanum, 12
   dentatum, 16
   dimorphum, 12
   dispersum, 16
   diversifolium, 12, 129
   ebeneum, 129
   eburneum, 16
   falcatum, 13
   filix-fœmina, 176
      crispum, 176
      depauperatum, 177
      Frizelliæ, 177
      multiceps, 177
      multifidum, 176
      plumosum, 177
      ramosum, 177
      Smithii, 176
   flabellifolium, 129
   flaccidum, 129
   fœniculaceum, 16
   fontanum, 132, 177
   formosum, 13
   fragrans, 16
   furcatum, 130
   germanicum, 132
   hemionitis, 131
   lætum, 13
   lanceolatum, 132, 177
   laserpitiifolium, 13
   lucidum, 130
   macilentum, 17
   macrophyllum, 17
   marginatum, 69
   marinum, 130, 178
      ramosum, 131
      sub-bipinnatum, 131
      trapeziforme, 131
   mexicanum, 17
   Michauxi, 178
   monanthemum, 13
   myriophyllum, 17
   nitens, 17
   nitidum, 17
   obliquum, 13
   obtusatum, 131
   obtusilobum, 14
   oligophyllum, 14
   palmatum, 131

INDEX.

Asplenium pinnatifidum, 132
    planicaule, 15
    polygodon, 131
    præmorsum, 17
    pulchellum, 14
    pumilum, 14
    radicans, 15
    rachirhizon, 15
    reclinatum, 131
    rhizophorum, 15
    ruta-muraria, 132, 178
    rutæfolium, 132
    septentrionale, 132, 178
    serra, 15
    serratum, 12, 15
    trichomanes, 132, 179
        depauperatum, 179
        incisum, 179
        multifidum, 179
    umbrosum, 16, 131
    Veitchianum, 16
    viride, 132
    viviparum, 16
    zamiæfolium, 17

BALANTIUM, 132
    culcitum, 132
Blechnum, 133
    attenuatum, 20
    australe, 17, 133
    brasiliense, 17
    cartilagineum, 20, 133
    cognatum, 17, 133
    corcovadense, 18
    glandulosum, 18
    gracile, 18
    hastatum, 20, 133
    intermedium, 18
    lanceola, 18
    longifolium, 18
    occidentale, 18
    orientale, 19
    polypodioides, 19
    punctulatum, 20
    serrulatum, 19
    spicant, 17
    triangulare, 133
    trifoliatum, 18
Botrychium, 179
    lunaria, 179
Brainea insignis, 20

CÆNOPTERIS JAPONICA, 151
Callipteris, 20
    malabarica, 21
    prolifera, 20
Campteria biaurita, 21
Campyloneuron, 36
Cassebeera, 22, 133
    cuneata, 22, 133
    dealbata, 23
    farinosa, 23
    geraniifolia, 134
    hastata, 134
    intramarginalis, 23, 134
    pedata, 24
    pulveracea, 23
Ceratodactylis, 24
    osmundoides, 24
Ceratopteris, 24
    thalictrioides, 25
Ceterach, 179
    officinarum, 179
Cheilanthes, 22, 26, 134
Cheilanthes alabamensis, 27
    argentea, 27
    cuneata, 22
    elegans, 29
    farinosa, 23
    frigida, 29
    hirta, 27
        Ellisiana, 27
    glauca hirsuta, 29
    intramarginalis, 23
    lendigera, 27
    micromera, 134
    microphylla, 28, 29
    micropteris, 134
    multifida, 29
    myriophylla, 29
    odora, 134
    pedata, 24
    Preissiana, 29
    profusa, 28
    radiata, 28
    Sieberi, 29
    spectabilis, 28
    squamosa, 29
    tenuifolia, 28, 135
    viscosa, 29
Cibotium, 29
    Barometz, 30
    Cummingi, 30
    princeps, 30

Cibotium Schiedei, 30
Circinalis, 31
  flavens, 90
  nivea, 91
  tenera, 91
Colysis, 31
  membranacea, 31
Coniogramma javanica, 62
Cyathea, 31, 135
  arborea, 31
  Cunninghamii, 135
  dealbata, 32, 135
  elegans, 33
  medullaris, 33, 135
  patens, 33
  Smithii, 135
Cyclopeltis, 33
  semicordata, 34
Cyrtogonium, 34
  crispatulum, 34
  flagelliferum, 34
Cyrtomium, 35, 136, 180
  caryotideum, 35
  falcatum, 136, 180
  Fortunei, 136
Cyrtophlebium, 36
  angustifolium, 36
  cæspitosum, 37
  decurrens, 36
  ensifolium, 37
  nitidum, 36
  phyllitidis, 36
  repens, 36
  rigidum, 37
Cystopteris, 137, 180
  bulbifera, 180
  fragilis, 180
    Dickieana, 181
  montana, 181
  sempervirens, 181
  tenuis, 137, 181

DAVALLIA, 37, 137
  bullata, 38
  canariensis, 137
    pulchella, 137
  decora, 38
  dissecta, 38
  elata, 38
  elegans, 38
  pentaphylla, 38
  polyantha, 38

Davallia pyxidata, 138
Dicksonia, 138
  antarctica, 138
  fibrosa, 139
  lanata, 139
  pilosiuscula, 201
  squarrosa, 139
Dictymia, 139
  attenuata, 139
Dictyoglossum, 39
  crinitum, 39
Dictyoxiphium, 41
  panamense, 41
Didymochlæna, 41
  truncatula, 41
Diplazium, 42, 181
  acuminatum, 42
  alternifolium, 42
  arborescens, 42
  coarctatum, 43
  decussatum, 43
  esculentum, 21
  integrifolium, 42
  juglandifolium, 43
  lasiopteris, 45
  marginatum, 69
  plantagineum, 43
  Serampurense, 21
  Shepherdi, 43
  striatum, 43
  subaltum, 44
  sylvaticum, 45
  thelypteroides, 181
  Thwaitesi, 45
Doodia, 45, 140
  aspera, 45
  blechnoides, 46
  caudata, 45, 140
  corymbifera, 46
  lunulata, 46, 140
  monstrosa, 46
Doryopteris, 46
  collina, 47
  palmata, 47
  sagittifolia, 47
Drymoglossum, 47
  lanceolatum, 48
  piloselloides, 48
Drynaria, 48, 140
  Billardieri, 140
  coronans, 49
  diversifolia, 49

INDEX.

Drynaria *irioides*, 82
  morbillosa, 49
  musæfolia, 49
  propinqua, 50
  pustulata, 140
  quercifolia, 50
  vulgaris, 97

ELAPHOGLOSSUM, 50
  apodum, 52
  callæfolium, 50
  conforme, 51
  crassinerve, 51
  frigidum, 52
  latifolium, 52
  lepidotum, 52
  longifolium, 52
  microlepis, 52
  muscosum, 52
  perelegans, 52
  scolopendriifolium, 52
  villosum, 52
Eupodium, 52
  Kaulfussii, 53

FADYENIA, 53
  prolifera, 54
Fern cases, construction and arrangement of, 204
  Stocks's, 207

GLEICHENIA, 54, 141
  circinalis, 142
  dicarpa, 142
  dichotoma, 55
  flabellata, 142
    læte-virens, 142
  furcata, 55
  glaucescens, 55
  hecistophylla, 142
  microphylla, 142
  rupestris, 142
  semivestita, 143
  speluncæ, 143
Goniophlebium, 55
  Catherinæ, 55
  colpodes, 58
  cuspidatum, 55
  dissimile, 58
  fraxinifolium, 58
  glaucum, 58
  harpeodes, 55

Goniophlebium incanum, 56
  lætum, 58
  menisciifolium, 56
  neriifolium, 57
  Lopholepis, 57
  owariense, 59
  piloselloides, 57
  rhagadiolepis, 59
  sepultum, 57
  subauriculatum, 57
  vacciniifolium, 58
  verrucosum, 58
Goniopteris, 59
  aspenoides, 60
  crenata, 59
  fraxinifolia, 59
  Ghiesbrechtii, 59
  gracilis, 60
  megalodes, 60
  obliterata, 60
  pennigera, 60
  prolifera, 60
  reptans, 60
  serrulata, 60
  tetragona, 60
GREENHOUSE FERNS, 117
  culture of, 119, 161
  soil for, 160, 162
  drainage for, 120
  potting, 121, 162
  watering, 122
  giving air to, 122
  summer management of, 163
  insects injurious to, 162
Gymnogramma, 61
  calomelanos, 64
  chærophylla, 64
  chrysophylla, 61
  Geardtii, 64
  javanica, 31, 62
  lanata, 64
  leptophylla, 64
  L'Herminieri, 64
  Martensii, 64
  ochracea, 64
  peruviana argyrophylla, 62
  pulchella, 62
    ramosa, 62
  rufa, 64
  speciosa, 64
  sulphurea, 62
  tartarea, 63

Gymnogramma tomentosa, 63, 64
    trifoliata, 63
Gymnopteris, 64
    aliena, 65
    nicotianæfolia, 64
    quercifolia, 64

HARDY FERNS, 165
    culture of, 166
        on rockwork, 166
        in pots, 166, 168
        on raised banks, 167
        in a fernery, 169
    propagation by spores, 170
        by division, 173
Hemidictyum, 69
    marginatum, 69
Hemionites, 65
    cordata, 67
    palmata, 66
    pedata, 67
Hemitelia, 67
    grandiflora, 68
    horrida, 68
    Hostmannii, 68
    speciosa, 68
Hewardia, 6
Humata, 69
    heterophylla, 69
    pedata, 69
Hymenodium crinitum, 39
Hymenophyllum, 70, 143, 181
    abruptum, 70
    asplenioides, 70
    ciliatum, 70
    cruentum, 70
    demissum, 143
    dilatatum, 143
    hirsutum, 70
    nudum, 70
    Plumieri, 70
    sericeum, 70
    tunbridgense, 181
    Wilsoni, 182
Hypoderris, 70
    Brownii, 71
Hypolepis, 72, 144
    repens, 72
        difforme, 72
    rugulosa, 144
    tenuifolia, 72

LASTREA, 144, 183
    canariensis, 144
    cristata, 183
    decomposita, 144
    decurrens, 184
    dilatata, 184
    elongata, 145
    filix-mas, 184
        cristata, 185
            angustata, 185
        paleacea, 185
        pumila, 185
        Schofieldii, 185
        spinulosa, 185
    Fœnisecii, 186
    Goldieana, 185
    Kaulfussii, 145
    marginalis, 185
    montana, 186
    noveboracensis, 186
    oreopteris, 186
    podophylla, 187
    recurva, 186
    Sieboldi, 187
    spinulosa, 187
    tenericaulis, 145
    thelypteris, 187
    uliginosa, 187
Lepicystis, 72
    incana, 56
    rhagadiolepis, 59
    sepultum, 58
Leptogramma, 73
    villosa, 73
Leucostegia. 73
    chærophylla, 74
    immersa, 73, 74
    pulchra, 74
Lindsæa, 74
    trapeziforme, 75
Litobrochia, 75, 145
    biaurita, 22
    denticulata, 75
    leptophylla, 76
    vespertilionis, 76, 145
Llavea cordifolia, 24
Lomaria, 145, 188
    alpina, 145, 188
    attenuata, 77, 146
    auriculata, 146
    Banksii, 148
    capensis, 146

Lomaria crenulata, 148, 188
  discolor, 148
  elongata, 148
  falcata, 77
  fluviatilis, 148
  Frazeri, 147
  gigantea, 77
  Gilliesii, 147
  lanceolata, 148
  magellanica, 147
  nuda, 147
  onocleoides, 78
  Patersoni, 148
  spicant, 188
    anomala, 189
    concinna, 189
    crassicaulis, 189
    imbricata, 189
    ramosa, 189
Lomariopsis sorbifolia, 112
Lonchitis, 78
  pubescens, 78
Lophosoria, 78
  pruinata, 7
Lorinsoria, 189
  areolata, 189
Lygodictyon, 78
  Forsteri, 79
Lygodium, 79
  articulatum, 80
  flexuosum, 79
  japonicum, 79
  palmatum, 79
  polystachyum, 79
  scandens, 80
  venustum, 80
  volubile, 79

MARATTIA, 80
  laxa, 80
  purpurascens, 80
Meniscium, 80
  palustre, 81
  simplex, 81
Microlepia, 81, 148
  novæ-zelandiæ, 148
  platyphylla, 82
  polypodiodes, 82
Microsorum, 82
Mohria, 149
  achilleæfolia, 149
  thurifraga, 149

Myriopteris, 27

NEOTTOPTERIS, 83, 149
  australasica, 149
  vulgaris, 84, 149
Nephrodium, 84
  articulatum, 85
  Hookerii, 85
  molle, 84
    corymbiferum, 84
  multilineatum, 85
  patens, 85
  terminans, 85
  truncatum, 85
  venustum, 86
Nephrolepis, 86
  acuta, 87
  davallioides, 86
  dissecta, 86
  ensifolia, 87
  exaltata, 86
  hirsutula, 87
  pectinata, 87
  splendens, 87
  tuberosa, 87
  undulata, 87
Niphobolus, 87
  angustatus, 89
  Gardnerii, 89
  lingua, 89, 149
  nummularifolius, 89
  pertusus, 89
  rupestris, 89, 150
  sphærocephalus, 89
  varius, 89
Nothochlæna, 89, 150
  distans, 150
  Eckloniana, 90
  flavens, 90
  lanuginosa, 151
  Marantæ, 90
  nivea, 91
  rufa, 91
  sinuata, 91
  squamata, 91
  tenera, 91
  trichomanoides, 91
  tomentosa, 91
  vestita, 151

ODONTOSORIA, 91
  aculeata, 92

214 INDEX.

Odontosoria tenuifolia, 92
Oleandra, 93
    articulata, 93
    hirtella, 93
    natalensis, 93
    neriiformis, 92
    nodosa, 92
Olfersia cervina, 93
Onoclea, 189
    sensibilis, 190
Onychium, 93, 151, 191
    auratum, 93
    lucidum, 151, 191
Ophioglossum, 191
    lusitanicum, 191
    vulgatum, 191
Osmunda, 191
    cinnamomea, 192
    Claytoniana, 191
    gracilis, 192
    interrupta, 191
    regalis, 192
    spectabilis, 192

PELLÆA, 22, 100
    hastata, 134
Phegopteris trichodes, 145
Phlebodium, 95
    aureum, 95
    glaucum, 95
    areolatum, 95
    decumanum, 95
    percussum, 95
    pulvinatum, 95
    squamulosum, 95
    venosum, 95
Phymatodes, 95
    Billardieri, 140, 152
    cuspidata, 97
    excavata, 97
    nuda, 97
    longifolia, 96
    longipes, 96
    longissima, 97
    peltidea, 97
    pustulata, 140, 152
    saccata, 96
    vulgaris, 96
Platycerium, 97
    alcicorne, 97, 152
    biforme, 100
    grande, 98

Platycerium stemaria, 99
    Wallichii, 100
Platyloma, 100, 153
    atro-purpurea, 153
    calomelanos, 100
    cordata, 153
    falcata, 153
    flexuosa, 100
    rotundifolia, 153
    ternifolia, 101
Pleopeltis, 101
    lycopodioides, 101
    membranacea, 31
    nitida, 101
    phymatodes, 97
    vacciniifolia, 101
    venosa, 101
Pœcilopteris, 34
Polyobotrya, 101
    cylindrica, 101
Polypodium, 103, 192
    alpestre, 192
    aureum, 95
    calcareum, 193
    dryopteris, 193
    effusum, 103
    hexagonopterum, 194
    lachnopodium, 104
    paradiseæ, 104
    pectinatum, 104
    phegopteris, 194
    phymatodes, 96
    plebejum, 154
    plumulum, 104
    Reinwardtii, 57
    sporadocarpum, 95
    subpetiolatum, 154
    trichodes, 104, 145
    vulgare, 194
        bifidum, 195
        cambricum, 194
        cristatum, 195
        dentatum, 194
        omnilacerum, 195
Polystichum, 154, 195
    acrostichoides, 195
    aculeatum, 195
    lobatum, 196
    angulare, 196
        cristatum, 196
        decompositum, 196
        dissimile, 196

INDEX. 215

Polystichum angulare grandidens, 196
    angulare lonchitis, 196
        polydactylum, 196
        proliferum, 196
        setosum, 196
        Wollastoni, 196
    anomalum, 105
    capense, 155
    concavum, 155
    coriaceum, 155
    flexum, 155
    mucronatum, 105
    ordinatum, 155
    proliferum, 105
    pungens, 156
    triangulum, 105
    vestitum, 156
Pteris, 105, 156, 197
    aquilina, 197
    arguta, 156
    argyræa, 106
    aspericaulis, 106
    cretica, 156
        albo-lineata, 156
    felosma, 107
    hastata, 134
    heterophylla, 107
    hirsuta, 107
    Kingiana, 156
    lata, 107
    longifolia, 107
    pungens, 108
    quadriaurita, 108
    rubra-venia, 108
    scaberula, 156
    semipinnata, 108
    serrulata, 108
        angusta, 156
    sulcata, 108
    tremula, 156
    trichomanoides, 91
    tricolor, 107
    umbrosa, 156

SAGENIA, 109
    coadnata, 110
    decurrens, 109
    hippocrepis, 110
    repanda, 110
Scolopendrium, 197
    vulgare, 198

Scolopendrium vulgare *angustifolium*, 198
    vulgare cornutum, 200
    cristatum, 200
    fimbriatum, 200
    fissum, 200
    fœcundum, 200
    glomeratum, 200
    macrosorum, 200
    marginatum, 199
    multifidum, 199
        furcatum, 199
    palmatum, 200
    polyschides, 199
    proliferum, 200
    reniforme, 200
    rugosum, 200
    subcornutum, 200
    supralineatum, 200
    undulato-lobatum, 200
    undulatum, 199
    variabile, 200
Sitolobium, 110, 201
    adiantoides, 110
    punctilobum, 201
Stenochlæna, 111
    Meyeriana, 112
    natalensis, 112
    scandens, 112
    sorbifolia, 111
    tenuifolia, 112
Stenosemia, 112
STOVE FERNS, 1
Struthiopteris, 202
    germanica, 202
    pensylvanica, 202

TÆNIOPSIS, 112
    graminifolia, 112
    lineata, 113
Todea, 158
    africana, 158
    hymenophylloides, 158
    pellucida, 158
    rivularis, 158
    superba, 158
Trichomanes, 113, 159
    anceps, 114
    Bancroftii, 114
    brevisetum, 160
    crispum, 114
    elegans, 115

Trichomanes Kraussii, 114
    muscoides, 114
    radicans, 160
        Andrewsii, 160
    reniforme, 160
    speciosum, 160
    trichoideum, 115
Vittaria lineata, 113
Woodsia, 203

Woodsia hyperborea, 203
    ilvensis, 203
    polystichoides Veitchii, 203
Woodwardia, 160
    areolata, 189
    japonica, 161
    orientalis, 161
    radicans, 160
        interrupta, 161

www.ingramcontent.com/pod-product-compliance
Lightning Source LLC
Chambersburg PA
CBHW031747230426
43669CB00007B/518